WHEN CITIZENS DECIDE

COMPARATIVE POLITICS

Comparative Politics is a series for students, teachers, and researchers of political science that deals with contemporary government and politics. Global in scope, books in the series are characterized by a stress on comparative analysis and strong methodological rigour. The series is published in association with the European Consortium for Political Research. For more information visit www.essex.ac.uk/ecpr

The Comparative Politics series is edited by Professor David M. Farrell, School of Politics and International Relations, University College Dublin, Kenneth Carty, Professor of Political Science, University of British Columbia, and Professor Dirk Berg-Schlosser, Institute of Political Science, Philipps University, Marburg.

OTHER TITLES IN THIS SERIES

When Citizens Decide

Lessons from Citizen Assemblies on Electoral Reform

PATRICK FOURNIER
HENK VAN DER KOLK
R. KENNETH CARTY
ANDRÉ BLAIS
JONATHAN ROSE

OXFORD
UNIVERSITY PRESS

OXFORD

UNIVERSITY PRESS

Great Clarendon Street, Oxford OX2 6DP

Oxford University Press is a department of the University of Oxford.
It furthers the University's objective of excellence in research, scholarship,
and education by publishing worldwide in

Oxford New York

Auckland Cape Town Dar es Salaam Hong Kong Karachi
Kuala Lumpur Madrid Melbourne Mexico City Nairobi
New Delhi Shanghai Taipei Toronto

With offices in

Argentina Austria Brazil Chile Czech Republic France Greece
Guatemala Hungary Italy Japan Poland Portugal Singapore
South Korea Switzerland Thailand Turkey Ukraine Vietnam

Oxford is a registered trade mark of Oxford University Press
in the UK and in certain other countries

Published in the United States
by Oxford University Press Inc., New York

British Library Cataloguing in Publication Data

Data available

Library of Congress Cataloging in Publication Data

Data available

Typeset by SPI Publisher Services, Pondicherry, India
Printed in Great Britain
on acid-free paper by
MPG Books Group, Bodmin and King's Lynn

ISBN 978-0-19-956784-3

1 3 5 7 9 10 8 6 4 2

Acknowledgements

A book that seeks to tell the story of unique institutions faces many challenges and ultimately depends on the help, advice, and cooperation of many. We are happy to acknowledge them here and to express our thanks to the many individuals whose contributions can be seen on virtually every page of this book.

This research on citizen assemblies started out as a single case study of what first appeared as a British Columbian experiment, but then expanded as it was replicated in the Netherlands and then Ontario, Canada. That resulted in the growth of our research team – to its considerable advantage – and to the time devoted to it. Thus, three of us expected to produce a provincial case study in 2006 or 2007, but five of us are now finishing a more complex and, we think, richer comparative study years later.

Our greatest obligation is to the 406 remarkable citizens who were members of the British Columbia (BC), Dutch, and Ontario citizen assemblies. They allowed us to observe them and agreed to fill out questionnaires – on thirteen separate occasions in British Columbia! – so that we could build a record of what they were thinking, saying, and doing throughout the phases of the assembly processes. They were acutely aware that these assemblies were making history and wanted to do so in a fashion that was transparent and subject to critical examination. Members wished that those who followed would learn from their experience. We hope that this book is faithful to those ambitions. We also hope that it demonstrates our admiration of these fellow citizens.

The chairs and staffs of the assemblies were responsible for establishing the institutional framework that allowed them to operate. In each case, their support for our ongoing research of their work was necessary and always freely given. It is perhaps invidious to single out any one in particular from these remarkable teams, but we would be churlish not to acknowledge, and thank again, Jack Blaney and Leo Perra in British Columbia, Jan van Schagen and Jacobine Geel in the Netherlands, and George Thomson in Ontario. They were always willing to take time from their onerous leadership responsibilities to support our research and we thank them, and their staff, for it.

Several other individuals deserve thanks for the special role they played in the development of the assemblies and our study of them. Gordon Gibson has rightly been recognized and celebrated as the designer of the citizen assembly. His insistence that they must be public, open, and transparent ensured that they would be accessible to researchers (as well as to fellow citizens). His gracious and reflective responses to all our questions have also improved our understanding. Campbell Sharman, a colleague at the University of British Columbia (UBC), was a major partner in developing the first (British Columbia) assembly programme, which proved the prototype for the others, and was a major support as we developed this research. David Farrell came to each of the assemblies as a visiting expert and author of its basic reference work (which was translated into Dutch for the Netherlands' assembly). We hope he has survived the autograph line-ups members subjected him to, a problem few textbook authors face. It was fitting testimony to the contribution his work made to the learning phase of the assemblies. In addition, his constant encouragements steered the manuscript to completion. Amy Lang came to the first British Columbia assembly meeting as a curious new sociology graduate student from the University of Wisconsin. Fascinated by her fellow Canadians' commitment to making deliberative democracy work, she decided to make it the focus of her PhD, staying through to the end, and then moving to watch and record the Ontario assembly, where she offered ongoing advice to the Ontario Secretariat.

Our understanding and interpretation of the citizen assemblies have been stimulated and enhanced by the work of others. Both Amy Lang and Bob Ratner were early observers and analysts of the British Columbia assembly. They were followed by Mark Warren and Hilary Pearse of the UBC who organized and led an international workshop to consider the BC experiment. Their work resulted in a rich edited collection entitled *Designing Deliberative Democracy*, and Warren has since collaborated with Archon Fung in the development of the *Participedia.com* website. Three members of the British Columbia assembly have written books about their experience from different perspectives. Jack MacDonald's *Randomocracy: A Citizen's Guide to Electoral Reform in British Columbia* explains just what and how the assembly set out to do and then why it came to its decisions; R.B. Herath's *Real Power to Real People: A Novel Approach to Electoral Reform in British Columbia* provides a detailed blow-by-blow account of what members went through; while Chuck Walker's *The Citizens' Assembly: Learning to Love BC-STV* offers a cartoonist's wickedly satirical account of his experience as an assembly member.

This book rests heavily on a number of different data sets. These include a number of surveys of the assembly members conducted across the distinctive phases of the assemblies' activities. Originally designed by Blais, Carty, and Fournier in British Columbia, they were subsequently replicated as completely as possible in the Netherlands and Ontario with the enthusiastic collaboration of Van der Kolk and Rose. In British Columbia, much of the independent administration and data collection was organized by Joel Schapiro of *Advanture Consulting*; in Ontario by Gail Motsi of the *Institute on Governance*; and in the Netherlands by Van der Kolk, administratively supported by Brinkman and financially supported by the Ministry of the Interior and Kingdom Relations. We record our thanks for their careful cooperation and the high standards of their work. Data on public opinion were collected to compare it with the views of the assembly members as well as to track the referendum campaigns and decision-making. Fred Cutler and Richard Johnston of the UBC were key collaborators in the design and analysis of this material. Cutler's contribution to this part of the project was so instrumental that he rightly deserves co-author credit for Chapter 8. The fieldwork was conducted by the Institute for Social Research at York University, under the direction of David Northrup, and was financed by the Canada Research Chair in Electoral Studies (at the Université de Montréal), several of the author's research grants from the Social Sciences and Humanities Research Council of Canada, and by the Centre for the Study of Democratic Institutions at UBC. Data on media coverage of the Canadian assemblies and referendum campaigns were collected by Stuart Soroka and his research team at the McGill Media Observatory, and in the Netherlands by Akkerman and Van Santen of the University of Amsterdam. We are deeply indebted to all, for without their help and belief that this data would be critical in developing a systematic account of citizen assemblies, it would not have been possible to write this book.

Preliminary versions of many of the analyses and observations in this book were initially rehearsed at a number of professional meetings organized by the American, Canadian, and Dutch Political Science Associations, the European Consortium for Political Research, as well as a host of public gatherings in North America and abroad. Early versions of several chapters were presented at a major international conference on the three citizen assemblies organized by Amy Lang for the Centre for the Study of Democratic Institutions at the UBC. In all cases, we benefited greatly from the questions, criticisms, and suggestions of those participating. Special mention goes to Stuart Soroka who, besides asking the first author at the end of each and every day during a fruitful sabbatical at McGill 'So, is the book finished?', graciously agreed to read the entire manuscript and provide invaluable feedback.

In addition, the authors acknowledge the Dutch Science Foundation (grant 311-99-006), the Fonds québécois de la recherche sur la société et la culture, and the Social Sciences and Humanities Research Council of Canada for their financial support, which enabled us to write this book.

Readers need to know that some of the authors are not simply observers and analysts of these assemblies. Many were, in different ways, intimately involved in the design, conduct, and work of the assemblies. Carty was initially seconded from the UBC to be the Director of Research for the BC assembly. In that role, he was directly responsible for creating and delivering the learning phase and facilitating the deliberative phase, but in fact he was involved in every aspect of the assembly from beginning to end as a key member of its leadership team. He subsequently consulted on the design and operation of the other two assemblies which he visited and spoke to. Rose was recruited from Queen's University to serve as Academic Director at the Ontario assembly where he led and directed the learning phase process and was deeply involved in the deliberative phase when assembly members constructed their recommended electoral system. Van der Kolk was one of the principal political science instructors involved in the learning phase of the Dutch assembly. All three appreciate the willingness of their universities to free them for that intensive involvement. Blais also spoke to the British Columbia and Ontario assemblies as an invited expert, focusing on the determinants of electoral turnout. All this involvement raised challenges for ensuring our analysis is as objective as possible, and we can only say we have been conscious of it at every stage of the research. Readers will judge how successful we have been. To aid in those efforts, we are happy to make the survey data available for anyone interested in secondary analysis.

Writing a book with four co-authors – some of whom are working in two other languages – is both difficult and rewarding. Each of us took initial responsibility for drafting different portions but, like a coalition cabinet, we assume collective responsibility for the total product.

And lastly, but certainly not least, our families have lived with us as we have lived with these assemblies since 2003. We thank them all for their forbearance and support, for this has been an experience which, as both citizens and scholars, we would not have missed for the world.

Table of Contents

List of Tables

List of Figures

List of Abbreviations

BC	British Columbia
BCCAER	British Columbia Citizens' Assembly on Electoral Reform
MMP	Mixed member proportional
OCAER	Ontario Citizens' Assembly on Electoral Reform
PR	Proportional representation
SMP	Single member plurality
STV	Single transferable vote

1

Power to the People?

And yet the reasons are utterly ludicrous which [the many] give in confirmation of their own notions about the honourable and good. Did you ever hear any of them which were not?

> Plato, *The Republic: Book VI* ($\approx$380 BCE)

(. . .) if the people are not utterly degraded, although individually they may be worse judges than those who have special knowledge – as a body they are as good or better.
Aristotle, *Politics: Book III* ($\approx$330 BCE)

And those people should not be listened to who keep saying the voice of the people is the voice of God, since the riotousness of the crowd is always very close to madness.

> Alcuin of York, letter to Charlemagne (798)

But as regards prudence and stability, I say that the people are more prudent and stable, and have better judgment than a prince; and it is not without good reason that it is said, 'The voice of the people is the voice of God'.
Niccolò Machiavelli, *Discourses on Titus Livius* (1531)

The voice of the people has been said to be the voice of God; and however generally this maxim has been quoted and believed, it is not true in fact. The people are turbulent and changing; they seldom judge or determine right.

> Alexander Hamilton, speech at the Constitutional Convention (1787)

(. . .) governments are more or less republican as they have more or less of the element of popular election and control in their composition; and believing as I do that the mass of the citizens is the safest depository of their own rights, (. . .) I am a friend to that composition of government which has in it the most of this ingredient.
Thomas Jefferson, letter to John Taylor (1816)

> The biggest argument against democracy is a five-minute discussion with the average voter.
>
> Sir Winston Churchill

The ultimate rulers of our democracy are not a president and senators and congressmen and government officials, but the voters of this country.
Franklin D. Roosevelt

> If the right people don't have power do you know what happens? The wrong people get it; politicians, councillors, ordinary voters. / But aren't they supposed to in a democracy? / This is a British democracy. / How do you mean? / British democracy recognizes that you need a system to protect the important things of life and keep them out of the hands of the barbarians.
>
> Sir Humphrey Appleby / Bernard Woolley, *Yes Prime Minister* (1988)

Listen, strange women lying in ponds distributing swords is no basis for a system of government. Supreme executive power derives from a mandate from the masses, not from some farcical aquatic ceremony.
Dennis (to King Arthur), *Monty Python and the Holy Grail* (1975)

Throughout human history, political thinkers, observers, and practitioners have debated the competence of citizens. The claims cited above illustrate the different perspectives of both ancient and modern philosophers (or philosophizers) on the capacity of ordinary people to make enlightened political decisions. In a letter written after his presidency, Thomas Jefferson observed that men naturally divide into two camps. On the one hand, there are those 'who fear and distrust the people, and wish to draw all powers from them into the hands of the higher classes' (Jefferson 1824). That view is exemplified by the citations that line up on the right side above. It sees the public as emotional, impulsive, thoughtless, selfish, deceitful, fickle, easily fooled, mistake-prone, cruel, violent, and fundamentally dangerous. Plato advanced this perspective in *The Republic*, comparing the affairs of state in democratic Athens with the state of affairs on a nautical vessel:

> Imagine then a fleet or a ship in which there is a captain who is taller and stronger than any of the crew, but he is a little deaf and has a similar infirmity in sight, and his knowledge of navigation is not much better. The sailors are quarrelling with one another about the steering – everyone is of opinion that he has a right to steer, though he has never learned the art of navigation and cannot tell who taught him or when he learned, and will further assert that it cannot be taught, and they are ready to cut in pieces anyone who says the contrary. They throng about the captain, begging and praying him to commit the helm to them; and if at any time they do not prevail, but others are

preferred to them, they kill the others or throw them overboard, and having first chained up the noble captain's senses with drink or some narcotic drug, they mutiny and take possession of the ship and make free with the stores; thus, eating and drinking, they proceed on their voyage in such manner as might be expected of them.

On the other hand, there are those 'who identify themselves with the people, have confidence in them, cherish and consider them as the most honest and safe' (Jefferson 1824). This more positive, or optimistic, view is reflected by the citations on the left side of the dialogue above. It considers people to possess the virtues of decency, honesty, justice, prudence, reliability, resourcefulness, trustworthiness, and wisdom. In his treatise on *Politics*, Aristotle disagreed with his mentor because he focused on the qualities of citizens as a collective rather than as individuals:

> The rule of many is upon the whole the best solution of these difficulties. The people, taken collectively, though composed of ordinary individuals, have more virtue and wisdom than any single man among them. As the feast to which many contribute is better than the feast given by one, as the judgement of the many at the theatre is truer than the judgement of one, as a good man and a fair work of art have many elements of beauty or goodness combined in them; so the assembly of the people has more good sense and wisdom than any individual member of it.

The relative power of these two strands of thought has varied over time, but they have continually coexisted. The pessimistic view dominated until the eighteenth and nineteenth centuries. Prior to this era, it was simply inconceivable to grant the population the opportunity to make important social decisions. Consequently, more than two millennia would pass after the Athenian democratic experience before popular sovereignty would re-emerge as a viable political alternative. And when democracy reappeared, it did so in a more limited fashion. For instance, a continuing ambivalence about the public's capacity led America's founding fathers to restrain the influence of the populace. Thus, they conferred the right to vote only on male landowners. Also, by dividing power among three distinct levels (executive, legislative, and judiciary), they sought to minimize the possibility that authorities would be swayed by the madness of the masses. And to this day, American citizens do not vote directly for the country's head of state and government – they instead vote for electors who then formally select the president.

These opposing visions about the competence of citizens still shape debates today, although the nature and tone of the exchanges have evolved. The more optimistic tradition carries on, now using a language different from that of Aristotle or Machiavelli. Contemporary scholars with this view generally recognize that most citizens are not politically sophisticated: they are sparsely interested, attentive, and informed about politics. These facts have, after all, been established incontrovertibly (Converse 1964; Luskin 1987; Delli Carpini and Keeter 1996; Fournier 2002). Nevertheless, public wisdom is possible because of two processes. At the individual level, citizens can take advantage of decisional heuristics –

affective and cognitive shortcuts and cues which allow them to simplify political choices and reach correct decisions (Lodge et al. 1989, 1995; Popkin 1991; Sniderman et al. 1991; Lupia 1994; Lupia and McCubbins 1998). At the collective level, aggregating individual opinions together tends to eliminate random off-setting errors and fluctuations and to capture the public's true sensible preferences (Miller 1986; Page and Shapiro 1992; Erikson et al. 2002). Book titles by authors that perpetuate this strand of thought are quite telling: *The Reasoning Voter*, *Reasoning and Choice*, *The Rational Public*, and *Motivated Political Reasoning*.[1] Indeed, Samuel Popkin puts the position bluntly by concluding: 'voters actually do reason about parties, candidates, and issues. They have premises, and they use those premises to make inferences from their observations of the world around them. They think about who and what political parties stand for; they think about what government can and should do. And the performance of government, parties, and candidates affects their assessments and preferences' (1991: 7).

Arguments from the more pessimistic side no longer call into question the legitimacy of popular sovereignty. Rather, they emphasize the biases and errors in public political decisions. Evidence shows that 'various and sometimes severe distortions can occur in people's political judgements. They hold inaccurate and stereotyped factual beliefs, hold their beliefs overconfidently, resist correct information, prefer easy arguments, interpret elite statements according to racial or other biases, and rely heavily on scanty information about a candidate's policy positions' (Kuklinski and Quirk 2000: 179). The result is that individuals and collectives make political choices which differ from the ones they would have made had they been informed (Bartels 1996; Delli Carpini and Keeter 1996; Althaus 1998, 2003; Luskin et al. 2002; Fournier 2006; Blais et al. 2009). And since elections and public opinion have an impact on the conduct of public policy (Blais et al. 1993, 1996; Erikson et al. 2002; Soroka and Wlezien 2010), there are real repercussions of this poor decision-making for democratic governance.

1.1 HOW CAN WE SHED SOME LIGHT ON THE POLITICAL COMPETENCE OF CITIZENS?

Debates about the competence of citizens have persisted over several thousand years, and they are unlikely to disappear overnight. In part, this resilience reflects the fundamentally ontological nature of the debate; where one sits and the

---

[1] These titles are half a world away from Gustave Le Bon's assertion, at the dawn of the twentieth century, that 'the arguments [crowds] employ and those which are capable of influencing them are, from a logical point of view, of such an inferior kind that it is only by way of analogy that they can be described as reasoning' (1896).

premises brought to the table largely determine how one reads the argument (Sniderman et al. 1991: 17).

This book proposes a different approach, one that is decidedly empirical. It looks as closely as possible at what ordinary citizens actually do when they are given the opportunity to make important political decisions. We recognize that situations where people play an influential role are rather unusual. However, such occasions are extremely revealing, providing us with important evidence about the inherent potential and limitations of citizens.

Modern democracies use representative institutions, so that the population does not exercise political power directly. Rather, the people designate representatives who govern in their name. Voters bestow their confidence, in a temporary and reversible fashion, on a group of delegates who are chosen via open competitive elections. It is those elected officials who determine which policies are established, modified, or abolished. Thus, citizens play a relatively small role in policymaking. They are sometimes consulted through various mechanisms, but their contribution to the legislative process remains limited. Even during a referendum, people can only accept or decline a proposal, they rarely control what is proposed. Furthermore, a person's single vote will not change the outcome of an election or a referendum.

Given that the stakes are so low, it makes sense for citizens to invest little time and effort in political matters (Downs 1957). However, the implicit assumption behind this logic seems to be that given a real chance to make a difference, people could and would live up to the challenge. But is that assumption valid? Are citizens more engaged and competent when they are offered a chance to play a decisive role in political decision-making? This question is quite possibly the central query in representative democratic thought.

Answering this question has not been possible because, in the absence of cases where citizens could contribute decisively to the development of public policy, we have lacked appropriate evidence. The situation has now changed. Three unprecedented democratic experiments have recently taken place. Instead of just voting, sanctioning, chastising, or being consulted, individual citizens were given the chance to spend a year developing a new political institution. Between 2004 and 2007, citizen assemblies on electoral reform were established in British Columbia, the Netherlands, and Ontario. In all three instances, governments entrusted a group of randomly selected citizens with the independent responsibility to design their political community's electoral system. In the two Canadian cases, the recommendations were the subject of a binding public referendum; in the Dutch case, the recommendation was delivered to the government.

Citizen assemblies are interesting stories in and of themselves. More significantly, they provide valuable insight into key questions about citizen competence and democratic politics. Under such extraordinary circumstances, the stakes are much higher than usual. Assembly participants had the opportunity to decisively influence politics. Do citizens behave differently in such a context? Do people get politically motivated and active? Does only a very interested group get involved?

Are the participants transformed in the process? Can citizens take reasonable policy decisions? Are they influenced by inappropriate factors? Can the larger public and political elites accept reforms designed by ordinary people? These are the kinds of questions that we address in this book.

1.2 HOW DID THE CITIZEN ASSEMBLIES WORK?

Only three citizen assemblies have been established up to this point. All three dealt with electoral system reform. All three involved similar processes. But each came to a different conclusion about what electoral system should be implemented in their respective jurisdictions. This section provides an overview of these citizen

TABLE 1.1 *Outline of the Three Citizen Assemblies on Electoral Reform*

	British Columbia	The Netherlands	Ontario
No. of participants	160	143 (140)	103
Gender split	50/50	50/50	50/50
Selection phase	Pool drawn randomly from voters' list; interested people signify their interest; participants picked randomly among interested		
Learning phase	Home study + 6 weekends (Jan.–Mar.'04)	Home study + 6 weekends (Mar.–June'06)	Home study + 6 weekends (Sep.–Nov.'06)
Consultation phase	50 public hearings, 1600 submissions (May–June'04)	18 public hearings, 1400 submissions (May–June'06)	41 public hearings, 1000 submissions (Oct.'06–Jan.'07)
Deliberation phase	6 weekends (Sep.–Nov.'04)	4 weekends (Sep.–Nov.'06)	6 weekends (Feb.–Apr.'07)
No. of meeting days	>26*	>20*	>24*
Existing system	SMP	List-PR	SMP
Reform proposal	STV	List-PR (change of details)	MMP
Destination of recommendation	Binding public referendum (May'05/May'09)	Report to government (Nov.'06)	Binding public referendum (Oct.'07)
Outcome	Narrowly failed/ failed decisively	Proposal rejected	Failed decisively

* The total number of work days depended on the number of public meetings attended by members (they generally attended several). Note that this total does not include days spent at home on reading, study, and research.

assemblies. Basic information about the process and the outcomes is presented in summary fashion in Table 1.1.

1.2.1 The British Columbia Citizens' Assembly on Electoral Reform[2]

The first citizen assembly was initiated with the unanimous support of the British Columbia legislature. Potential members were chosen at random from the voters' list and contacted by mail. They were asked to indicate their willingness to take part in the process and to attend an information meeting. Thus, self-selection was clearly part of the selection process. Among interested participants, one man and one woman were picked for each electoral district, literally drawn from a hat: seventy-nine men, seventy-nine women.[3] These individuals came from various backgrounds, ethnic communities, and occupations. They were given a clear and precise mandate: the assembly could recommend maintaining the existing electoral system (single member plurality) or propose the adoption of any other system (even one not in use). If the assembly came to the conclusion that a new system should be put in place, it was to formulate a specific reform proposal which would be submitted to the population for approval in a referendum. If the public agreed with the proposal, the new electoral system would take effect by the following election. Thus, the assembly had real power; its recommendation would be put directly to the electorate, and it could not be shelved even if the government was not happy with it.

To accomplish these responsibilities, a three-phase year-long process was designed and implemented. The first phase was learning. Typical of ordinary citizens, assembly members knew very little about electoral systems at the start of the whole process. They were assigned reading material and received a six-weekend crash-course on electoral systems in Vancouver during the first months of 2004. Lectures and discussions occurred in plenary and small-group sessions. The second phase was consultation. Fifty public hearings, each attended by four to sixteen different assembly members, were held across the province. Anyone could come and argue for or against any electoral system. In addition, a website was set up to encourage public proposals for reform and 1600 proposals were received from all over the world. At the end of those public consultations, members held another weekend session to share, digest, and discuss what they had heard. Finally, there was a deliberation phase. It consisted of six weekends in the fall. Members first identified their core values, the key features they believed an electoral system should

---

[2] A detailed description can be found in the technical report of the British Columbia assembly (BCCAER 2004). For accounts by members, see Herath (2007), MacDonald (2005), and Walker (2005). Warren and Pearse (2008) provide an academic analysis of the assembly.

[3] One man and woman from British Columbia's aboriginal communities were subsequently selected when it was discovered that none had emerged through the regular district-level process.

contain. This set of values narrowed the list of potential systems to consider. They were left with single member plurality (SMP; the current 'first past the post' system), and two alternatives: single transferable vote (STV), and mixed member proportional (MMP).[4] Members then spent two weekends constructing detailed models of the alternate systems they thought might be appropriate for the province. Finally, they debated the merits of their alternatives in comparison with the existing process and decided that the STV was the best electoral system for the province.

The referendum on the assembly's proposal took place on 17 May 2005 at the time of the provincial general election. The legislature had previously set two thresholds for success: 60 per cent support province-wide, with a majority in 60 per cent of constituencies. Following a campaign where party competition for office overshadowed discussion of the reform proposal, the referendum did not clear one of the two bars. STV garnered a majority in 97 per cent of constituencies (all but two districts), but was supported by only 58 per cent of the voters province-wide. Sensing the assembly's recommendation might not have benefited from a complete debate, the government decided to hold another referendum on the same proposal on 12 May 2009, again coinciding with a provincial election. This time, STV failed decidedly: receiving 39 per cent across the province, with a majority in no more than 9 per cent of the districts.

1.2.2 The Netherlands' Electoral System Civic Forum (Burgerforum)[5]

The Dutch *Burgerforum* was the second citizen assembly. The *Burgerforum* was comprised of 143 individuals, drawn from a group of 1732 who self-selected themselves from a random pool of 50,400 invited eligible voters. While clearly inspired by the British Columbia innovation, the Dutch assembly compressed their schedule of activities into nine months from March to November 2006. The learning phase on electoral systems was spread over six weekends (in The Hague and Zeist), and it overlapped a public consultation phase which involved eighteen local meetings in May and June. Four weekends in the fall were then dedicated to the decision-making phase.

This was the only citizen assembly for which an SMP electoral system did not represent the status quo. Elections in the Netherlands are conducted under (semi-) open-list proportional representation (list-PR). Rather early in their deliberation phase, the Dutch assembly opted to retain the same type of system, so most

[4] STV is a form of preferential PR where voters are able to rank order as many candidates as they choose in electoral districts that return more than one candidate to the legislature. MMP is a mixed system that typically gives electors two votes, one for a local candidate in an SMP component, and one for a list of party candidates that is then used to compensate for the lack of proportionality in the SMP part of the system. For an accessible description of these options, see Appendix 1 and Farrell (2001).

[5] A detailed description can be found in the technical report of the *Burgerforum* (2006 proces verslag; also available in English on the DVD that accompanied the final proposal).

discussions turned on potential (if substantial) modifications to it. In the system ultimately recommended, voters would still cast one vote, either for a specific candidate from one of the party lists (as currently) or for a party list. Under the proposal, citizen preferences would exert increased influence over which list candidates get elected, since votes for specific individuals would garner more weight than they currently do. The assembly also proposed a revision to the method by which residual seats are allocated.

The *Burgerforum*'s set of recommendations was not presented to the population in a binding referendum. Rather, it was submitted to a new government, elected while the assembly was working. On 18 April 2008, the State Secretary of the Interior and Kingdom Relations sent a letter to parliament, stating that the government would not implement the proposal of the citizen assembly.

1.2.3 The Ontario Citizens' Assembly on Electoral Reform[6]

The Ontarian experience mirrored the pattern set in British Columbia. The selection process combined randomness with self-selection. The learning phase hinged around six residential weekends in Toronto during the fall of 2006. The consultation phase relied on public meetings and written submissions. And the deliberation phase, in the spring of 2007, saw the assembly identify its objectives, construct two alternative electoral systems, and then come to a decision. The Ontario gender-balanced assembly was the smallest of the three: it contained 103 citizens, one for each of the provincial legislature's electoral districts.

After examining all options, this assembly's shortlist contained the same electoral systems as British Columbia's: SMP (the status quo), STV, and MMP (the two alternatives). Ontario citizen assembly members, however, opted to recommend MMP. The particular version of MMP they designed would give voters two votes, one for a local district candidate (this SMP component filling 70 per cent of the seats) and one for a political party (this component to allocate the remaining 30 per cent of the seats).

This reform proposal was also the subject of a binding referendum in October 2007, held at the time of a provincial general election. Again, the legislature had set a double threshold: 60 per cent of voter support across the entire province, and a majority in at least 60 per cent of districts. Neither was reached. Only 37 per cent voted in favour of the recommendation, and in only 5 ridings out of 107 did it garner a majority.

---

[6] For an extensive account, see the technical report (OCAER 2007*a*).

1.3 WHAT MADE THE CITIZEN ASSEMBLIES UNIQUE?

Citizen assemblies are intended to be instances of direct, participatory, and deliberative democracy. First of all, their design echoes one of the important institutions of
Athenian direct democracy from the sixth century BCE. The fundamental political
body in Athens was the *ecclesia* (assembly). All citizens in good standing – that is,
males with military training – could attend to vote on important decisions (e.g. war,
legislation, criminal trial). Meetings of the assembly were held regularly though not
frequently: once a month initially, and up to once a week during the fourth century
BCE. The day-to-day operations of government, however, were managed by a less
well-known institution: the *boule* (council). This council was composed of 400
individuals (later 500) who met on a daily basis. Council members were drawn by
lot among citizens who had declared themselves eligible by placing their name
written on a piece of pottery in a large designated jar. Mandates lasted for one year
and a person could serve twice during his lifetime. In compensation for absence
from their regular occupation, members of the *boule* were exempt from military
service for the year, and were paid for attendance. The council supervised the
republic's finances, bureaucracy, military resources, foreign relations, construction,
commerce, and social welfare. Most importantly, it prepared and wrote legislation
that would then be sanctioned by the assembly.

In many ways, modern citizen assemblies resemble the Athenian council much
more than their namesake. A citizen assembly and a *boule* both work for approximately one year, both are filled through a combination of self-selection and
randomness, both have members remunerated for their service to the community,
and both need to have their major recommendations approved (sometimes by the
wider electorate). Although modern citizen assemblies have fewer participants,
meet less frequently, and have narrower responsibilities than their ancient counterparts, the similarities are nevertheless striking.

Recent decades have witnessed the appearance of a myriad of projects associated
with participatory democracy. These mechanisms seek to augment public engagement and participation in decisions. One study inventoried over 100 different types
(Rowe and Frewer 2005), including citizen juries/*planungszelle*, consensus conferences, deliberative polls, and participatory budgeting. Citizen assemblies stand out as
constituting the most extensive modern form of collective decision-making by
common folk. It is the only method of citizen policymaking that combines all the
following characteristics: a relatively large group of ordinary people, lengthy periods
of learning and deliberation, and a collective decision with important political
consequences for an entire political system. Table 1.2 compares the main features
of the three citizen assemblies with the other principal participatory institutions.[7]

---

[7] For more detailed descriptions of these processes, see Crosby (1995), Crosby and Nethercut (2005)
on citizen juries; Dienel and Renn (1995), Hendriks (2005) on *planungszelle;* Joss and Durant (1995),
Hendriks (2005) on consensus conferences; Luskin et al. (2002), Fishkin and Luskin (2005) on
deliberative polls; and de Sousa Santos (1998), Cabannes (2004), Novy and Leubolt (2005) on
participatory budgeting. For a compilation of such institutions, see www.participedia.com.

TABLE 1.2 *Different Forms of Citizen Involvement*

	Citizen juries/*planungszelle*	Consensus conferences	Deliberative polls	Participatory budgeting	Citizen assemblies
Developed by (first instance)	Dienel (Ger.) Crosby (the United States, early 1970s)	Danish Board of Technology (1987)	James Fishkin (the United States 1994)	City of Porto Alegre, Brazil (1989)	Gordon Gibson (Canada 2002)
No. of citizens	12–26	10–18	100–360	30–50	103–160
No. of meetings	4–5 days	7–8 days	2–3 days	Varies, often quite intensive	20–30 days
Selection method	Random selection	Random + self-selection	Random selection	Election	Random + self-selection
Activities	Information + deliberation	Information + deliberation	Information + deliberation	Consultation + deliberation	Information + consultation + deliberation
Result	Collective position report	Collective position report	Survey opinions	Budgetary allocations	Detailed policy recommendation
Destination of proposal	Sponsor and mass media	Parliament and mass media	Sponsor and mass media	Local public officials	Government and public referendum

First, citizen assemblies involve more participants than most other forms of participatory democracy. For instance, citizen juries and consensus conferences typically consist of a dozen or two individuals. Around thirty to fifty elected delegates are actively involved throughout the participatory budget process.[8] Only deliberative polls have clearly exceeded the number of participants found in the assemblies.

Second, the length of learning and deliberation activities in citizen assemblies is unparalleled with proceedings spanning some nine to twelve months. Participants met for the equivalent of at least ten deliberative polls. As a result, citizen assembly members could rely on incomparable amounts of time for learning, discussion, and debate with many weeks available for each of these distinct tasks. Only participatory budgeting can rival citizen assemblies in terms of the number of meetings, but they rarely involve extensive learning activities.

Third, the three citizen assemblies had to collectively build a detailed institutional design from scratch. Rather than expressing individual preferences in a survey or voting on a set of predefined options as in deliberative polls, each assembly's membership had to reach a collective agreement on the concrete specifics of an electoral system.

Fourth, a citizen assembly proposal had important weight, both in terms of mandate and procedure. On the one hand, these three groups were entrusted with the responsibility to devise a cornerstone of representative democracies. Electoral systems have a crucial impact on the distribution of power by translating individual preferences expressed as votes into an allocation of seats in parliament that in turn determines which party or parties form the government. On the other hand, the assemblies' recommendations would be taken seriously. One was to go directly to the government, and the other two were to be the subject of a binding public referendum. Both the substance of the decision each assembly had to make and what would become of that decision were politically significant. Only cases of binding participatory budget decisions match the political relevance of citizen assemblies, though the two deal with quite different policies and polities: concrete budget allocations in local communities versus the institutional allocation of power during national and provincial elections.

Finally, unlike deliberative polls, assembly participants do not constitute a strictly random sample of the population. They are drawn randomly from among those who demonstrated interest within a random sample of voters. Citizen assembly architects presumed that it is very difficult to have people commit to such extended proceedings without some element of self-selection. Later, we will examine whether this matters or not.

Citizen assemblies are also exercises of deliberative democracy. Work in that area was developed by political theorists (e.g. Manin 1987; Cohen 1989, 1996;

---

[8] Participatory budgeting total tallies are often very impressive (up to 40,000 participants). But these numbers include everyone who attended a consultation meeting.

Habermas 1989, 1996; Dryzek 1990, 2000; Fishkin 1991, 1995; Gutmann and Thompson 1996, 2004; Elster 1998). Various real-world applications of the principles have included: conversations about public affairs among neighbours or co-workers (Mutz 2002, 2006; Cramer-Walsh 2003), discussions among naturally occurring groups such as town hall meetings (Mansbridge 1980) or school parent organizations (Rosenberg 2007), and experimental studies of exchanges and reflection in small groups of university students (Druckman and Nelson 2003; Druckman 2004; Mendelberg and Karpowitz 2007). Many of the contrasts we have noted between citizen assemblies and other participatory mechanisms apply equally to these examples of deliberative democracy. The deliberation practised by the citizen assemblies was of a much more considerable and decisive nature.

The three cases might be called 'deliberation-on-steroids'. They present the most favourable environment for deliberative effects. So our analyses should capture the maximum impacts of such processes. Moreover, citizen assemblies constitute a litmus test for the consequences of deliberation. If potential effects cannot be uncovered in these three extensive applications, then it would be difficult to imagine a context where they would manifest themselves.

1.4 WHAT QUESTIONS DO THE CITIZEN ASSEMBLY EXPERIENCES HELP US ANSWER?

This book deals with three unique real-life instances of ordinary people exercising decisive political power. These extraordinary experiments are fascinating in their own right. They can also help us to address some core questions in the study of democratic politics.

1.4.1 Why do governments delegate power to citizens?

Citizen assemblies, especially on the question of electoral reform, are exceptional occurrences. It is one thing for political parties and governments to grant citizens a say in institutional design, but it is quite another for them to give up control over the rules of the game by which they compete for their own livelihood. It may make sense for public officials to try to pass the buck when facing difficult, divisive, or unpopular choices. Letting people pick the electoral system does not. Doing so defies the dominant view that political parties seek to shape the electoral rules in order to maximize their seats and power (Benoit 2004; Colomer 2005; Pilet 2007; Blais and Shugart 2008). From that perspective, political parties should only support the establishment of an assembly if they anticipate gaining something from its recommendations. We are thus driven to consider the possibility that politicians are not solely motivated by seat maximization but also by ideological conceptions or ethical principles (Van der Kolk 2007; Bowler et al. 2008). Chapter 2 analyses both the reasons behind the existence of these citizen assemblies and their functioning. *Why did three governments decide to institute a citizen assembly? How did the assemblies work? Why were they organized in such a way? Were they set up to fail?*

1.4.2 How do the participants react to the process?

Chapter 2 also examines the overall reactions of the participants to the entire process. *Did they engage in the proceedings? Did they learn about the issues at hand?* If the stakes are indeed high and the deliberative process does work effectively, behaviour might well be different in citizen assemblies than in everyday political life. To begin with, assembly participants should be highly motivated to invest time and effort into the project and to do a good job. While free-riding might be the norm in politics as usual, a citizen assembly provides a strong set of incentives to get fully involved. Also, the assembly process provides ample opportunities to learn, think, and talk. Therefore, if motivation and opportunity are combined (Luskin 1990), the result should produce individuals with greater civic involvement and competence than normally observed.

1.4.3 Does it matter who does (and does not) participate?

No political activity entails universal participation. There are always people left standing on the sidelines, whether the behaviour is voting in an election, signing a petition, marching in a demonstration, becoming a member of a political party, joining a community or protest group, working for a campaign, or being elected as a delegate for constituents. Participation varies both in terms of scope and sources of exclusion. The first variation is obvious: the proportion of citizens who vote is vastly superior to the proportion who become members of a legislature. The second variation speaks to the reasons for abstention: people do not participate because they do not want to (they lack interest), because they cannot (they lack time and/or money), because they were not asked (they lack an opening), or various combinations of all these (Verba et al. 1995). The consequence is a socio-economic participation divide: research indicates that participants tend to be more educated, more wealthy, and older (Wolfinger and Rosenstone 1980; Blais 2000; Putnam 2000). Most importantly, this unequal participation results in biased representation and responsiveness (Downs 1957; Verba et al. 1995; Bartels 2008). Consequently, authorities disproportionately hear and respond to relatively privileged citizens.

When a real-world deliberative democracy experiment is attempted, the organizers generally take great strides to minimize obstacles to participation and to maximize representativeness. They can offer monetary incentives and compensations to offset potential losses of income, and childcare services to free-up parents' schedules. However, one difficulty is never fully surmountable: self-selection. All deliberative processes involve some self-selection, even those identified as relying on random selection (Table 1.2). Deliberative polls try to convince all their potential participants contacted by telephone to take part in the weekend activities, but everyone is free to decline and many in fact do. In citizen assemblies, self-selection was even more extensive. Invitations to information meetings were distributed randomly and participants were drawn randomly among those interested, but, as in Athens, no one was offered a position unless they had expressed their interest. Is self-selection problematic for deliberative democracy?

We probe the role that self-selection and the resulting degree of representativeness played in our three cases. *How well did citizen assemblies represent the voting age populations? Were their socio-demographic traits, attitudes, and behaviours similar? Was the outcome dictated by the composition of each assembly? Were participants biased against the status quo? Did they favour one particular option from the start?* These questions are explored in Chapter 3.

1.4.4 How good are citizens' political judgements?

In their natural habitat, citizens' opinions exhibit instability, incoherence, and even whimsicality. First, individual opinions often fluctuate greatly over time (Converse 1964; Feldman 1989; Zaller and Feldman 1992). If one asks a person a question one day, and then repeats the same question a few weeks or months later, one is likely to obtain different answers, even on central and salient issues. People appear to respond randomly, as though they were 'flipping a coin' (Converse 1964: 243).[9] Second, individual opinions are also weakly structured (Converse 1964; Butler and Stokes 1974; Luskin 1987; Kinder 1998). There is a lack of empirical consistency across conceptually related attitudes of the same level (e.g. issue positions), and between conceptually related attitudes of different levels (e.g. values and issue positions). Elites may have structured belief systems, but John and Jane Q. Public rarely do.[10] Finally, the public's collective opinion, while allegedly more stable and reasonable, can sometimes be swayed dramatically by transient factors. Why should support for spending on defence increase during international crises (Page and Shapiro 1992: ch. 6)? Why should president Bush's

---

[9] Debates do persist about whether the instability is attributable to the nature of respondents' attitudes (Converse 1970, 1980; Luskin 1987; Zaller 1992) or of their measurement (Achen 1975; Erikson 1979; Judd and Milburn 1980; Ansolabehere et al. 2008), but evidence of individual instability remains ubiquitous.

[10] Again, objections have tended to focus on the role of measurement error (Judd and Milburn 1980; Hurwitz and Peffley 1985, 1987; Ansolabehere et al. 2008). Nevertheless, the dominant position is that incoherence in political opinions is rampant among the citizenry.

job performance rating jump by a whopping 40 percentage points in the days following 9/11?[11] Why should governments be punished for acts of nature such as droughts, floods, and shark attacks (Achen and Bartels 2002)? Why should a person's mood affect his evaluations of political candidates (Ottati et al. 1989)? The sensitivity of opinions to changes in context is often understandable, but 'not necessarily rational' (Kuklinski and Quirk 2000: 161).[12]

In citizen assemblies, developed opinions should be of higher quality. This improvement hinges on the competence that participants are expected to attain during the process. If assembly members become informed and sophisticated, then their views should also exhibit greater stability, coherence, and steadfastness. These expectations stem from research which 'suggests that more-informed citizens (. . .) are more likely to hold stable opinions over time (. . .), are more likely to hold opinions that are ideologically consistent with each other (. . .), and are less likely to change their opinions in the face of new but tangential or misleading information (. . .) but more likely to change in the face of new relevant or compelling information' (Delli Carpini 2005: 35).

In this book, we thoroughly investigate the quality of opinions in citizen assemblies. Chapter 4 examines the dynamics of preferences relating to electoral systems during the almost year-long proceedings. *When did preferences develop and crystallize? How did they evolve over time? Was there individual and collective volatility? Was movement driven by sensible forces?* Then, in Chapter 5, we turn our attention to the structure of individual and collective decisions reached by the assemblies. *Were preferences consistent with members' values and objectives? Did the level of consistency improve over time? Was consistency only present among the most informed participants? Did the assemblies make reasonable decisions?* Lastly, in Chapter 6, we consider the possibility that the assemblies were affected by external influences. *Did lobbying from political parties determine the outcome? Were assemblies influenced by biases of the expert teaching staff or the chair? Did they simply follow the advice expressed by the public during consultations? Were they coerced by a few persuasive assembly members?* Together, these three chapters ascertain the degree of competence exhibited by citizen decision-making in extensive deliberative processes.

---

[11] This type of reaction, labelled a rally-around-the-flag effect, frequently occurs when a country is attacked or commits its troops to combat (Mueller 1973, 1994). As the personification of the nation, the leader suddenly merits new respect and moral support. While this effect has been specified and explained, it nevertheless constitutes a blatant overreaction to events.

[12] In a similar vein, the construction of the questionnaire – the format, formulation, and order of items – can have a substantial influence on responses (Schuman and Presser 1981; Schwarz and Sudman 1992; Tourangeau et al. 2000). The survey does not simply measure crystallized opinions, it also shapes them.

1.4.5 Does participation produce better citizens?

Advocates of deliberative democracy have made interesting arguments about the consequences of political participation and deliberation (Pateman 1970; Thompson 1970; Mansbridge 1999; Gastil 2000; Morrell 2005). The claim is that they can improve citizens. Participation, particularly the more demanding forms, ought to develop social virtues such as democratic character, political awareness, political efficacy, a sense of cooperation, and a sense of community. However, empirical analysis of the effects of participatory and deliberative activities is limited and provides mixed findings. Evidence from deliberative polls indicates that people who take part do become more efficacious, sociotropic, and trusting (Fishkin and Luskin 1999; Luskin and Fishkin 2002). Conversations with diverse social networks enhance broadmindedness and tolerance (Mutz 2002, 2006). But the idea that election and campaign activities increase political efficacy has only been partially supported (Finkel 1985, 1987). And there are those who seriously question the impacts of such processes. Hibbing and Theiss-Morse (2002) argue that the positive effects of participating and deliberating are actually mostly limited to instances when substantial agreement already exists. Indeed, during 'normal' political circumstances, the effects may be negative, rendering participants infuriated and antagonistic.

Chapter 7 asks whether or not participation in a citizen assembly fosters citizenship. We determine the actual impact of involvement in this most intense deliberative process on various attitudes and values unrelated to the narrower question of electoral system preferences. *Did assembly members become more interested in politics, more active in politics, more civic-minded, more open-minded, more tolerant, and more trusting?* If the participants' views were not systematically transformed during the almost year-long proceedings, then the claims of beneficial and/or detrimental effects are probably tenuous.

1.4.6 Can uninformed citizens, political parties, and governments trust informed citizens?

Traditional systems of representative democracy are thought to be suffering from crises of legitimacy. People are experiencing political malaise: they express greater distrust of governmental institutions and authorities (Nevitte 1996; Nye et al. 1997; Norris, 1999; Pharr and Putnam, 2000; Hibbing and Theiss-Morse 2001, 2002; Dalton 2004), and engage less in various forms of political participation (Blais 2000; Gray and Caul 2000; Putnam 2000; Franklin 2004). While the sources of this political discontent and apathy have not been clearly identified, these symptoms have been documented as increasing over the last decades across various countries around the world.

Part of the rationale for embracing participatory and deliberative democracy is to inject some popular legitimacy into policymaking (e.g. Cohen 1989; Habermas

1996; Dryzek 2001; Gutmann and Thompson 2004). Yet the impact of the three citizen assemblies is questionable, for while they generated three different reform proposals, none were implemented. In the two Canadian cases, the proposals did not pass the referendum requirements set by the legislature; and the Dutch government simply ignored the other. Why? Should we conclude that citizen assemblies are bound to fail?

Chapter 8 explores how the assemblies' decisions were received by key political actors (governments, political parties, interest groups, media, and the public) in an attempt to account for their lack of success. *Were voters unaware that 'ordinary citizens' had proposed the reforms? Were they suspicious of the assembly's legitimacy? Did the public fear change? Did politicians try to undermine the endeavour? Did the media ignore or attack the citizen assembly and its recommendation?* We need to answer these questions to ascertain the value of citizen decision-making as a political tool.

1.4.7 Whether, when, and how should we let citizens decide?

The final chapter ties everything together. It returns to the general theoretical themes outlined in this section. We review and expand the insights provided by the various chapters about the logic and limits of power sharing, the benefits and pitfalls of participation, and the competence of citizens. The lessons that emerge are relevant for scholars and students interested in electoral systems, deliberation, public policy, institutions, political behaviour, and democracy.

1.5 WHAT DATA DO WE USE TO ANSWER OUR QUESTIONS?

Our analyses rely on many sources of data (see Table 1.3). First, and most importantly, there are surveys of assembly members themselves. Participants in all three citizen assemblies were interviewed with self-completed pen and paper questionnaires on numerous occasions. Assembly members were surveyed thirteen separate times in British Columbia, five times in the Netherlands, and four times in Ontario. In each case, the interviews spanned the entire process, with a baseline questionnaire completed before members met for the first time, and a post-assembly survey after all the work had been accomplished. The surveys varied in length: some contained upwards of 200 items, while others were composed of only a few questions. They covered a host of values, attitudes, and opinions. Significantly, question wording and ordering were almost identical across the three cases. These surveys allow us to uncover what the participants of the citizen assemblies were thinking before, during, and after key moments of the proceedings. We use them throughout the book.

Content analyses of media coverage were conducted for all three cases. Every story in the main national and regional newspapers that mentioned electoral reform, electoral systems, or the citizen assembly was collected and coded. The British Columbia data spanned seven newspapers and seventeen months, the Ontario data covered ten newspapers and thirteen months, while the Dutch study included all major newspapers, some popular magazines, as well as some radio and television broadcasts over a period of sixteen months. All three studies encompass the entire assembly process (including the Canadian referendum campaigns). The Canadian content analyses were directed by Stuart Soroka at McGill University's Media Observatory, while the Dutch examination of media coverage was carried out by a research team at the University of Amsterdam (Akkerman and van Santen 2007). These data provide information about the reactions of stakeholders throughout the proceedings and about the messages to which referendum voters were exposed.

Since the ultimate fate of two of the assembly reform proposals hinged on the support of the population, we conducted public opinion surveys during the three Canadian referendums. In British Columbia in 2005, a total of 2634 21-minute computer-assisted telephone interviews (CATI) were conducted over four months.[13] The survey started as a weekly rolling cross-section at the time when every household received a copy of the assembly's report, and intensified to a daily

TABLE 1.3 *Data Employed in this Book*

	British Columbia	The Netherlands	Ontario
Assembly members data	13-wave panel	5-wave panel	4-wave panel
Media data	17-month content analysis	16-month content analysis	14-month content analysis
Public opinion data	4-month rolling cross-section (before the referendum)	Limited cross-sectional poll data	1-month rolling cross-section (before the referendum)
Evaluation reports and other documents	Available	Available	Available

[13] The principal investigators of the 2005 British Columbia Electoral Reform Referendum Study were André Blais, R. Kenneth Carty, Fred Cutler, Patrick Fournier, and Richard Johnston. The fieldwork ran from 17 January to 16 May 2005. It was conducted by the Institute for Social Research at York University under the direction of David Northrup. The response rate is 51.9 per cent.

rolling cross-section during the last two weeks of the campaign. Four years later, during the second British Columbia referendum on STV, 1039 respondents were questioned over the last four weeks of the campaign, and the sample was released dynamically on a daily basis.[14] In Ontario, a daily rolling cross-section of 1352 interviews was performed during the month-long official campaign period.[15] With these survey data, we can assess the nature of the public's opinions and knowledge concerning electoral reform and the citizen assembly, and track their evolution over time up until referendum day. In the Netherlands, no referendum was held. The only opinion poll data were collected in July 2006 (a few months after the assembly started). They deal with the campaign organized to inform people about the *Burgerforum* and public views towards the Dutch electoral system. When appropriate, we also draw upon general population statistics and results from national electoral studies.

A fourth data source consists of the evaluation reports, the teaching materials, and the technical reports produced by the citizen assembly organizations. This extensive documentation is crucial for describing how each assembly was structured and unfolded.

Armed with these diverse sources of evidence, we aim to provide a rigorous account of the three citizen assemblies and to draw the general lessons to be derived about citizens, governance, and democracy.

---

[14] The principal investigators of the 2009 British Columbia Referendum Study were R. Kenneth Carty, Fred Cutler, and Patrick Fournier. The Institute for Social Research surveyed from 16 April to 11 May 2009. The response rate is 41.5 per cent.

[15] The principal investigators of the 2007 Ontario Referendum and Election Study were André Blais, R. Kenneth Carty, Fred Cutler, Patrick Fournier, Richard Johnston, Scott Matthews, and Mark Pickup. Interviews were administered from 10 September to 9 October 2007 by the Institute for Social Research. The response rate is 45.5 per cent.

2

Why Citizen Assemblies and How did they Work?

It is axiomatic in government that hornets' nests should be left unstirred, cans of worms should remain unopened, and cats should be left firmly in bags and not set among the pigeons. Ministers should also leave boats unrocked, nettles ungrasped, refrain from taking bulls by the horns, and resolutely turn their backs to the music.

Sir Humphrey Appleby, *Yes Minister* (1982)

It is one thing to let citizens decide. It is quite another to determine how they might go about it. When the idea to have a citizen assembly on electoral reform was first advanced, no one knew how it might be done for the simple reason that it had never been done before. In this chapter, we turn to considering why the assemblies were created and how they functioned. Only once this has been accomplished can we answer our questions about citizen competence and decision-making. Though the three assemblies had much in common, each reflected the distinctive context of its own political community. By describing in some detail the structure and operation of the citizen assemblies, we can develop a more complete understanding of the unique cases around which this study revolves. The material in this chapter also serves as a launching pad for those that follow. As it discusses how these assemblies worked, it raises issues that will be explored more extensively later on: notably the representativeness of the participants, the influence of the staff on decisions, the impact of lobbying and public consultations, and the reasons behind the rejection of the proposals by voters and governments.

Perhaps the most surprising thing about the assemblies is that they were citizen assemblies on *electoral reform*, a subject which politicians typically want to control themselves. Thus, we begin with a consideration of the origins of the assemblies before turning to an analysis of how they were organized and operated. The subsequent discussion then traces the assemblies' activities chronologically through their selection, learning, consultation, deliberation, and decision-making phases before turning to the aftermath.

2.1 ELECTORAL SYSTEM CHANGE

Much of the scholarly literature on electoral systems has traditionally focused on their impacts upon phenomena such as levels of voter turnout, the number and nature of competing political parties, or the stability of legislatures and governments. However, in recent decades, researchers have started addressing the question of electoral system change (see e.g. Shugart 1992; Bawn 1993; Remington and Smith 1996; Boix 1999; Benoit 2004; Rahat 2004; Colomer 2005). In this line of research, it is the electoral system itself that is to be explained. The dominant strand in this work assumes that disciplined political parties try to shape the electoral systems to their advantage. The presumption is that their preferences are mainly centred on maximizing legislative seats and government power. In a paraphrase of Duverger's law, this theory has been described as the 'micro-mega rule': large parties prefer small legislatures, small district magnitudes, and small quotas, while small parties prefer large legislatures, district magnitudes, and quotas (Colomer 2004: 3). But others have strongly questioned the usefulness of assuming simple rationality, the predominance of seat-maximizing motivations, or the central position of unitary political parties (Van der Kolk 2007). Electoral systems change cannot always be studied apart from choices over other issues. In some instances, political parties prefer substantial changes that do not affect the distribution of seats (directly), parties sometimes split over electoral system change, and certain politicians are clearly motivated by ideological conceptions rather than seat-maximizing calculations (Bowler et al. 2008).

Our comparative study deals with three states that decided to take up the issue of electoral system change. By instituting a citizen assembly, each took the issue out of the hands of political parties and reduced their capacity to advance the narrow power-maximizing opportunities so beloved of political scientists theorizing about the process. Our three stories may add to our understanding of electoral system change by focusing on motivations that are not simply guided by seat maximization. They also reveal something of the values and orientations ordinary citizens bring to thinking about the appropriate principles that ought to govern such system changes.

2.2 ORIGINS OF CITIZEN ASSEMBLIES

Why were citizen assemblies instituted? By whom? How did they proceed? Answering these questions tells us something about the context in which each assembly was created and the decisions that ordered them. Although all three occurred within months of each other, they were not created independently. The

British Columbia assembly was the first and the precedents it set, and the lessons it offered, had direct and immediate impacts on the other two. We open with it.

2.2.1 British Columbia

British Columbia's political system had long been bipolar: its competitive two-party system is a classic instance of the effects of a 'first-past-the-post' system, as described in Duverger's law. Since the 1950s, elections in the province had been dominated by two parties: until 1990 by Social Credit and a social democratic party (the Co-operative Commonwealth Federation later reorganized as the New Democrats), and since then by the New Democrats and the BC Liberals. These two large parties benefited from this system and any change to a proportional one would not be in their obvious electoral interest. That made the creation of a citizen assembly to consider electoral reform particularly unexpected and quite remarkable.

Why would a party in government relinquish one of its most important powers – deciding the rules by which it is elected to the legislature and office – to a body that was untested and unpredictable? This question surely must have been on the minds of many in premier Gordon Campbell's government when he announced the formation of the world's first modern citizen assembly. Campaigning in opposition, Campbell had promised a review of the electoral system as part of a larger programme of democratic renewal. His platform explicitly proposed the creation of a Citizens' Assembly on Electoral Reform whose recommendations would be subject to ratification in a public referendum. In opposition, Campbell and his Liberal party appeared to have little to lose by advocating reform to a system that seemed to be dysfunctional. During the previous (1996) election, the party had received the greatest share of the popular vote but won fewer seats than the New Democrats who were returned to power. That led many Liberals to clamour for change. Then, at the next election, the legislative opposition was effectively eliminated when the Liberals won all but two seats in the legislature with only 57 per cent of the vote. That confirmed a perception that the system was broken and change needed to be seriously considered (Carty et al. 2008).

Campbell directed his government on the basis that its campaign promises had to be honoured. The government immediately tied its hands and eliminated one of the premier's powerful political weapons by fixing, for the first time in Canadian history, the date of the next election. Thus, it was no surprise when, one year into his mandate, Campbell announced the government's intention to create a Citizens' Assembly on Electoral Reform. While policy proposals may reflect strategic interest, rational calculation, or necessary accommodations among coalition partners, this policy initiative had simpler foundations. Campbell had promised to do it when running for office. And when asked why he chose a citizen assembly as the vehicle, he reportedly said 'because it's the right thing to do' (Gibson 2008). While it is not clear whether Campbell had any considered views on the issue of electoral reform itself, there seems little doubt that the new premier was centrally responsible for the establishment of the citizen assembly.

Given that there had never been a citizen assembly of this sort, the government did not know how to go about creating one. Premier Campbell asked Gordon Gibson, a prominent political commentator and former politician, to prepare a report on the creation, composition, and selection of a citizen assembly.[1] Gibson's *Report on the Constitution of the Citizens' Assembly on Electoral Reform* (2002) laid the foundation for the British Columbia experiment and, as it developed, the subsequent citizen assemblies. Comprehensive in scope, the report discussed everything from the staffing requirements to the core processes of selection, public consultation, learning, and deliberation, and developed a working budget for the proposed assembly. Gibson recognized two principles – independence and legitimacy – as necessary for a citizen assembly and detailed how these potentially conflicting principles could be reconciled. Perhaps most crucially, his report clearly anticipated and discussed the importance of having an assembly that was recognizably representative of the population. Though he contemplated the possibility that some screening of potential assembly members might take place by fellow citizens or eminent persons such as judges, he ultimately decided against it and recommended a random selection process that would allow the invited to opt out. Gibson's faith in the capacity of his fellow citizens would prove to be justified and constitutes a profoundly important legacy of his report.

Gibson's recommendations around the terms of reference and structure of the assembly were unanimously approved by the provincial legislature in April 2003. However, the make-up of the assembly differed in two important respects from his proposals. First, the government decided to double its size, with two members from each electoral district rather than the one Gibson recommended. This allowed for an easy adoption of gender parity, since one man and one woman could be drawn from each district. The second change was to leave it to the chair to decide if there were to be vice-chairs, and in the end none were appointed. To enhance the legitimacy of the assembly, at least in the eyes of the political and party elites, a special committee of the legislature was created to vet the assembly's chair and senior staff and to be available to offer all-party support to the assembly.

The government also moved to make good on the second part of their electoral reform by introducing, and passing, a bill to provide that any recommendation of the assembly would go to public referendum at the time of the next provincial general election (already fixed by law for May 2005). While referendums cannot be binding under Canadian constitutional provisions, the government made a firm commitment that, if it passed (and the government was returned), the proposal would be implemented. At the same time, the premier made it clear that neither he

---

[1] Gordon Gibson was a well-respected fellow of a national think tank located in British Columbia and a regular commentator on current events. In the past, he held the Liberal party's only seat in the British Columbia legislature at a time when the party occupied a very minor role in provincial affairs.

nor his party would be taking any position on an assembly recommendation in order to clear the way for a discussion of its merits independent of the government's partisan interests or views. This position, from which Campbell never deviated, would prove to have important implications when a referendum actually took place. One other aspect of the referendum plan would prove significant. The legislature decided that there should be a high and double acceptance standard. In practice, this meant that to pass a referendum would require 60 per cent support province-wide and a majority in 60 per cent of the electoral districts. The former was justified by the fact that the very structure of the democratic process was at stake, the latter allegedly to protect the rural areas from the heavily populated urban areas in the south-western corner of the province. While many in the government caucus thought the second would be the highest hurdle, the opposite ultimately proved to be the case, evidence perhaps that sitting politicians may not always know their electorates.

2.2.2 The Netherlands

A variety of different proposals for electoral reform had been attempted over the previous fifteen years prior to the creation of the Dutch citizen assembly. Traditional mechanisms of electoral system change had been tried, including commissions and expert studies. But none of these conventional procedures led to substantial changes in the electoral system, which has been in use since 1917 (Van der Kolk 2007). The political party D66 (Democrats 66) made its membership in the 2003 coalition government contingent on advancing the issue. However, when a legislative proposal to change the electoral law designed by the D66 minister De Graaf failed because of lack of support within the coalition, he resigned from the cabinet. His successor from D66, Alexander Pechtold, decided to take a new track. A number of civil servants working on the file had heard about the British Columbia assembly when attending a conference of political scientists in California that had been organized to discuss the De Graaf proposal. They reported this to Pechtold who subsequently announced in July 2005 the creation of a Dutch version – the *Burgerforum*. He believed that this would enable him to find a way to change the electoral system while strengthening the image of his party as being the most 'democratic'. Within the government, his plans were reluctantly accepted as the price of keeping D66 in the coalition.

As in British Columbia, the Dutch assembly followed a period of careful thought and preparation. Initial discussion and planning went beyond the specifics of the proposed assembly's mandate. Experts offered advice about the structure and format as well as the administration and external communication functions of the assembly. An additional 100 stakeholders from 'political, policy sectors, municipal authorities and the scientific, educational and communications sectors' also delivered input on a range of issues that culminated in a discussion with the minister (Van Schagen 2007: 4). Significantly, the planning team also decided to consult closely with the British Columbians, and a delegation of four public servants (who ultimately administered the assembly) travelled to meet with both organizers and members of the first assembly. The result led them to model the *Burgerforum* on the British Columbia experience; adopting its multiphase process (selection–learning–consultation–deliberation), a random selection mechanism for ensuring that assembly members had diverse backgrounds, and the appointment of a strong and prominent independent person to assume the role of chair.

The plans for the Dutch civic forum differed in one important political way from its Canadian counterparts. The government decided that any recommendations from the assembly should simply be submitted to government. There was no intention to present it to the public in a referendum. No doubt, the country's unhappy experience with the unsuccessful referendum on the European treaty in 2005 played a substantial role in this decision (Aarts and Van der Kolk 2006).

2.2.3 Ontario

The origins of the Ontario Citizens' Assembly on Electoral Reform are similar to those of British Columbia. Like that assembly, the Ontario version was created largely because the leader of an opposition party believed that one of the most fundamental institutions of democracy ought to be examined by an independent body and he had campaigned for office on the issue. When they won a majority government in 2003, the Liberals brought in a number of changes related to democratic renewal including a ban on partisan government advertising, campaign finance reform, and fixed election dates. They had also promised to create a citizen assembly to examine the issue of electoral reform. Premier Dalton McGuinty followed Campbell's example by proposing to hold a binding referendum on the assembly's recommendation. McGuinty saw electoral reform not as an end in itself but as one way to renew sliding public confidence in democratic institutions. Although the announcement came one year into the government's mandate (before the Netherlands' *Burgerforum* was instigated), the assembly only began during the third year of the government's term and reported in its fourth. As a result, the Ontario citizen assembly started and ended its activities after the Dutch assembly.

Ontario's context differed from that in its sister province to the west. The province's multiparty competition had produced significant policy lurches. A centrist Liberal minority government (1987) had been quickly followed by a New Democratic left-wing majority government in 1990 and then a sharp swing to the right under a majority Conservative government in 1995. This had been produced by its 'first-past-the-post' electoral system, but the province had not suffered the same series of electoral anomalies (wrong winners and lopsided majorities) as British Columbia. For critics of the idea to hold a citizen assembly, this meant that there was less of a warrant to hold one. And unlike in British

Columbia, the report of the Select Committee of the legislature that recommended the citizen assembly in Ontario was not accepted unanimously by the parliament. With only the Liberals and New Democrats publicly in favour of considering electoral reform, for some the assembly appeared to be nothing more than the consequence of an ill-conceived party promise and a waste of tax dollars.

Ontario's all-party Select Committee replicated Gibson's planning work. As in British Columbia, its proposed assembly was designed to ensure it would be independent of the government and free to recommend any model for electing members of the legislature, including an endorsement of the status quo. Its membership was to be representative of the province (including, as in British Columbia, some aboriginal representation), and chosen on the basis of existing electoral districts. Any proposal for change would have to be 'described clearly and in detail', only limited by being consistent with the Constitution of Canada. This provision, copied from the British Columbia plan, ensured that in the event of a referendum, voters would know precisely what alternative electoral system was being proposed.[2]

It was always intended that any assembly recommendation would go to the public in a referendum, but the Select Committee rejected the hurdles imposed in British Columbia and proposed that the threshold for any referendum should simply be the traditional majority of 50 per cent + 1. The government appears to have been less sure; it ultimately decided to adopt the double standard that had been established in British Columbia: 60 per cent province-wide, with a majority in 60 per cent of the districts.

2.2.4 Why a citizen assembly?

In none of our three cases does the decision by a government to launch an electoral reform initiative appear to have been the result of party calculation of its long-term strategic interests. However, it is clear that the initiating party in each instance hoped to garner the benefits of 'act contingencies' by portraying itself as a party of progressive change (Shugart 2008: 16). In both Canadian provinces, opposition party leaders adopted electoral system change as a campaign issue (part of wider democratic reform agendas), and then felt obliged to be seen to keep their promises. In the Netherlands, electoral reform had always been an integral part of D66's identity – it was even made a condition of their coalition participation – and the party was determined to demonstrate it could produce results.

But none of this necessarily entailed a citizen assembly. Indeed, no government had ever resorted to using one before. In British Columbia, the first to do so, the decision to create such an assembly appears to have been the result of a mix of factors. One man had promised to put electoral reform on the front burner, but neither he nor

---

[2] Thus, the assembly could not simply recommend, for example, proportional representation. It was instructed to spell out the details of the specific system being proposed.

his party had very considered opinions on the subject or any preferred system. They might, of course, have resorted to appointing a committee of experts, but the country had spent the previous decade in a fruitless and painful attempt to revise the constitution, and those failures had led many to question the usefulness of leaving such subjects to the political class and their usual experts. In British Columbia, some commentators and activists were advocating constituent assemblies for such work, and premier Campbell's decision to propose a citizen assembly reflected those debates. It is also clear that Campbell accepted the proposition that politicians were in a conflict of interest on the subject of electoral rules. He argued that such decisions ought to be the prerogative of the people and that it was simply right to leave it to them. The result was his decision to ask Gibson to tell him how to do it.

It was the success of the British Columbia Citizens' Assembly that provided both the Dutch and Ontario electoral reformers with an alternative reform process. In the Netherlands, the failure of old approaches meant that D66 ministers were looking for new approaches and were open to suggestions from political scientists that they might consider the British Columbia model. In Ontario, a new government, priding itself on its democratic instincts, was anxious to find new ways to engage citizens and found the British Columbia example a ready-made template. In neither of those two cases was there an easy unanimous support for an assembly, but in both, launching an assembly appeared to be one way to deal with existing political commitments.

There seems a measure of serendipity, or at least accident, in this story. For one thing, had Gordon Campbell not been the leader of the BC Liberals, the first citizen assembly would probably never have been created. Also, had the British Columbia assembly never existed or if it had been deemed a failure, it seems unlikely that either the *Burgerforum* or the Ontario assembly would have occurred. Or, if they had, they would likely have taken some different shape or direction. The demonstration effect of the British Columbia assembly was considerable, indicating that citizens could play an important role in choosing an institution as significant as their electoral system. It established the principle of randomness as a cornerstone of selection and recognized the importance of an in-depth education programme serving as the basis for their decision-making. All three assemblies differed in a number of ways – size, length of time, and the existence of a possible referendum – and in the balance of this chapter, we examine the similarities and differences in their structures and operations.

2.3 ORGANIZATION

The Gibson Report, which laid the foundation for the first citizen assembly, recognized that such an undertaking would require substantial support and assistance. One could not expect to put a group of strangers in a room and ask them to come to a well thought-out decision about whether to recommend a new electoral system, a question to which most had probably never given any thought. The members of an assembly would need to meet, learn, consult, deliberate, and decide over many months. For the learning phase alone, rooms would have to be booked, a curriculum devised, briefing material selected, speakers recruited, and a flexible agenda that members could take ownership of created.

Central to this infrastructure would be the chair of the assembly. Describing the necessary leadership, Gibson noted: 'He or she will have multiple duties – to be the public face of the Assembly, to manage the budget voted by the Legislature for the purpose, to see to the employment and general guidance of other staff, to exercise discretionary powers conferred by the mandate and, most importantly, to assist in guiding the work of the Assembly by facilitating relationships among the Members and securing adequate outside advice' (2002: 21). A primary responsibility would be to recruit people responsible for research, learning, administration, and communications.[3] Ultimately, each assembly depended upon a staff of about a dozen individuals.

2.3.1 The chairs

The British Columbia chair was nominated by the government, confirmed by a legislative committee, and then his appointment was unanimously ratified by the legislature (as Gibson had recommended). In both Ontario and the Netherlands, statutory instruments were used to appoint their respective chairs. While one might expect that the chair of a citizen assembly would be chosen from among its regularly selected membership, none of these assemblies adopted that principle. This reflected the governments' recognition that creating and managing a unique and diverse organization (with no help from the government in order to maintain independence) would require an individual with proven leadership skills as well as immediate credibility with political parties, interest groups, and the media. Thus, while all three chairs were technically members of the assembly who could vote, it would be a misunderstanding of the role of the chair to see him or her as a 'regular' assembly member.

All the chairs came from quite different backgrounds. British Columbia's chair, Jack Blaney, was a former university president with a distinguished record as an adult educator. He was particularly attracted to the assembly as an exceptional exercise in adult learning. The Dutch chair, theologian Jacobine Geel, was the only female chair. A columnist and television host, she was drawn to the project as an exercise in citizens' dialogue. In Ontario, George Thomson was a former deputy minister and family court judge. He had considerable experience in providing

---

[3] In the Dutch case, some of this responsibility was shared with a permanent civil servant who provided much of the initial planning and then the operational administrative leadership of the *Burgerforum*.

educational programmes for the legal community through his involvement in Canada's National Judicial Institute.

As one would expect, these different backgrounds affected their leadership styles and how they worked with members as well as staff. Thomson recognized that his training as a lawyer meant he was most familiar with position-based negotiation and that for the assembly he had to shift to a process that would privilege value- and interest-based deliberation and discussion. Geel believed that her lack of knowledge of the subject allowed her to focus on the process dimensions of the assembly's work. Blaney approached the role in an inherently optimistic fashion. His experience running adult education programmes (and perhaps even universities) had convinced him that 'if you believe in people, they'll always come through'. Both Thomson and Blaney sought to establish personal relationships with each member, calling them several times to ensure they were as engaged as they could or wanted to be. All three agreed that their biggest challenge was to keep the assembly processes moving in order to complete their task within the required time frames. In each case, the chairs played a pivotal role in establishing an environment where individuals with different skill sets could flourish.

There was one other important characteristic that the chairs shared: none had any substantive expertise in the policy area and none knew much about electoral systems as they started. This greatly strengthened their capacity to act as impartial leaders of their assemblies for no one could argue that they brought any preconceived opinions or preferences to the projects. At the same time, it meant that they, like the assembly members, were dependent upon the individual(s) charged with directing the learning phase that would lead to the final deliberative sessions.

2.3.2 Research/academic staff

In addition to the chair, the other staff person with regular contact with assembly members on substantive questions was the research/academic director. In this context, teaching about electoral systems required expertise in the subject matter but no commitment to, or recognizable preference for, any particular system. He – in all three cases, principal teaching was done by a male political scientist – had to develop and deliver the curriculum without leading assembly members to a specific conclusion. In British Columbia, the chair appointed R. Kenneth Carty the research director after consulting with informants around the province, a decision which was endorsed by a legislative committee that had to approve the assembly's senior staff positions. In the Netherlands, Jan van Schagen, a civil servant who held a PhD and worked in a university, was chosen to be the in-house academic director, though the teaching was done by external consultants: two professors, one in political science and one in law (Henk van der Kolk and Henk Kummeling). In Ontario, three candidates were interviewed and Jonathan Rose was selected by the chair and executive director.

Thus, in each case, the assemblies relied on academic political scientists to provide leadership for the learning phase. Although this was done in-house, each assembly sought external expertise and advice on the curriculum from political scientists familiar with electoral systems, deliberation, and organizational behaviour (BCCAER 2004: 121; OCAER 2007*a*: 182; Van Schagen 2007: 37). In British Columbia and the Netherlands, teaching was divided between two individuals (with one having primary responsibility), while in Ontario time constraints led that assembly to rely on one. In British Columbia and the Netherlands, people with a record of scholarly publications on electoral systems were employed, and they had relative autonomy in the creation of the learning curriculum. By contrast, Ontario deliberately chose an instructor who was not a specialist on electoral systems, and the development of the curriculum was a more collaborative exercise with the chair and an academic advisory group playing a more hands-on role than in the other cases.

The central issue for any organization that supports a deliberative group is its impartiality. As Gastil notes, good deliberation is dependent on a 'balanced presentation of alternative perspectives' (2006: 1). Was this achieved in the three citizen assemblies? Did members believe that the presentation of material was biased? Did they feel that the staff had their own preference? Were they led to some preordained conclusion? Answers to these kinds of questions are central to an assessment of the success of the assemblies. We return to them, and to the neutrality of the chair and teaching staff, in Chapter 6.

2.4 SELECTION PHASE

The selection procedure was a critical element in the assembly process, for it was designed to produce the representative character that was considered essential to establishing their legitimacy. All three used random selection from official records to provide names for the initial letters of invitation and then again to choose members from those who indicated a willingness to participate. The aim of using random selection in two stages was to produce assemblies as representative as possible of the population. According to British Columbia's Terms of Reference, the membership was 'to be broadly representative of the adult population of British Columbia, particularly respecting age, gender and geographical distribution'.[4] In Ontario, fifty-two members were to be female and fifty-one members were to be male. Without specifying any parameter, the founding regulations did

---

[4] Age, gender, and geography were adopted as criteria because they were the only characteristics available on the voters' list – the only province-wide listing of citizens available from which to draw a sample.

mention that the composition of the assembly was to be a representative body of electors. Elections Ontario designed a process to take the electorate's age distribution into account. In a letter to parliament, the Dutch minister of Administrative Renewal asserted: 'for the legitimacy of the proposal produced by the *Burgerforum*, it is important that the assembly is made up broadly. Ideally, the members of the assembly should form an exact mirror image of Dutch society.'

The selection process started with a stratified sample from the voters' lists in British Columbia and Ontario and the Municipal Personal Records Database in the Netherlands. Stratification was based on geography (electoral districts in British Columbia and Ontario; provinces in the Netherlands) and gender. In Canada, there were also provisions for aboriginal representation: one of the Ontario members had to be aboriginal, while a change was made to the original design in British Columbia to add two aboriginal members (bringing the total to 160).

An invitational letter was sent to the initial large sample of individuals (see Table 2.1). It stated that the recipient had been randomly selected as a potential participant in a citizen assembly on electoral reform. If they were interested, individuals were asked to respond indicating as much and their availability to attend a local information and selection meeting where their name would be included in the pool of eligible citizens. The letter pointed out the historic nature of the project, the time commitment expected of the members, and the chance to serve their province or country. As Table 2.1 shows, positive response to these initial letters was around 7 per cent. So the vast majority of people invited were not interested and/or available.

Those who expressed interest were strongly motivated to participate. In Ontario, over 95 per cent of individuals who were invited to attend a selection meeting accepted the invitation, notwithstanding the great distances many would have had to travel (OCAER 2007a: 43–4). For some, this amounted to a three-hour drive. In British Columbia, where distances would have been greater (in

TABLE 2.1 *Selecting Members for the Assembly*

	British Columbia	The Netherlands	Ontario
Source	Voters' list	Kiesregister	Voters' list
Size of the electorate	2.3 million	12.1 million	8.0 million
Initial letters	23,034	50,400	123,489
Positive responses	1715 (7.4%)	3121 (6.2%)	7033 (5.7%)
Invited to attend meeting	1441	3121	1253
Invitations accepted	1105	—	1196
Attended selection meeting	964	2042	—
Expressed willingness to serve	914	1732	—
Number of meetings	27	9	29
Members selected	158 (+2)	140 (+3)	103

some cases involving overnight journeys over mountains in late fall and early winter), over 87 per cent of those who confirmed they would attend a selection meeting did so (BCCAER 2004: 35–6). The very high degree of attendance at those meetings was common to all three assemblies.

Once at a selection meeting, prospective members heard presentations on the expectations and obligations of membership. They were told that prior knowledge was not a precondition and were reassured that most others had little or no knowledge of electoral reform. Members of the assembly secretariat staff conducted these meetings, answered questions, and allayed any concerns potential members might have about their knowledge or ability. At the end of the meeting, those present were given the opportunity to withdraw, but very few did. In British Columbia and the Netherlands, over 85 per cent of those who attended the information sessions agreed to submit their names for the drawing.[5] The meetings in British Columbia and Ontario concluded with names being drawn from a hat or ballot box. In Ontario, alternates were also chosen in case anyone dropped out prior to the first meeting (none was required). In the Netherlands, the members were selected after all the meetings were held. To publicize the *Burgerforum*, this was done in an Internet broadcast, but the first draw had to be annulled when it was discovered that the company organizing the draw had made some errors in the provincial stratification. A second draw, this time in the presence of the Minister, was more successful.

In Chapter 3, we return to the question of how successful this process was in producing representative assemblies. That will allow us to consider the reasons for seeking representativeness and the meaning it brought to the assemblies.

2.5 LEARNING PHASE

Most citizens in democracies know little about the intricacies of electoral systems – indeed many have a very limited understanding of their own system, let alone that of others. In this regard, the members of the three citizen assemblies on electoral reform were quite typical, and they freely recognized as much. When asked at the start of their work 'how informed about electoral systems do you feel?', the average member gave himself or herself a failing grade. On a 0–10 scale, British Columbians scored 4.4, Ontarians 4.3, and the Dutch just 2.9 (though their question asked about 'foreign electoral systems').[6] An extensive learning phase

---

[5] We do not have comparable data for the Ontario assembly but, impressionistically, the proportion was also high there.

[6] When asked only about their national electoral system, the Dutch average was higher at 5.8.

was thus necessary before any debate about the most appropriate electoral system could take place. All three citizen assemblies were planned accordingly.

2.5.1 Structure and content

Each assembly devoted six (residential) weekends, spread over several months, to the learning phase (though in the Dutch case some of this training overlapped with the consultation phase). These learning weekends required members to travel from their homes and stay together in hotels.[7] As Table 2.2 shows, there was considerable similarity in the curriculum of all three, in part because both the Netherlands and Ontario started with the British Columbia programme and made appropriate modifications to suit the context within which they were working. The British Columbia model reflected many of the suggestions offered in the original Gibson Report (2002: Appendix 3).

An in-depth learning phase was needed not only to allow sufficient time to understand the implications of different voting systems but also to convey the complexity of the topic. Electoral systems can be understood in two broad ways. One way is to see them through their constituent elements or their *mechanics*. This is usually understood as the district magnitude (the number of representatives per electoral district), the ballot structure (whether the electoral choice is categorical or ordinal, and whether the choice is for a party or a candidate), and the formula

TABLE 2.2 *The Assemblies' Learning Curriculum*

	British Columbia	The Netherlands	Ontario
Weekend 1	Introduction to the Citizens' Assembly	Elements of an electoral system	Introduction to the Citizens' Assembly
Weekend 2	Elections and parliamentary government	Electoral system families	Political representation/ government and the legislature
Weekend 3	Plurality and majority systems	Consequences of electoral systems	Plurality and majority systems
Weekend 4	PR and mixed systems	Some learning and consultation	PR and mixed systems
Weekend 5	Changing electoral systems	Some learning and consultation	Electoral systems around the world
Weekend 6	Options for public discussion	Some learning and consultation	Simulations/system design

---

[7] In Canada, this could involve (winter) journeys of several hours to Vancouver and Toronto respectively. The smaller distances in the Netherlands allowed Dutch members to get to their meetings in The Hague and Zeist more easily.

(whether the winners are decided by plurality, majority, or proportional rules). Alternatively, electoral systems can be understood by their outcomes or *consequences*. This approach considers the different modes of representation under different systems and the consequences they have for the character of democracy, answering questions such as: How likely is a system to produce majority or minority governments? Will there be a greater likelihood of single-party or multiparty governments? How many and what kind of parties are likely to gain representation under particular systems? Is representation likely to be interest-based or territorially based? Both of these approaches had to be taught if assembly members were to fully understand the mechanics as well as the consequences of the decisions they were to make. Members would have to comprehend how electoral systems trade off competing goods and that no one system can deliver everything (Katz 1997).

The curriculum was very similar in the two Canadian assemblies. Both began the learning phase with an introduction to Westminster-style parliamentary government, explaining the functions of parliament, the party system, and principles of representation. Weekends 3 and 4 were dedicated to an examination of the broad families of electoral systems (plurality, majority, proportional representation (PR), and mixed). Examples were described according to both their outcomes (what kind of government and legislature are produced) as well as their mechanics (ballot structure, district magnitude, and formula). Unlike a citizens' jury, the learning programme did not rely on advocates for specific systems. Rather, the staff outlined the strengths and weaknesses of each in a neutral fashion. The assessments used criteria commonly used to analyse electoral systems, such as the extent to which they offer voter choice, stable government, effective parliament and parties, accountability, and increased voter participation. In the penultimate weekend of the learning phase, members heard from international experts on electoral systems who described the features of systems in different countries, as well as some of the lessons from places – such as New Zealand – that had recently changed their electoral system. In the final week in British Columbia, members turned their attention to preparing a report that could be widely distributed as a basis for the public consultations to follow. In Ontario, no such preliminary report was required and their final week was devoted to simulations showing members how changing variables of a system affect electoral results. In both cases, the chairs reminded members that the assemblies were still in the 'data collection' phase of their work and discouraged them from making a precipitous choice. As Chapter 4 indicates, however, this does not mean that some members had not already developed private preferences.

The content of the training in the Dutch assembly utilized three main modules: the (mechanical) elements of electoral systems, the combination of those elements in different families of systems, and the consequences of each of these families. Quizzes, voting simulations, as well as presentations by members of the Dutch parliament complemented the formal lectures. As with the other assemblies, a members-only website complemented formal learning in the classroom. Whereas this learning phase was discrete in the Canadian cases, in the Netherlands it spilled over into the following period when the *Burgerforum* was holding its public consultation meetings.

There was a common structure to these learning weekends. They usually began with a welcome from the chair who made an opening statement, allowing members to raise any questions about outstanding issues, the weekend's curriculum, or other business. Days would begin at 9 or 9:30 in the morning and go on until after 4 in the afternoon, with breaks for refreshments and lunch. Plenary lectures – usually by the academic director/chief research officer – laid the foundation for broad themes or key concepts. They were followed by small-group sessions of constantly varying composition. These sessions were moderated by specially trained graduate students in political science (British Columbia) or political science and upper-year law students (the Netherlands and Ontario). In all three assemblies, these facilitators would meet before the weekend with the secretariat's academic team to go over the proposed plans for the small-group sessions. Activities were designed to stress active learning and interaction among the members within the groups. Often, the purpose of the small-group sessions would be to reinforce ideas of the plenary, but occasionally the groups would report back on an issue they had discussed. These sessions were designed partly as tutorials, and also recognizing that people learn in different ways and in different venues.

With such a varied group of participants, few of whom had the foundation usually expected when learning about electoral systems, teaching methods and materials had to be appropriate for adult learners. Quoting Albert Einstein, one member in Ontario described the material as having to be as 'simple as possible but not simpler'. While much of the discussion was necessarily somewhat abstract and theoretical, such as the meaning and nature of representation, other elements were inevitably highly detailed and specific, such as the calculation of the Hare quota. Every assembly used the same text as the basis for its programme. Given its organization, breadth, and clear approach, David Farrell's *Electoral Systems: A Comparative Introduction* (2001) served as the primary textbook. In the Netherlands, the *Burgerforum* staff had it translated into Dutch for their members. While the book is both rigorous and remarkably well written, one British Columbian took it upon himself to 'translate' it into what he believed was more accessible prose (to the 'ordinary person'). In Ontario, Farrell's book was supplemented by a sixty-page book commissioned for the project. It discussed the families of electoral systems and evaluated them in light of the assembly's mandate and principles. A third book, *Electoral System Design: The New International IDEA Handbook* (2005), was used as a supplementary text in Ontario to provide visual representations of ballots, brief narratives of recent elections, and for its compendium-like structure.

The texts were not the sole source of academic material. Recognizing that a book is not the best form of information for many, fact sheets, presentations, summaries, government reports, and bibliographies were an integral part of the data members received. This amounted to a wealth of information in a variety of forms. Ballots were obtained or reproduced in all three assemblies to help provide tangible illustrations of how voting took place in other countries. Interactive, hands-on techniques such as simulations (Ontario and the Netherlands) or quizzes (the Netherlands) complemented lectures and other didactic methods. Members could (and often did) ask the academic staff questions on the members-only website. Informal evening sessions that were held in all three jurisdictions provided a valuable opportunity to review the lessons learned during the day. These ad hoc meetings were often organized and run by members themselves, allowing them to take ownership of their learning and encouraging the very important function of peer teaching.

One of the consequences of a residential learning programme (where members are away from family and friends for a weekend at a time) is the creation of nodes of expertise. Members who were computer literate ran simulations of election results and altered design variables to see how the outcomes might change. Others who had a propensity for data collection would develop spreadsheets that could be sorted according to different variables. Still others acted as librarians, searching out information and resources to share with other members. And individuals who favoured learning through conversation talked through material with colleagues.

2.5.2 Did members learn?

Our evidence indicates that citizen assembly members learned a great deal about the subject of their mandate. First, they were asked to gauge their own knowledge of electoral systems on a 0–10 scale. The means are reported in Table 2.3. Scores in the

TABLE 2.3 *Factual and Self-Reported Knowledge, Start and End of Learning Phase*

	British Columbia		The Netherlands		Ontario	
	Start	End	Start	End	Start	End
Self-reported ratings (0–10, mean)						
Information about electoral systems	4.4	8.1	—	—	4.3	8.3
Information about national electoral system	—	—	5.8	8.1	—	—
Information about foreign electoral systems	—	—	2.9	6.6	—	—
Factual knowledge (% correct)						
Country where candidate with most votes wins	64.0	90.0	47.2	76.7	64.9	91.6
Country with two votes (party, candidate)	14.7	68.7	40.0	94.8	14.4	74.7
Country where voters rank candidates	5.3	78.7	20.8	72.4	17.5	78.9
Country with proportional representation	27.3	85.3	20.0	51.7	23.7	84.2

baseline questionnaire, before the first meetings of the assemblies, were rather low, most below the scale's midpoint. By the end of the learning phase, members of each of the assemblies reported a much greater confidence in their knowledge of electoral systems. The means almost doubled, increasing by more than 3.5 points in each case (with the not surprising exception of Dutch reported knowledge of their domestic system, though that too showed a marked improvement).

Of course, this greater sense of confidence might be a misguided feeling resulting from participation in the intensive information sessions that were a virtual political science boot camp. However, more objective evidence also shows that many assembly participants became very informed about electoral systems. Several times during the assembly process, we asked them questions to measure their factual knowledge. These questions challenged them to name (*a*) a country where ('like in Canada') the candidate with the most votes wins; (*b*) a country where people have two votes, one for the party they prefer and one for the local candidate they prefer; (*c*) a country where voters get to rank the candidates in their order of preference; and (*d*) a country where they have PR ('like in the Netherlands'), that is, the percentage of seats a party gets is about the same as the percentage of votes it got. Table 2.3 presents the percentage of correct answers to these four knowledge questions at two moments for each assembly: before the assembly began its activities, and during the mid-year break after the completion of the learning phase.

As the data reveal, assembly members initially knew very little about other electoral systems. In the first wave survey, the only item that received close to a majority of correct answers was naming a country using 'first past the post' (typically, members cited the United States or the United Kingdom). Perhaps that is not startling for Canadians, since they use that system and are close to the United States. But this was also the most well-known item in the Netherlands. Knowledge of other items was dismal. Rarely more than a quarter of assembly participants could name a country with two votes, a country that ranks candidates, or a country with PR.[8] By the end of the learning phase, however, knowledge levels had drastically improved. In many instances, the proportion of correct answers jumped by more than 50 percentage points. Among each assembly, a majority, often overwhelming, could accurately name an example of each electoral system. In only one instance did less than two-thirds of assembly members respond correctly: just half the Dutch participants could name another country using PR. This may reflect the fact that discussions in the Dutch assembly often stressed that PR in the Netherlands is quite unique, thus inciting people to state they did not know a 'similar PR system'. Overall, knowledge generally reached close to four-fifths of respondents.

---

[8] Though many Dutch *Burgerforum* members could also name a country with two votes, perhaps due to the close proximity of Germany's MMP system.

Thus, both self-reported measures and more objective knowledge tests tell a similar story. Anecdotal evidence also indicates that many participants became quite proficient about the topic. They were asking very tough questions and having highly sophisticated discussions. Technical conversations and debates continued during breaks, meals, social outings, and on web forums. Observing the assemblies, it was hard not to be impressed with the capacity of citizens to learn, absorb, and understand the intricacies of a subject to which most had given little, if any, prior thought.

How did participants learn? What worked? What did not? We cannot answer these questions decisively, for their programmes involved multiple elements – personal study, plenary lectures, and small-group discussions – that overlapped over time. A tentative indication is provided by self-reports. The British Columbia and Ontario assembly members were asked at the end of the learning phase how useful they thought different elements of the programme had been to their personal learning. Similar questions were given to the Dutch members at the conclusion of the whole process. Table 2.4 suggests that formal presentations by experts – both on the staff and visiting – were the most useful activity in helping members accumulate and integrate information. The two other central components of the formal learning programme – small-group discussions and personal study – were also considered important activities. The various forms of conversations with staff, members, and other people, whether in person or online, were rated as less useful.

But however they learned, it is clear that many assembly members became very knowledgeable about electoral systems and how they worked. The extent to which this new information translated into non-erratic and structured preferences about electoral systems is explored in Chapters 4 and 5 respectively.

TABLE 2.4 *Usefulness of Activities for Learning*

	British Columbia	The Netherlands	Ontario
Plenary lectures by staff	6.3 (1)	6.5 (1)	6.4 (1)
Plenary talks by visitors	5.9 (2)	5.7 (3)	6.0 (2)
Small-group discussion sessions	5.8 (3)	6.0 (2)	5.6 (3)
Personal study	5.5 (4)	5.7 (4)	5.6 (4)
Informal conversation with other members	5.3 (5)	—	5.3 (7)
Plenary discussion by whole assembly	4.7 (6)	4.9 (5)	5.3 (5)
Informal conversations with staff	4.7 (6)	—	5.3 (6)
Conversation with family, friends, neighbours	4.7 (8)	4.9 (6)	4.6 (8)
Discussion on the web forum	3.9 (9)	4.0 (7)	3.8 (9)

Members were asked to 'rate the following activities in terms of what was most useful for learning'. The scale spanned 1–7, where '1' means least useful and '7' means most useful. Means are reported (with ranks in parentheses).

2.6 CONSULTATION PHASE

By the end of the learning phase, assembly members had developed the knowledge they would need to begin their analysis and assessment of their society's electoral system needs. But that was just the first half of their preparation. They had yet to know their fellow citizens' opinions about electoral reform. The Gibson conception of the assembly process also involved these representative citizens consulting widely with those they represented. Included in their terms of reference and mandate was an instruction to do just that – to hold a series of consultations so that there could be public input into their deliberations and decision-making.

Scholars of deliberative democracy take public consultation to be an essential part of decision-making. Gutmann and Thompson (2004) make the theoretical argument that deliberative democracy demands a public and transparent process in order to establish the authenticity and legitimacy of the exercise. From a practical perspective, Catt and Murphy see the need for public consultation as a consequence of recognizing 'the policy-making process as a forum for weighing competing preferences and priorities rather than as a procedure for uncovering hidden and incontestable truths' (2003: 408). Consulting is thus used to improve the policy process by increasing the information or the range of perspectives available to decision-makers. Essentially, public consultation is intended to serve several purposes. It can strengthen relationships between decision-makers and citizens thereby increasing the legitimacy of the policy (Barber 1984); it can allow the public an opportunity to provide input into policy options (Arnstein 1969); and it can broaden the range of stakeholders involved in policy development (Irvin and Stansbury 2004).

All three assemblies organized a broad and vigorous consultation programme. In British Columbia, a decision was made (by the staff) to ensure there would be an opportunity for all interested citizens to participate in a meeting within a reasonable distance of their home. Responding to demand, some of it stimulated by the assembly members in their local communities, fifty public hearings were ultimately organized across the province in May and June 2004. By the time they were completed, assembly members had heard 363 separate presentations from the 2851 attendees (BCCAER 2004: 71–9). In Ontario, forty-one meetings (plus four outreach focus groups for some hard-to-reach social segments) were held over the winter months from November 2006 to January 2007. They featured 501 formal and informal presentations made by the 1973 citizens in attendance (OCAER 2007a: 85–9). Both these assemblies' meetings were structured to connect citizens to the assembly, so each one included a number of assembly members who could report what they heard to their colleagues.[9]

---

[9] In British Columbia, members voted to have an additional full weekend meeting at the end of the consultation stage to discuss what they had heard in the public hearings. At this meeting, held in the northern part of the province, there was also a full review of the web submissions that had been received to that point.

In British Columbia, members attended at least one meeting in some part of the province they had never previously visited in order to expose them to the diversity of views that characterize the province's population. The central focus of most of these public meetings was the presentations made by the public and the question/discussion period they invariably prompted. Secretariat staff took minutes and ensured that summaries of the sessions appeared on the assemblies' websites.

Electoral systems are complex, and detailed discussion can quickly descend to confusing detail. So it is not surprising that, aside from a few presentations by electoral system enthusiasts, most presentations centred on broad themes (such as the nature or desirability of local representation) or principles (such as proportionality). In both provinces, the majority of presentations favoured some kind of change: 92 per cent of the presentations in British Columbia advocated some type of reform, while in Ontario the proportion was 90 per cent (BCCAER 2004: 75; OCAER 2007b: 2–3). It seems clear that individuals concerned with the organization and fairness of the province's electoral politics saw these hearings as an opportunity to express their views. Few favouring the status quo bothered to attend.

The Dutch assembly's consultation phase, which went from May to August 2006, was different from the other two. There, consultation took the form of eighteen regional debates attended by 740 citizens. Twelve of these were organized in collaboration with the Dutch Centre for Political Participation. Each meeting was structured around a main debate question asked at the beginning and the end of the evening: 'Are you of the opinion that changes need to be made to the electoral system of the Second Chamber?'. Six agree/disagree propositions supplemented this primary question and allowed those attending to articulate their views about the electoral system (Van Schagen 2007: 20–1).

In addition to the public meetings, the assemblies constructed websites which individuals could visit to learn about assembly activity. The sites also allowed visitors to send written submissions on either specific models of electoral systems or simply expound on the values that they believed should underpin any decision. By posting submissions as they were received, the sites created an ongoing public debate. In some instances, individuals reading others' submissions were motivated to either argue with them or reconsider their positions in subsequent contributions. For example, the British Columbia site (www.citizensassembly.bc.ca) had almost 51,000 different visitors from 151 countries. Ultimately, 1603 formal submissions were received, summarized, and reviewed by groups of assembly members. In Ontario, 1039 proposals were submitted (www.citizensassembly.gov.on.ca). In many cases, the submissions were brief or repetitive – one common format in the British Columbia assembly simply read 'I like MMP' – suggesting they came from an organized group, but members soon found their way to those with more detail. The Dutch assembly attempted an innovative real-time consultation session online where members of the public could interact with assembly members via the Internet. The Web was also used to facilitate early discussion among assembly members themselves on a members-only Web forum. It proved a valuable tool as

TABLE 2.5 *Views about the Consultations*

	British Columbia	The Netherlands	Ontario
Public meetings were helpful	89.8	86.0	96.8
Public meetings were informative	84.9	85.0	95.7
Public meetings were interesting	93.8	93.5	96.8
Public meetings were repetitive	85.3	49.4	64.4
Online submissions were informative	86.2	—	86.4
Online submissions were repetitive	96.6	—	90.6

Numbers are percentages.

they began the task of filtering information and ideas in anticipation of the deliberation phase.

Table 2.5 reveals something of the assembly members' responses to the consultation phase. Though they believed (and sometimes complained) that the submissions at the hearings and on the Web were often very repetitive, they also found the process interesting, informative, and helpful. In the two Canadian cases, meetings across such geographically large political systems provided an important opportunity for members to raise awareness of the assembly in their communities and to hear what interested fellow citizens had to say. It may also have helped to make the assembly more legitimate, giving it a public face, and demonstrating that this was a genuinely independent citizen-driven endeavour.

If members found the meetings helpful, one important element of this was to instil confidence in their newly acquired expertise. When confronted by citizens advocating some electoral change, many members quickly discovered that they now knew far more about the actual specifics of the systems being discussed than those making the presentations. The public hearing process, at least in Canada, left the members with an increased sense of personal legitimacy, reinforcing how well prepared they were for the task of deliberation. The widespread call for change that the Canadians heard was understood as just that, and members felt free to use their new knowledge to determine just what sort of system would generate desirable changes.

Did the consultation phase have a decisive impact on the assemblies? Were their final decisions influenced and shaped by all they heard and read in this phase of the proceedings? This possibility is investigated in Chapter 6.

2.7 DELIBERATION AND DECISION-MAKING PHASE

The learning phase provided the necessary foundation of knowledge for deliberation. During this period, no electoral system was excluded as the merits and limitations of each family and type were explored. The consultation phase that followed was important as a legitimating exercise, but it too was not about any specific alternative because none yet existed. Up to this point, members had not even begun to deliberate formally as a body, since they had not been required to express preferences nor make decisions. It was assumed that, as in other deliberative exercises, individuals do not start with a clear and coherent understanding (Button and Ryfe 2005: 28). Preferences were to emerge and take shape during the deliberative discussions. The story of when preferences developed and what factors motivated them is discussed elsewhere in this book (Chapters 4 and 5 respectively). Here, we sketch out the issues, votes, and decisions of the deliberation phase in each assembly.

A distinctive feature of the assemblies was that they had to come up with a specific policy recommendation. Unlike deliberative polls which are mainly about capturing informed private preferences, the assemblies were designed to make a recommendation on the basis of a collective preference. Each assembly had to go beyond simple deliberation and find an aggregative procedure for identifying its preference and articulating a recommendation. Since procedure matters in shaping the outcome of any aggregative process, it is important to note what procedures were adopted by the assemblies and then reflect on the participants' evaluation of them.

The route from deliberation to decision followed a similar path in all three assemblies. It started with a discussion of the important values the electoral system should meet, then narrowed the consideration of electoral system options to those that met the identified criteria, moved to constructing detailed models of these options, and then concluded by evaluating alternatives against the existing system to make a final decision. Of course, agreeing how to decide over the options was important in all three assemblies. Each one agreed that an absolute majority would be the formal decision rule for final decisions, but each sought an outcome that reflected a broader consensus and fostered continuing discussion rather than (parliamentary-style) debate in an attempt to reach it.

In British Columbia, the deliberation phase began with members prioritizing the values they deemed important in an electoral system. Three were identified as central: voter choice, proportionality, and local representation. The academic staff suggested that these three values were compatible with some system families but not others. The assembly therefore decided to dismiss majoritarian systems (which do not deliver proportional results) and list-PR systems (which are at odds with local representation). This left them with mixed member proportional (MMP) and the single transferable vote (STV) as the system types best able to incorporate all three of the valued dimensions. To evaluate the appropriateness of such different systems, which can take many forms in practice, the assembly decided to construct a version of both that might plausibly be recommended to the public. That process took two weekends. Constructing a model STV system was not difficult, as it largely involved decisions about district magnitude and ballot structure. Creating an MMP model took a bit longer, since some fifteen or sixteen separate, but interrelated, decisions had to be made about its two parts (the local district side and party list side) as well as the rules linking them. At each stage of the model-building process, assembly members were returning to their considerations of voter choice, proportionality, and local representation, discussing how their decisions were congruent with them, and what trade-offs among them were involved. It has to be said that the strong preference of many for voter choice (see Chapter 4) led to a particularly complex MMP model.

By the fourth weekend of the deliberative phase, the assembly was ready to choose between its two alternative systems. Whichever system came out ahead would then be compared with the existing single member plurality (SMP) system. Members first met in small groups to start their conversation and rehearse their arguments. In the following plenary session, the discussion was structured with individuals making the case, in turn, for one of the systems and then the other. The debate was not only extensive, principled, passionate, but also respectful and conducted at a high level, with several participants arguing the assembly should rally behind the consensus position. At its conclusion, it was decided to hold a secret ballot that saw STV preferred to MMP by a 4:1 ratio (123 31). The assembly returned the next morning to consider the merits of STV as opposed to the current system. After another discussion and debate, the vote was 142–11 in favour of the STV model. The final decision was to determine whether they felt confident enough to recommend the proposed STV system to the public, thus ensuring a referendum. There was little doubt about that outcome – 95 per cent of assembly members voted to do so.

In the Netherlands, the assembly members began by selecting the strong and weak aspects of the current system and identifying the main functions of a desired electoral system. The most important statements centred on proportionality, simplicity, the existence of a single nationwide district, and the place of political parties. By contrast, regional representation and a reduction in the number of parties were seen as substantially less desirable. All members were invited to suggest alternative electoral systems after the consultation phase and in the first weeks of the deliberation phase. The staff merged all proposals into four alternative systems. Members were invited to amend this list, and a few took advantage of this possibility. The assembly ended up with six alternatives, all of which were proportional: three modifications of the present system, an MMP system, a system which would allow voters to express a preference for coalitions, and a rather complex system in which parts of the legislature were elected every two years.

Because the Dutch civic forum had to choose between several options, it was decided to use a sequential run-off voting system, where the option receiving the fewest votes would be eliminated in subsequent balloting. This would go on until two options were left, these two would be discussed extensively, and the winning option would compete with the status quo. Members quickly dropped the more complicated systems and the MMP system. The three remaining options were all basically straightforward list-PR systems. Partly because of strategic voting, the assembly then decided to reject a system where voters would have been allowed to cast a party vote and a preferential vote for a candidate of another party. In this rejected system, the preferential vote would not have affected the distribution of seats but would have changed the distribution of seats within parties. Because a large group supporting the option that was ultimately selected was afraid of this alternative, some tactically shifted their support to their second preferred choice for one round.

The Dutch assembly thus ended up with two options: one list-PR system introducing a choice between a party vote and a vote for a candidate, and another keeping the current system with some minor modifications (i.e. changing the formula from d'Hondt to Hare). The first system was favoured with 83 per cent of the votes. In the final decision, this alternative competed with the status quo and was selected with the support of 88 per cent of *Burgerforum* members.

In Ontario, the identification of the assembly's values resulted in the selection of the same three criteria as in British Columbia (local representation, proportionality, and voter choice). To advance their discussion, members determined which systems they thought best represented those values. This was done using a preferential vote where members ranked all electoral systems. The result was much the same as in the first assembly, with MMP and STV (in that order) identified as the two most preferred alternatives. At that stage, the assembly proceeded to design models of those two electoral systems that they believed would be suitable for their province. Ontario members had a different set of design opportunities than their British Columbian colleagues, for they were not constrained by the size of the existing legislature. This made constructing an MMP system somewhat more complex but at the same time somewhat easier. It now involved extra (potentially controversial) decisions about the total size of the legislature but that, in turn, made the trade-offs between local representation and proportionality potentially less onerous. The assembly wrestled until the last minute with tricky technical questions about 'overhang' seats, but it finally agreed on an acceptable MMP model. There was less difficulty with its STV model, about which fewer members seemed enthusiastic.

As in British Columbia, the assembly's key debate came down to a discussion about the comparative merits of the two alternative systems. In this instance, however, MMP prevailed by a 3:1 margin (75–25). When compared with the existing system, the Ontarians also preferred their alternative (86–16). Ultimately, 92 per cent of assembly members voted to recommend MMP to the population in a referendum.

In all three assemblies, the concluding vote showed overwhelming support for the final recommendation. But it is important to ask if the participants believed these outcomes had been achieved reasonably. Some of our survey data, reported in Table 2.6, speak to this issue. First, very lopsided proportions felt that all assembly members had an equal opportunity to express themselves during the discussions. They also clearly believed that their views were treated respectfully by their peers. And in Ontario, where participants were also asked to judge the fairness of the decision process, most responded positively. Finally, crushing

TABLE 2.6 *Views about the Deliberations*

	British Columbia	The Netherlands	Ontario
Every member had an equal opportunity to present their views (%)	92.0	77.7	92.8
Members showed respect for each other and their opinions (1–5)	4.6	—	4.6
The decisions were taken fairly (1–5)	—	—	4.6
Very or somewhat satisfied with the assembly's decisions (%)	95.9	86.8	96.9

The first and fourth items were measured in the post-assembly questionnaire. For the second and third items, we report averages of all measures during the deliberation phase (1 = strongly disagree, 5 = strongly agree).

majorities were satisfied with the decisions that had been taken by the assemblies. Most impressively, satisfaction with the assembly's decisions topped 80 per cent among those who were on the losing sides of the debates (i.e. those who voted for a different alternative system and those who voted for the current system). The fact that those whose preference had not been endorsed by the assembly rallied to the wider group's decision suggests members considered the deliberative and decision-making process had been conducted in a just and equitable way.

Citizen assemblies have been presented as an ultimate application of deliberative democracy. According to the ideal, participants in a decision-making body should exchange arguments about preferences, should refer to some general principles, and should adjust previously held opinions according to these arguments and principles. This sketch suggests the citizen assemblies met many of the deliberative democrats' expectations, but we will return to examine the evolution of preferences over time and the sources of movement (in Chapter 4), the relationships between these final decisions and the principles that allegedly drove them (in Chapter 5), and the role of outside influences (in Chapter 6).

2.8 INTERESTED AND ENGAGED CITIZENS

All three citizen assemblies were charged to do something that had never been accomplished before: take a group of ordinary citizens and challenge them to assess their political communities' electoral system and, if they found it wanting, to propose a concrete alternative. All three completed the task on schedule and within budget, and they produced reports that commanded a broad basis of support. Here, we briefly consider the members' responses to the challenge they were offered and speculate on some of the basic reasons that explain them.

It is clear that the prospect of serving on a citizen assembly generated some excitement even before it had ever gathered. This was evident at local selection meetings. Some individuals whose name was picked randomly at the end of the evening reacted as if they had won the jackpot: jumping up and down, screaming or crying with joy. Those who had come long distances only to be disappointed by not being chosen sometimes appealed to organizers to place them on an alternate list. An uninformed spectator would never have guessed that this recruitment process was for a project that would lead these men and women to spend weeks of their lives away from friends and family working on what many might see as a dry and complex policy topic. Thus, it seems clear that when offered such an opportunity to contribute to important public decisions, some people are motivated to invest large amounts of time and effort.

Moreover, it appears that all three assemblies managed to maintain this high motivation among their members throughout the very long proceedings. There are several indications of this. Organizers of the first citizen assembly anticipated that they might have a number of dropouts, especially when participants came to realize the extent of the sacrifice and effort they were going to have to make. Still, only one person quit in British Columbia, while in Ontario there was not a single withdrawal. In the Netherlands, the civic forum ended with six fewer members than the 143 it started with: four quit for personal reasons, while two left at the beginning because the process was too time-consuming for them. Also, attendance was near perfect. It hovered around 95–99 per cent in all three assemblies. Members missed meetings for only the most compelling reasons – getting married, delivering a baby, having an operation, or burying a loved one. The woman who missed a meeting because she was giving birth was back at the following session two weeks later and received a great round of applause from her colleagues. Furthermore, assembly members quickly became actively involved in 'extracurricular' activities at their own initiative. They gave media interviews, wrote op-ed letters to the press, and made presentations to local community groups and schools. One individual had large signs put on his pickup truck advertising the British Columbia assembly as he travelled up and down Vancouver Island.

A high level of enthusiasm for the assembly work is also apparent in the responses of members to our surveys. Table 2.7 shows that, over the entire span of the proceedings, great proportions of individuals felt that the project was important, that they were not wasting their time, and that the next step was exciting. More tellingly, even at the end of the year-long process, when participants knew exactly how much time and effort had been required of them, views remained very positive.

Only a handful regretted getting involved (2 per cent in British Columbia and 6 per cent in Ontario), and overwhelming majorities would be willing to join another citizen assembly on a different topic (92 per cent in British Columbia and 90 per cent in the Netherlands). In all three cases, these evaluative data indicate a very high degree of appreciation among the members for their assembly experience.

TABLE 2.7 *Enthusiasm of Assembly Members*

	British Columbia	The Netherlands	Ontario
The work of the assembly is important (1–5)	4.9	—	4.9
This session was well worth my time (1–5)	4.8	—	—
Looking forward to the next session (1–5)	4.9	—	4.8
Regrets joining the citizen assembly (%)	2.4	—	5.6
Would join another citizen assembly (%)	91.9	90.4	—

For the first three items, we report averages for the entire process (1 = strongly disagree, 5 = strongly agree). The last two items were measured in the post-assembly questionnaire.

So how can we account for the motivation, interest, dedication, and enthusiasm exhibited by assembly members? While the attraction of 'making history' by being the first to participate in a citizen assembly was an obvious source of pride for many members, this account of the structure and process, along with our own observation of the proceedings, allows us to suggest some of the factors that might be critical to their high level of engagement:

• *Random selection*

Selected through a process based on randomness, albeit one that provided for the opportunity to self-select out, members developed a strong sense of legitimacy. The assemblies attracted members with high levels of motivation.

• *Important task*

Electoral systems have important consequences that echo through the entire political system. Assembly members knew they were charged with a policy problem that was central to the health of their democracy. This provided a relevant and motivating challenge with serious stakes.

• *Significant power*

Members perceived that the assemblies had real influence and power. They were not simply engaged in public relations or consultations. In British Columbia and Ontario, any recommendation for change would automatically go to public refer- endum. In the Netherlands, the *Burgerforum*'s report would be delivered directly to the nation's cabinet.

• *Independence from government*

Freed from any government control or management, the citizen assemblies were confident that they were masters of their own proceedings and the solutions that would emerge from them. This encouraged purposeful participation.

• *Effective leadership*

A strong independent chair, with no interest in the substantive issue, created cooperative working and social relationships among the members that allowed them to spend the extended periods of time necessary for the successive phases of the project.

• *Community building*

An extensive residential context provided ample opportunities to socialize, trade joyous and less happy stories about life, and understand each other's perspectives. Assembly meetings actually became a crucible where new friendships were forged.[10] These personal bonds mattered as well in sustaining interest.

2.9 WHAT HAPPENED AFTERWARDS?

All three citizen assemblies came to an end, after their deliberative phase, with the production of final reports outlining their activities and final decisions. In the two Canadian cases, they made recommendations for a major change in the electoral system, while the Dutch *Burgerforum* suggested only minor alterations. The next stage would involve implementation of the recommendations. In British Columbia and Ontario, as the respective governments had promised, the reports triggered a referendum at the time of the subsequent provincial general election. The acceptance threshold was exceptionally high, with Ontario following British Columbia's precedent of a double standard (60 per cent support province-wide and a majority in 60 per cent of the constituencies). In neither case did the referendum question engage the public, which was more preoccupied with the issues of the election. Campaigning politicians in both provinces mostly ignored the question. Despite this lack of attention, the assembly's proposal was endorsed by 58 per cent of the British Columbian electorate (and a majority in all but two electoral districts) in 2005. The government, returned with a smaller vote share, decided that the proposal deserved another chance and promised to rerun the referendum in 2009 at the time of the next general election. In this second instance where some public funding was provided to both sides, STV attracted much less support: only 39 per cent of voters (with a majority in eight districts). This result mirrors the outcome of the 2007 referendum in Ontario, when MMP garnered only 37 per cent

---

[10] This is epitomized by the fact that more than half of British Columbia's assembly members attended a conference in January 2009 to celebrate the fifth anniversary of the inaugural meeting. Many considered this a 'family reunion which they could not miss for the world'. In Ontario, three reunions have ensured members stayed connected.

province-wide and obtained a majority in only 5 of the 107 electoral districts. Both provinces have no immediate plans to revisit the issue of electoral reform.

In the Netherlands, the *Burgerforum*'s recommendation – never destined for voters – also had a frosty reception. Initially, D66 had the political clout to put electoral reform on the agenda and to instigate a citizen assembly, even though no other party had a real appetite for electoral system change. However, the political landscape changed drastically while the assembly was working. During the proceedings, the coalition government fell, the D66 ministers (including Pechtold) left the government, and an election was called. When the assembly's report was released, no government had yet been formed. One did emerge a few months later, but D66 was not part of it. Given the structure of partisan and coalition interests, there was no prospect for electoral reform in the Netherlands, even of the modest sort proposed by the *Burgerforum*.

While all three citizen assemblies unfolded without a major problem, all three reform proposals failed to be implemented. Why? We will tackle this question in Chapter 8.

2.10 CONCLUSION

Electoral reform is a subject that closely touches the interests of active politicians, and so it took a set of idiosyncratic circumstances – a succession of particularly dysfunctional electoral outcomes and the unformed democratic instincts of an opposition politician suddenly in office – to create a citizen assembly in which ordinary voters were given the power to design the electoral system. The precedent of British Columbia's assembly meant that the model was available when Dutch and Ontario politicians were seeking a mechanism to consider the issue.

Gibson's careful plan for a four-stage multi-month process worked. It was neither quick nor cheap, but the result appears, at this initial stage of the analysis, successful. Having sketched the ways in which these three assemblies were organized and operated, we can now turn to a more detailed consideration of just who these citizens were as well as why they decided as they did. The balance of the book will be devoted to examining the nature of participation, the dynamics of preferences, the quality of decision-making, the impact of the exercise on citizenship, and the reactions of other political actors.

3

Who were the Participants?

In democracy everyone has the right to be represented, even the jerks.

Chris Patten, *London Evening Standard* (2 May 1991).

In the construction of the three assemblies, there was a strong emphasis on the importance of their 'representativeness'. All selection procedures used a random selection process to send initial invitations and then to pick members from among those individuals willing to participate. In each case, the purpose of adopting the random selection principle was to create an assembly membership that was as representative as possible of the wider society (see Section 2.4). For instance, the Terms of Reference of the first assembly mandated that the participants were 'to be broadly representative of the adult population of British Columbia'. Elections BC, which maintained the provincial voters' list, argued that random selection would provide 'a reasonable cross-section of the population reflecting an appropriate mix of ethnicity, education and economic status'.

Notwithstanding the efforts to use random sampling in the various stages of the selection process, self-selection was also a central element: only those who expressed an interest could take part. Although the stratification of the initial sample (using region, gender, and, in some cases, age) avoided visible differences between population and sample, self-selection could have led to distortions of the 'mirror image' of the electorate that the assemblies were intended to be.

Critical questions are raised. Where does the idea of representativeness come from, and why was it important? How well did the assemblies represent the general public? Did self-selection undermine the process? What consequences can be attached to (not) having a representative body? In this chapter, we start answering these questions by briefly discussing the notion of representation by lot as compared with representation by election. We argue that representation by lot is by no means a new form of political representation and that it derives its representative character from other sources than elections. Subsequently, we outline the similarities and differences between the respective populations and the assemblies, as well as examine the potential consequences of any differences. We conclude this discussion by considering the extent to which the representative character of the assemblies was perceived by the members as a critical element legitimating their activity.

3.1 CAN RANDOMLY SELECTED INDIVIDUALS REPRESENT OTHERS?

'Representation has only been associated with the system of election (. . .) never with lot' writes Bernard Manin in his study of the foundations of modern representative democracy (1997: 8). Despite the strong relationship Manin sees between representation and elections, the idea that other mechanisms can underpin representation is accepted by others. For example, Hanna Pitkin, in her account of descriptive representation, notes that various authors propose using representative sampling to select representatives (1967: 73–91). She points out that some scholars argue that random sampling is to be preferred to elections because it is more likely to produce a parliament that reflects the population of ordinary citizens. More recently, others have also argued for the use of lotteries for representative systems (McCormick 2006).[1]

In practice, though, the use of lotteries in politics has always been limited. And the idea of full random sampling has never been particularly popular. For example, Manin shows that in Athens, which is often characterized as using lotteries to fill offices, the process was restricted to citizens who expressed interest in holding office (see Section 1.3). Also, inclusiveness in Athens, the extent to which people were allowed to participate, was limited to a small group (Smith and Wales 2000: 56). Only citizens were allowed to acquire a representative function. Children, women, slaves, foreigners, and their descendants were not.

In all three citizen assemblies, some groups were also excluded. People below the voting age were disqualified.[2] In British Columbia and Ontario, elected representatives and some party officials were barred from membership. In the Netherlands, the rules disallowed members of the Electoral Committee, of the Ministry of the Interior, and of the national and European parliaments from taking part in the assembly, but members of local councils and party officials were not excluded. In each case, the main reason for barring these officials seems to have been to ensure the assembly's independence from government. Recommendations were to reflect the views and preferences of the public, not the politicians who would compete under any proposed electoral system.

Recognizing that these restrictions compromised an absolute random selection, the more significant challenge to assembly representativeness was self-selection: the final membership draws were limited to people who demonstrated their willingness to join the citizen assembly. Perhaps only individuals who cared for

---

[1] For a proposal of combining lotteries with elections in order to ensure descriptive representation, see Amar (1983). Barber also defends lotteries in his book *Strong Democracy* (1984).

[2] This was to be consistent with electoral laws which exclude members of the population on grounds such as age and citizenship.

the topic or had an axe to grind threw their name into the hat. We need to ask if self-selection distorted the representativeness of the assemblies.

How are we to evaluate representation through self-selection and lot as compared with representation through elections? One way is by focusing on different aspects of representation and using them to compare representation by lot with representation by election. Following previous work, we distinguish five types:[3]

- *authorization*: individuals have the right to represent others through some accepted procedure;
- *responsibility*: individuals represent others by being obliged to explain some decisions and by accepting possible sanctions;
- *symbolization*: individuals are accepted as representative of others;
- *description*: individuals are representative by being like (in some respects) the others represented; and
- *substantive*: individuals represent others by acting according to their wishes and/or interests.

A democratically elected legislature is deemed representative mainly because it is *authorized* to act as a consequence of its members being selected by clearly defined electoral procedures. It is also representative because citizens are able to hold the assembly members *responsible* in subsequent elections. Some legislatures acquire a certain *symbolic* representation, although many parliaments face low levels of confidence and trust. Ideally, there is also some similarity between the legislative assembly and the public, although full *descriptive* representation is generally neither attained nor desired. It is not attained because assemblies and populations often differ substantially – many legislatures have disproportionately few women or members of minority groups. It is seldom desired, for parliaments are also expected to be wiser and more informed than the electorate at large. However, in some instances, even the central elements of a legislature's representative character – authorization and responsibility – can be relatively deficient. Warren argues that 'democratic linkages between citizens and representatives can and do break down in numerous ways' and people 'are increasingly likely to believe that representative linkages are not working well' (2008: 52–3). Electoral procedures and results are occasionally contested, and the capacity to hold officials accountable is questionable. In sum, elections are often rather blunt instruments of democratic control.

Citizen assemblies appear to provide an alternative to the deficiencies in the representativeness of elected bodies by focusing on other aspects of representation. The representative character of citizen assemblies is mainly built upon the

---

[3] The prime source for a discussion of the various aspects of representation is Pitkin (1967). Brown (2006) argues that different representative bodies can stress different aspects of representation. Others too have studied which aspects of representation are relevant for different representative bodies (Mansbridge 2003; James 2008: 121–6; Warren 2008: 67–8).

concepts of *descriptive* and *substantive* representation. The descriptive part is obvious: the selection process is designed to produce an assembly that reflects the society from which it is drawn. As a consequence, the assembly is expected to have preferences that are more congruent with those of the general population than those of elected politicians. Therefore, assembly designers expected that assemblies would also be better able to substantively represent the population. Descriptive and substantive representation, along with *authorization* through lottery and self-selection, would also legitimize an assembly through *symbolic* representation. In the citizen assemblies, the final aspect of representation – *responsibility* – was less important. Though one might argue that the assemblies as a whole were also held accountable, for in two cases their decisions were subject to popular referendum, while in the third case the advice was delivered to government for evaluation by elected representatives.[4]

The citizen assemblies were thus designed to represent the population, albeit in a different way than legislatures do. Descriptive representation was to increase both their substantive and symbolic representational dimensions. At the same time, however, the assemblies were intended as deliberative bodies whose participants would be open to reconsider and change their opinions, a premise that seems to run contrary to the idea of pure descriptive representation. Our question is to what extent the three citizen assemblies actually met the criteria of descriptive representation.

3.2 COMPARING ASSEMBLIES AND POPULATIONS

The selection of members in the three assemblies started with random sampling from lists of voters. All drawn individuals were sent a letter asking them to participate in the process. Among each of the different communities, the same proportion – about 6–7 per cent – responded positively indicating an interest in participating (see Table 2.1). In all three selection processes, the intention was to choose equal numbers of men and women. And in each case, geographical representation – constituencies in British Columbia and Ontario, provinces in the Netherlands – was fully assured by using those units as strata in the sampling procedure. In addition, in British Columbia, explicit attention was paid to the representation of age groups.[5] All other characteristics were largely left to random selection.

---

[4] Pitkin sees an inherent tension between description and accountability; people cannot be held accountable for what they are.

[5] In Ontario, the initial sample was also stratified by age, but this criterion was not used in the subsequent steps that led to the selection of members.

The comparisons in this chapter use data from statistical offices and election studies to describe the populations. For the assemblies, we rely on the first survey conducted among the participants. Comparing three assemblies with three populations is far from simple. Not all data sets were designed to be comparable. Some information from the election studies was only collected among a subset of the initial sample, making inferences to the population at large difficult. In some instances, the evidence only allows us to make comparisons for one or two assemblies. The data, therefore, have to be interpreted with care.

3.3 WERE THE ASSEMBLIES REPRESENTATIVE IN TERMS OF SOCIO-DEMOGRAPHIC CHARACTERISTICS?

Given that the sampling process that underlay assembly invitations was strongly organized around gender and geographical representation, it is not surprising that men and women were represented equally and that all geographical units were well represented. The effort to represent all age groups, however, was a little less successful. The two cases where age sampling was less strictly applied (the Netherlands and Ontario) produced assemblies that better reflected the population's age distribution (Table 3.1). In British Columbia, both the youngest and the oldest age groups were under-represented. In the Netherlands, only the oldest age group was

TABLE 3.1 *Socio-Demographic Characteristics of the Population and the Participants*

	British Columbia		The Netherlands		Ontario	
	Pop.	Ass.	Pop.	Ass.	Pop.	Ass.
Age (year)						
18–24	11	7	11	11	12	11
25–39	26	24	26	32	27	23
40–55	32	35	30	31	30	32
56–70	17	28	21	23	20	26
71+	14	6	13	4	11	12
Country of origin						
Canada	73	74	—	—	71	74
Other	27	26	—	—	29	26
Education						
No high school degree	28	5	9	1	22	2
Bachelor/university	19	44	26	57	20	44
Average no. of organizational memberships	2.0	2.1	—	—	1.8	1.8

Apart from the last row, numbers are percentages.

under-represented; about 13 per cent of the Dutch population is older than 70, while only 4 per cent in the assembly belonged to this age group. By comparison, Ontario's assembly replicated the age distribution of its population quite well. The number of people born abroad – about a quarter of the Canadian voting-age population – was almost completely matched in the two Canadian assemblies.[6]

When studying descriptive representation, one has to decide which character-istics of individuals are relevant. One approach is to concentrate on socio-demographic variables known to be related to political participation. Research in-dicates that age and education are two central determinants of participation (Wolfinger and Rosenstone 1980; Blais 2000; Franklin 2004). Individuals participate because they can, because they want to, and because they have been asked to (Verba et al. 1995). Since these factors are so predominant among older, better-educated, and more socially connected people, participants are more likely to come from these groups. We have already indicated that the population's age breakdown was reproduced relatively accurately in the assemblies. What about the other two factors?

Were assembly members more educated than the populations they came from? University training provides the simplest comparative measure of education across the assemblies and populations.[7] On average, members of the assembly were far more educated than the general population (see Table 3.1). Across British Columbia, the percentage of people with a university degree was 19 per cent, among assembly members it was more than twice that at 44 per cent. In Ontario, the figures were similar: 20 per cent (population) as compared with 44 per cent (assembly). In the Netherlands, which has a different type of educational system, 26 per cent of the population was trained at this level, while the number was over twice as large in the *Burgerforum* (57 per cent). And the proportions of individuals without a high school degree were dramatically lower in all assemblies than among the wider populations.

Did assembly members exhibit more social capital? No. Their average number of memberships in civic organizations – an indicator of the extent of social network integration – is almost identical to the population data.

In terms of socio-demographic profiles, it appears that the main discrepancy between the assemblies and the populations concerned education levels: assembly participants were much better educated. This difference is also uncovered in deliberative polls, the process that makes the most strenuous efforts to attain strict

---

[6] The population figures are drawn from census statistics: 2001 for British Columbia and 2006 for Ontario.

[7] To measure the level of education in the Canadian population, we use census data for the population over 15 years old (from Statistics Canada). The Dutch population data were collected from Statistics Netherlands and cover individuals aged between 15 and 64 (thus including people not having finished their studies yet and excluding a large part of the older population). The appropriate categories that amount to university graduates were collapsed in the British Columbia and Ontario assembly questionnaires. The equivalent Dutch assembly categories include 'HBO' and university. In the table, we also find comparisons across the lowest level of education. The lowest level in Canada is no high school diploma, while in the Netherlands, it is having only 'basisschool'.

TABLE 3.2 *General Attitudes and Behaviours of the Population and the Participants*

	British Columbia		The Netherlands		Ontario	
	Pop.	Ass.	Pop.	Ass.	Pop.	Ass.
Political interest						
Low (0–2)	19	1	16	8	14	3
Medium-low (3–5)	30	24	33	31	30	14
Medium-high (6–8)	33	50	23	40	40	59
High (9–10)	18	25	28	21	15	24
Satisfaction with democracy						
Very satisfied	12	1	7	8	16	10
Fairly satisfied	42	46	69	70	49	67
Not very satisfied	30	46	20	19	24	21
Not satisfied at all	13	7	4	2	7	2
Government does not care						
Strongly agree	24	11	—	15	22	11
Somewhat agree	37	40	44	47	38	31
Somewhat disagree	27	35	56	35	28	40
Strongly disagree	11	13	—	3	10	16
Turnout	71	95	80	98	57	96

Numbers are percentages.

representativeness. While the participants of deliberative polls generally resemble those contacted but who did not participate, both groups tend to be more educated than the general population (see Fishkin et al. 2009, App. A1; Farrar et al. 2010, App. A). This difference, however, need not be problematic if the attitudes of participants are similar to those of the general public. We thus examine whether this was true or not in the case of the three citizen assemblies.

3.4 WERE THE ASSEMBLIES REPRESENTATIVE IN TERMS OF ATTITUDES TOWARDS POLITICS?

In this section, we compare the political views and behaviours of assembly members, as expressed in the first baseline questionnaire, with those of a representative sample of the population as revealed in the nearest national election study.[8] We start by

---

[8] This is the 2004 Canadian Election Study for British Columbia, the 2006 Canadian Election Study for Ontario, and the 2006 Dutch Parliamentary Election Study for the Netherlands.

looking at general attitudes towards politics. If citizens are interested in politics, we would expect that they would be more willing to participate. Were assembly members more politically interested than the average person? Not surprisingly, they were (see Table 3.2).[9] Very few assembly members indicated little or no interest in politics, while between 15 and 20 per cent of the populations admitted as much. At the other end of the scale, the assemblies contained a larger proportion of highly interested individuals than the population in two of the three cases.[10]

Perhaps more directly relevant are attitudes towards politicians and the government, for they may shape preferences regarding electoral systems. Two competing expectations can be formulated. The first is that assembly members have a more positive outlook towards politics than the general public, given that they are more politically interested and there is a connection between interest and positive attitudes. But alternatively, it may be that members are more negative than the population, for they may have been predominantly (self-) selected from among the ranks of those who think politics can and should be improved. If both factors are at work, they may even cancel each other out.

The results of our analysis are ambiguous [11] On the one hand, in the two Canadian assemblies, sentiments towards the state of democracy were slightly more negative than among the public at large: members claimed to be a bit less satisfied with the way democracy currently works. In the Netherlands, though, there was no substantial difference between the two groups.[12] On the other hand, traditional indicators of cynicism and efficacy exhibited the reverse pattern. Canadian assembly members reported more positive attitudes about government and politicians than the general public, while *Burgerforum* participants held more negative views than the population. Statements like 'the government does not care about what people like me think', 'those elected soon lose touch with the people', 'all parties are basically the same', and 'politicians are ready to lie to get elected' were supported less frequently by the British Columbia and Ontario assembly members than by their fellow citizens. For their part, Dutch assembly members were more likely than their compatriots to think that 'people like me have no influence on government policy', that 'MPs do not care about the opinions of people', and that 'political parties are only interested in votes not opinions'.

---

[9] Instead of political interest, we used a slightly different question in the Dutch case in order to facilitate comparison with the Dutch population: 'When there is national news in the newspaper, for example about problems in the government, how often do you read it?'.

[10] Overall, on a 0–10 scale, the assemblies and populations differed by an average of 1.5 points.

[11] Note that the population data were not collected at the same time as the assembly data, and the observed differences could be a consequence of changes in context.

[12] In the Canadian assembly questionnaires, this question was positioned right before the 'satisfaction with the electoral system' item, so this result may have been a consequence of the close proximity of the latter.

TABLE 3.3 *Electoral System Opinions of the Population and the Participants*

	British Columbia		The Netherlands		Ontario	
	Pop.	Ass.	Pop.	Ass.	Pop.	Ass.
Satisfaction with current electoral system						
Very satisfied	5	1	13	3	14	2
Fairly satisfied	53	34	74	67	61	52
Not very satisfied	35	55	12	28	21	45
Not at all satisfied	7	9	1	2	4	1
A majority of seats without a majority of votes						
Acceptable	17	9	—	—	27	8
Not acceptable	62	76	—	—	56	73
A party that gets 10% of votes should get 10% of seats						
Strongly agree	8	31	—	—	12	19
Somewhat agree	40	39	—	—	35	46
Somewhat disagree	22	12	—	—	27	17
Strongly disagree	7	8	—	—	7	3

Numbers are percentages.

Finally, we inspected two central political behaviours: turnout and vote choice. Almost all assembly members reported having voted in the previous election (95 per cent or more). Official turnout statistics suggest that 20–43 per cent of citizens failed to show up at the ballot box. So it seems clear that those abstainers also shied away from the assembly process.[13] In addition, the partisan preferences of assembly members differed from those of the entire electorate. We compared the distribution of reported party support in the most recent election among assembly members with the actual election results. In British Columbia, the absolute differences added up to just 6 percentage points. But at 23 and 17 points, the totals were higher in the Netherlands and Ontario.[14] However, there does not seem to be a clear pattern to these deviations, for in both British Columbia and the Netherlands the largest parties were under-represented, while the governing party was over-represented in Ontario.

These data reveal that there were notable differences between the political attitudes of the populations and those of the assemblies. With the exception of greater levels of interest and turnout among the assembly memberships, though, the direction of these differences varied across the three cases.

---

[13] Since turnout is likely over-reported in a survey, the real difference with actual turnout may have been smaller.

[14] These are the summed absolute differences between percentages in the assembly voting for a party and actual support in the last election according to voting records divided by 2.

3.5 WERE THE ASSEMBLIES REPRESENTATIVE IN TERMS OF ATTITUDES TOWARDS ELECTORAL SYSTEMS?

Given their mandates, the most important potential biases in these assemblies are to be sought in their members' attitudes towards electoral systems. Such bias could have directly influenced the outcome of the process. The simplest attitude to examine is satisfaction with the current electoral system.[15] In all three assemblies, members were less satisfied with their existing system than the population (see Table 3.3). The differences were considerable. In British Columbia, where a clear majority of the population was content with 'first-past-the-post' (58 per cent), most assembly participants expressed dissatisfaction (64 per cent). In the other two cases, both groups were on the happier side of the fence, but the assembly majorities were slimmer. Only 13 per cent of the Dutch population was dissatisfied with open-list proportional representation (list-PR), while 30 per cent of *Burgerforum* members shared that opinion. In Ontario, three-quarters of the public was pleased with the status quo, compared with only about half of the assembly members. This suggests that assembly participants may have been more inclined towards electoral reform than were average citizens.

Although the populations were generally satisfied, the Canadians did not like some of the features of their electoral system. Most British Columbians (62 per cent) and Ontarians (56 per cent) thought it was unacceptable for a party to 'win a majority of seats without winning a majority of votes' (an inherent feature of single member plurality). Among the assemblies, this sentiment was even more widespread (76 and 73 per cent respectively). Both groups also agreed with the general principle of proportionality. The public in British Columbia (48 per cent) and Ontario (47 per cent) believed that 'a party that gets 10 per cent of the votes should also get 10 per cent of the seats', and even larger proportions of assembly members subscribed to the proposition (70 and 65 per cent). Despite being satisfied with the current electoral system, many Canadians, both inside and outside the assemblies, desired a system that would generate more proportional electoral outcomes.

In the 2006 Dutch Parliamentary Election Study, respondents were only asked about the desirability of a more regionally based system. Less than half the population said that regional differences were not sufficiently reflected in parliamentary elections (43 per cent). As the Dutch assembly process started, a majority of its participants supported the idea that better representation of regions in parliament was needed (67 per cent). This gap between the two groups proved

---

[15] The question was about the Canadian system in the population survey. Since provincial and national electoral systems are comparable, we can safely assume the attitudes will be similar. The question in the Dutch Parliamentary Election Study was 'How satisfied are you with the way members of Parliament are currently elected?'. Dutch members were asked: 'How satisfied are you with the functioning of the current electoral system?'.

to be inconsequential, since support for a district-based electoral system was not strong enough to advance such a proposal to the decision-making phase.

In sum, there seems to have been a bias in favour of change in all three citizen assemblies. Assembly members were less satisfied with the existing electoral system than their respective populations. But higher levels of public satisfaction were tempered by dissatisfaction with certain aspects of the electoral system. Moreover, especially in the two Canadian cases, assembly members and the general population favoured changes in the same direction.

3.6 DID THE BIASES MATTER?

Compared with the populations, citizen assembly members were better educated, more interested in politics, and less satisfied with the current electoral system in all three cases. These biases may have had consequences for substantive representation if these characteristics were also related to opinions about the most desirable electoral system.

Since it was impossible to ask for the participants' views about systems they had never heard of, we only started capturing their preferences at the conclusion of the learning phase. We use this first measurement, recognizing the possibility that members' initial preferences may have already been changed by this time. To analyse the relationship between members' characteristics and electoral system preferences, we focus on comparisons between the four electoral systems that received the most attention in the assemblies: single member plurality (SMP), single transferable vote (STV), mixed member proportional (MMP), and list-PR.

Did participants with a higher level of education, a higher level of political interest, and a less positive attitude towards the current voting system have substantially different opinions about electoral systems? And more specifically, did they have stronger preferences for a particular system that is a departure from the status quo? Table 3.4 presents the bivariate relationships between these three variables and relative evaluations of electoral systems.

In British Columbia, education and satisfaction with the current system were negatively correlated to the relative preference of SMP (the status quo) to STV (the ultimate reform proposal). However, it should be noted that even among those having low levels of education, STV was preferred to SMP. The effect of a more representative assembly would thus have been small. In addition, there seems to have been a relationship between education and a preference for STV relative to both MMP and list-PR. The background of this difference is still unclear. In Chapter 5, we will see that assembly members who favoured a simple system resisted STV. It may be that these individuals were less educated, a proposition we explore in Chapter 6.

TABLE 3.4 *Relationships between Variables and Initial Preferences for Electoral Systems*

	SMP > STV	SMP > MMP	SMP > list-PR	STV > MMP	STV > list-PR	MMP > list-PR
British Columbia						
Education	−0.14*	n.s.	n.s.	0.22**	0.19**	n.s.
Political interest	n.s.	n.s.	n.s.	n.s.	n.s.	n.s.
System satisfaction	−0.16*	n.s.	−0.24**	n.s.	−0.14**	−0.19**
Netherlands						
Education	n.s.	n.s.	n.s.	n.s.	n.s.	n.s.
Political interest	n.s.	n.s.	−0.12*	0.16**	n.s.	−0.17**
System satisfaction	n.s.	n.s.	n.s.	n.s.	n.s.	0.17**
Ontario						
Education	n.s.	−0.19*	−0.26**	n.s.	n.s.	n.s.
Political interest	n.s.	n.s.	n.s.	n.s.	n.s.	n s
System satisfaction	−0.20**	n.s.	n.s.	n.s.	n.s.	n.s.

** Significant at 0.05; * significant at 0.10. Numbers are Kendall tau-b. The data are based on rankings (B preferred to A, indifferent, or A preferred to B).

In the Netherlands, education – the most important difference found between the population and the assembly – was not related to system preferences. Nor were more subtle divergences between different variants of list proportional representation (open, closed, or free) linked to education.

In Ontario, a relative preference for proportional electoral systems over the status quo was somewhat more visible among the higher educated participants, for education was connected to higher rankings of both list-PR and MMP than SMP. Still, this variable did not point to one particular favourite system.

So, apart from British Columbia where those with a higher level of education liked STV more than MMP from the start while those less educated had the reverse ranking, the representational deficiencies we observe in the assemblies were not substantially associated with differences of opinion regarding the various electoral system families considered.

3.7 HOW DID THE ASSEMBLIES PERCEIVE THEIR COMPOSITION?

This brings us to a final observation about how the question of randomness and representativeness was seen by the participants. Assembly designers intended that these groups would derive their legitimacy from a random selection process that would produce an assembly of ordinary citizens. To what extent was this true?

The members of the first assembly, in British Columbia, accepted the claim that they were representative because of random selection. Though some initially wondered if they were individually representative of their area as opposed to being collectively representative of the province, most ultimately opted for the latter position. They also adopted randomness as the acceptable basis for action. Thus, when it was decided, on a couple of occasions, to appoint a committee – to choose the presentations to be heard on the first day of the deliberative phase, or to select the members who would present the final report to the government – all agreed that the right way to select the committee was by random draw. Randomness was considered very important by the members and it legitimated their capacity to speak for the people of British Columbia.

Within the Dutch assembly, there were some discussions about whether the *Burgerforum* was indeed able to 'stand for and act for' the Dutch population. Some members saw themselves as mere delegates and suggested the assembly should conduct a study among the people to find out what they wanted. However, the chair stressed the idea that the assembly should act 'on behalf of' the public, and this was ultimately accepted by the membership. In the work of the *Burgerforum*, the idea of randomness was not an operating principle, and committee construction mostly depended on a self-selection mechanism.

In Ontario, the representative character of the assembly became an important identifying characteristic, largely because the chair would often repeat the claim to both the members and the media. The members probably hoped that, as a representative sample of the public, their recommendations would have traction. The phrase 'random selection of Ontarians' or an equivalent was occasionally mentioned in the media, but neither to support nor impugn their recommendations.

The extent to which the representativeness of the assemblies had consequences in the Canadian referendums on their recommendations is discussed in Chapter 8.

3.8 CONCLUSION

In this chapter, we have shown that, despite the emphasis on randomness and despite a careful reflection of gender, region, and, to some extent, age, there were some differences between the populations and the citizen assemblies. In all three cases, assembly members were more educated than the voting-age population from which they were drawn. Education, however, was not significantly and systematically linked to preferences concerning electoral systems. There were also gaps between the assemblies and their respective populations on certain political attitudes. Members expressed greater interest in politics and less satisfaction for the current voting system. Nevertheless, ratings of major electoral system families did not differ substantially in consistent ways across levels of interest and satisfaction.

There is an issue about whether these attitudinal discrepancies between the assemblies and the populations stem from the inherent limitations of the selection process or from some natural evolutionary process. On the one hand, it is entirely possible that the random draw among a self-selected pool resulted in a group of individuals who were different – more interested and more reform-oriented – than typical citizens. When recruiting individuals to spend a year working on a public policy proposal, it seems unrealistic to expect to attract a perfectly representative group. On the other hand, these biases could have been the consequences of the preliminary deliberative activity of newly identified members. Our baseline survey was administered before the formal work of the citizen assembly had begun, but quite some time after the participants were first selected – approximately two months in the Canadian cases, and about two weeks in the Netherlands. It is possible that the views of individual members evolved during this period. Perhaps people who have committed to extensive public work on a particular topic start to think about that subject, to do some research on their own, and to bring up that topic when chatting with acquaintances. During these many weeks, interest in politics might have been enhanced and attitudes towards electoral politics might have been nudged in the direction of change. This possibility might help explain why attitudinal gaps between population and assembly for political interest and satisfaction with the current system were smallest in the Netherlands where the period between the selection and our baseline questionnaire was shortest. We simply cannot rule out one hypothesis over the other. Reality is probably a mixture of both.

The logic and the legitimacy of the citizen assemblies depended on them being representative. It is clear that, at least on some dimensions, they were not. Nevertheless, had these departures from perfect representativeness not existed, had the composition of the assemblies perfectly mirrored the populations, there is no persuasive evidence that the outcomes of the citizen assemblies would have been any different. In Chapter 4, we examine the dynamics that led to their final decisions.

4

How did the Decisions Come About?

> The decisions affecting matters of general interest come to by an assembly of
> men of distinction, but specialists in different walks of life, are not sensibly
> superior to the decisions that would be adopted by a gathering of imbeciles.
> The truth is, they can only bring to bear in common on the work in hand those
> mediocre qualities which are the birthright of every average individual.
>
> Gustave Le Bon, *The Crowd* (1896)

As we have seen in previous chapters, three structurally similar citizen assemblies
on electoral reform came to three different conclusions. In two cases – British
Columbia and Ontario – they recommended a major change. Although the two
Canadian assemblies both decided that their single member plurality (SMP)
system ought to give way to a form of proportional representation (PR), they
clearly differed on what sort of PR system was desirable. For its part, the Dutch
Burgerforum called for a modest change to the ballot, but essentially recommended the Netherlands maintain its existing system. This would seem to refute
critics' claim that if citizens are put to work for an extended period they will
inevitably recommend some major change, if only to justify their time and effort.
In this chapter, we trace the dynamics of assembly members' preferences throughout the proceedings to explore how they came to such different outcomes.

During a year-long deliberative process, opinion stability is unlikely, and one
should expect some inter-temporal dynamics. But different types of instability are
possible. On the one hand, there is evidence of extreme individual attitude change:
citizens' views about political issues often fluctuate over time, almost to the point
of appearing like random responses (Converse 1964; Feldman 1989; Zaller and
Feldman 1992). On the other hand, the literature on deliberative democracy – both
empirical and theoretical – clearly argues that learning, discussion, and thought
engender more enlightened preferences (cf. Luskin et al. 2002; Mutz 2002, 2006).
As the embodiment of 'deliberation-on-steroids', citizen assemblies should be
more likely to exhibit the second type of movement. The extensive knowledge-
acquisition and decision-making phases of our three cases ought to have led to
progressive and systematic – rather than flimsy and haphazard – opinion change.
Is this expectation valid?

This chapter documents the path taken by assembly members' views on electoral systems. It ascertains when preferences emerged, whether they moved afterwards, how volatile they were, and whether the movement was steered by comprehensible factors.

4.1 THE STARTING POINT

In each assembly, the existing electoral system inevitably provided members with a benchmark. It was the system with which they were most familiar, and the one against which any recommendation would have to be measured. One might expect that an impact of the assembly's learning phase would be some alteration in members' attitudes about their own system as they gained knowledge about the wide variety, and comparative merits, of alternative ways of conducting elections. This proved to be the case in two of the assemblies. In both British Columbia and Ontario, the two instances of plurality systems, the proportion expressing satisfaction 'with the way the electoral system works in [their province]' was never particularly high to begin with, but it dropped sharply over the course of the learning stage. In British Columbia, it was halved, from 35 to just 19 per cent, while in Ontario the proportion satisfied fell from 54 to 33 per cent. It would seem that the more Canadian participants learned, the less satisfactory their own system appeared to them. By contrast, the Dutch members went into their assembly far happier, 70 per cent were fairly or very satisfied with their electoral system, and learning about other systems led to even more of them expressing satisfaction (82 per cent).[1]

Interestingly, the more frequent tracking of members' opinions in British Columbia indicates that most of the decline in satisfaction with the province's current system had occurred by the second weekend of the learning phase, before other electoral systems had been examined. The earliness of this shift suggests that more knowledge about the status quo was the key explanation, rather than in-depth information about the various other options.

At the beginning of the assembly process, in a questionnaire administered before the first meeting, we could not enquire about participants' opinions on the variety of electoral systems, simply because they lacked knowledge of the multiple alternatives. But we did ask them if they preferred one electoral system for their jurisdiction (province/country). The vast majority of assembly members

---

[1] This Canadian decline in expressed satisfaction with the working of domestic electoral systems was not matched by a similar decline in satisfaction with the state of (domestic) democracy. That said, the Dutch consistently expressed higher levels of satisfaction with their democracy than did the Ontario members who, in turn, were more satisfied than the British Columbians.

claimed that they had no preferred system in mind. 90 per cent in both British Columbia and Ontario, and 83 per cent in the Netherlands.

The learning phase changed this initial state of affairs. By its end, the proportions reporting no preference had dropped to slightly less than half (47 per cent in British Columbia, 46 per cent in the Netherlands, and 44 per cent in Ontario). How quickly did the preferences emerge during the information-acquisition sessions? The more detailed British Columbia data provide some indication. The percentage with a favourite system increased from 10 per cent before the proceedings, to 25 per cent in the third (of six) learning weekends, to 39 per cent in the fourth, to 53 per cent after the public consultations. Thus, the opinions were forged gradually over the many weeks of the first part of the process.

The preferences that had begun to materialize reveal that the assemblies were starting to move in different directions. Among the Dutch, already highly disposed to favour their existing system, no other system commanded substantial support. In both Canadian provinces, the members who had developed a preference through the learning phase were not rallying to their current plurality systems. In Ontario, a very large majority (about 80 per cent) of the decided claimed to support a mixed member proportional (MMP) system, suggesting that an incipient consensus had become apparent by the end of this phase. In British Columbia, the half of the assembly's membership which had developed a preference was divided between those favouring the single transferable vote (STV) and those opting for an MMP system.

At the end of the learning phase, the assemblies had successfully accomplished one of their major tasks – teaching their members enough about electoral systems so that they could make assessments about them and begin to deliberate in a thoughtful and informed way about possible alternatives. As we have seen, this process appears to have left the members of the two Canadian assemblies more unsatisfied with their existing systems and so predisposed to seek an alternative. Dutch members exhibited the reverse pattern, they seem to have learned little that reduced their confidence in the country's current system or fostered a debate that was likely to lead to any major change.

4.2 CHANGING VIEWS OF ELECTORAL SYSTEMS

After the learning phase, members knew enough about the distinctive elements of a range of different electoral systems, and how they incorporated various representational principles, to come to initial judgements about them. Table 4.1 records their estimations of 'how good' members thought 'each system would be' for their community. The evaluations ranged from 'very bad' to 'very good' (on a 1–7 scale), and were captured at three critical junctures in the assembly process: at the

TABLE 4.1 *Average Ratings of Electoral Systems*

	British Columbia			The Netherlands			Ontario		
	T1	T2	T3	T1	T2	T3	T1	T2	T3
Majority, two ballots	3.0	2.8	2.8	3.0	2.7	2.6	3.5	3.3	4.0
Majority, preferential ballot	3.4	3.7	3.4	3.1	2.8	2.8	4.0	4.1	4.3
Plurality, single member (SMP)	2.9	3.1	2.9	3.2	2.8	2.7	3.4	3.6	3.5
Plurality, multi-member	3.3	3.3	3.1	—	—	—	3.9	3.7	3.7
Proportional representation, open-list	5.3	4.9	4.5	5.6	5.8	6.0	4.9	4.7	5.0
Proportional representation, closed-list	3.8	3.5	3.2	4.3	4.8	4.4	4.4	4.2	4.9
Single transferable vote (STV)	5.1	5.2	6.2	3.9	3.2	3.2	4.8	4.4	4.6
Mixed, proportional (MMP)	5.4	5.4	5.2	5.2	5.0	4.4	5.9	6.1	6.5
Mixed, parallel (MMM)	4.2	3.6	3.6	4.4	4.1	3.8	4.2	4.7	4.5

Scores on 1–7 scales: very bad to very good. Three points in time: T1 is the end of the learning phase, T2 is the midpoint, and T3 is after the final decision.

end of the learning phase, at the midpoint (after the consultation phase), and after the completion of the final recommendation and report.

Assembly members were obviously able and willing to discriminate among electoral systems. The ratings they gave used much of the available scale and a number of systems – primarily the majoritarian and plurality types – regularly got what might be considered failing grades in the bottom half of the range. Indeed, their ratings suggest that most of the Canadians consistently thought almost any other (proportional) system was better than their existing SMP regime. The Dutch agreed.

The data also suggest that assembly members became, if anything, more discriminating over the life of the process, as the range of scores given to the various types of systems (i.e. the difference between the highest and lowest ratings) steadily increased, growing from the learning phase through the following stages and reaching a maximum at the end of the assemblies' work.

There were, however, some important differences between the assemblies. Dutch and Ontario assembly members appear to have travelled a similar path. Three features characterize the evolution of assessments of electoral systems among these two assemblies. First, the system that got the largest average rating at the end of the learning phase continued to be rated highest in subsequent evaluations later in the process. Second, the average score given to their most highly rated system grew at each successive stage. And third, the strength of their preference for this system (as measured by the difference between its score and the score of the second best rated system) also grew in each following survey. To put it simply, assembly members in the Netherlands and Ontario seem to have settled on a view that identified the best system by the end of the learning phase, and then just consolidated and strengthened that preference over the consultation and deliberation phases. In the Netherlands, this meant that debate quickly focused around suggestions for modest change (open-list PR). In Ontario, the emergence of widespread support for MMP essentially transformed the deliberative phase into a design exercise exploring this system's different variables.

The assembly in British Columbia had a quite different experience. Not one of the three conditions that characterized the evolution of system ratings in the other two assemblies marks its pattern. There was no steady growth in the ratings members gave to highly rated systems, nor was there any systematic consolidation of apparent preferences. Most significantly, the system with the highest initial average rating (MMP) was not the one most preferred at the end. Instead, the deliberative phase witnessed a major change in the order of system rankings and saw the emergence of STV as the assembly's most highly rated electoral system.

To help focus on the choices assembly members made, we can isolate the key alternatives each ultimately dealt with in their deliberative phase. In the Dutch case, it was staying with a form of open-list PR or shifting to an MMP system that would provide some greater degree of local representation. In the two Canadian cases, it was a choice between which of the two proportional alternatives, MMP or STV, would be recommended. The charts in Figure 4.1 record the proportions of members who rated one of these two alternatives higher than the other, or indicated that they were indifferent between them. They illustrate that there were striking differences in the evolution of these assemblies' evaluations of competing systems.

Ontario assembly members' relative rankings appear to have been unmistakable from the beginning. A substantial majority gave the mixed member alternative

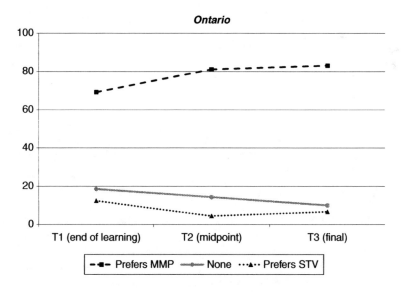

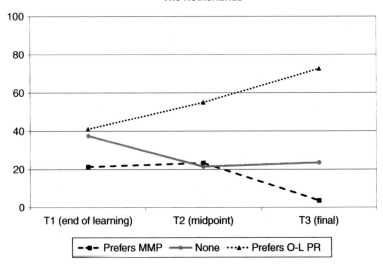

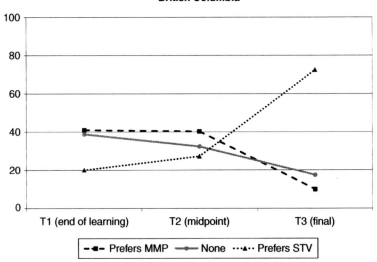

FIGURE 4.1 Evolution of Members' System Rankings

their highest rating as early as the end of the learning phase (69 per cent), and that number only grew as the comparatively small proportions of those with no preference (19 per cent) and those who preferred STV (12 per cent) shrank. It is difficult to see in this profile much evidence that the deliberative phase did anything but rally the minority to the inevitable final decision.

The Dutch chart indicates that there were twice as many members as in Ontario who were still indifferent at the early stages of the process (38 per cent). However, as time went on, many of those individuals appear to have recognized the country's basic satisfaction with its existing commitment to a highly national form of proportionality. Similarly, the initial modest support for MMP (21 per cent) dropped decisively during the deliberations. By the end of the proceedings, open-list PR was far and away the most highly rated system of a large majority of the membership.

It seems reasonable to conclude that the deliberative phase was not critical in either of these two assemblies – the main decision had effectively been made before the members got to this stage. Deliberations simply reinforced existing preferences. Of course, aggregate relative stability could be masking massive individual volatility. But that was not the case. In both the Netherlands and Ontario, majorities of assembly members gave electoral systems very similar evaluations over time. For instance, 77 per cent of *Burgerforum* participants gave open-list PR essentially the same score after the learning phase and at the end of the process. Similarly, 82 per cent of Ontarians provided MMP ratings which did not change over the many months between T1 and T3.[2]

The British Columbia chart suggests that its membership went through a more complex transformation during its deliberative phase. It appears that at the end of the learning phase, twice as many members rated MMP higher than STV (41 per cent as opposed to 20 per cent), while about 40 per cent rated them equally. Although the numbers expressing no preference between the two slowly declined, the proportion ranking STV first did not exceed those giving the highest rating to MMP until the deliberation phase during which it grew dramatically. When did STV surpass MMP? At the end of the second deliberative weekend, after an STV model was designed for British Columbia, assembly members were asked to rank order five electoral systems. For the first time, STV was ranked higher than MMP, and by a ratio of 2:1 (66 per cent versus 31 per cent). The design of an MMP model the following weekend did not reverse this pattern, and ultimately the assembly decided to recommend an STV electoral system.

This account reveals what the assembly members were thinking about different electoral systems and how that changed (or not) as they worked through the successive stages of their process. It does not tell us why they were making those judgements or the balance of considerations that led to them (we explore these questions in Chapter 5). But there is a puzzle to explain. Why was there, in the British Columbia assembly, a drastic shift in the assessments of the two proportional alternative systems that produced the final proposal of STV? Our first candidate is the dynamics of the importance that members attached to a series of principles relating to the features and consequences of electoral systems.

---

[2] We count scores as the same if respondents gave a rating that was identical or that differed by only one point.

4.3 THE SHIFTING IMPORTANCE OF CRITERIA FOR JUDGEMENT?

Citizens who knew little about the workings of different electoral systems were unlikely to evaluate them in any narrow technical or legalistic way. They started with a focus on the values they believed an acceptable electoral regime ought to articulate as a basis from which to compare and assess alternatives. There are many criteria by which electoral systems are conventionally judged by political scientists, politicians, and activists, and assembly members were seemingly prepared to consider them all. Table 4.2 reports their assessments of the importance of a set of different criteria from the end of the learning phase to the completion of their work. Assembly members were not systematically asked to choose among the criteria or to rank order them, but they were invited to rate each separately on a seven-point scale where '1' represents the opinion that the criterion was 'not important' and '7' that it was considered 'extremely important'. We can draw several observations from this evidence: most values were rated highly; there was little change in the importance members attributed to them; and the lack of temporal dynamics implies they cannot explain the shift in system preferences in British Columbia.

First, even after a long and arduous learning and deliberative process, these citizens were genuinely reluctant to rate any of these criteria as unimportant. The average ratings are very high, with little differentiation among them. Over time, the difference between the highest- and lowest-rated criteria actually shrank in both the change-oriented British Columbia and Ontario assemblies. In none of the assemblies did any single criterion ever fall into the lower half of the scale. It is also difficult to identify any criteria as obviously trumping others, despite the fact that all electoral systems involve quite explicit trade-offs among these very values and

TABLE 4.2 *Average Importance Assessments of Criteria for Judging Electoral Systems*

	British Columbia			The Netherlands			Ontario		
	T1	T2	T3	T1	T2	T3	T1	T2	T3
Effective government	6.1	5.8	6.1	6.2	6.0	6.1	5.9	5.8	6.2
Electoral accountability	5.8	5.9	6.0	6.3	6.1	6.1	5.8	5.7	6.0
Parliamentary check on government	6.0	5.8	6.0	6.3	6.2	6.2	5.9	5.7	6.1
Fair representation of parties/groups	5.9	5.4	5.8	5.7	6.0	5.8	6.0	6.0	6.4
Democratic political parties	5.6	5.2	5.4	5.9	6.0	5.9	5.2	5.1	5.6
Choice for the voter	6.2	6.0	6.2	6.0	6.1	6.2	5.8	5.8	6.5
Identifiable local representation	5.1	4.8	5.4	4.5	3.8	4.0	6.0	6.1	6.2
Encouragement to participate	6.0	5.6	5.8	5.7	5.4	5.4	5.0	5.4	5.9
Equality of the vote	5.7	5.5	5.9	6.2	6.5	6.4	—	—	—
Simplicity	—	—	4.2	5.5	5.9	5.9	4.8	5.1	5.6

Scores on 1–7 scales: not important to extremely important. Three points in time: T1 is the end of the learning phase, T2 is the midpoint, and T3 is after the final decision.

that assembly members were quite prepared to differentiate the systems themselves (Table 4.1). It is striking, however, that voter choice emerged at the end of the deliberative process as the highest-rated value in both Canadian assemblies and one of the most highly rated among Dutch members. This is a value that typically gets little attention in the political science literature.[3] That members of all three assemblies should all rate it so highly suggests that citizens bring a distinctive perspective to the debates about electoral systems, a viewpoint that emphasizes the interests of voters and the nature of the choice they are offered on their ballots.

A second striking feature of these value assessments is how little they changed over the course of the respective assembly experiences. Readings taken at three important points in the life of the assembly hardly moved at all. In the case of the British Columbia and the Netherlands assemblies, some scores climbed marginally while others fell a bit. In Ontario, every criterion was actually rated modestly higher at the end of the process. This aggregate steadiness mirrors similar individual-level stability in value ratings. On average, across assemblies and criteria, 75 per cent of members gave each value the same importance rating from the first to the last measurements (T1 and T3).[4] The evidence indicates that these kinds of fundamental judgemental orientations were not significantly altered by the assemblies' lengthy deliberations.

One value that moved somewhat over time was local representation. This idea – central to the difference between majoritarian and proportional systems, and generally portrayed as one of the principal virtues of SMP systems – was one many members struggled with. Initially, lower scores in both British Columbia and the Netherlands testify to the lower consensus about its importance. Its shifting ratings (falling then rising slightly in both those assemblies) reflected members' greater willingness to change their minds about the place it ought to have in electoral system design.

Most importantly, the third lesson drawn from an examination of the members' declared values is that their movement over time in British Columbia does not lead to any direct or easy prediction of what electoral system they would prefer between MMP and STV. To explore this further, we concentrate on a few specific criteria. Three particular criteria are directly tied to specific electoral system design issues: proportionality ('fair representation of parties'), vital to questions of the appropriate formula; local representation, critical to the issue of district magnitude (the number to be elected in a given electoral district); and voter choice, important for questions of ballot form. There is a potential tension among these values. For instance, strengthening the proportional dimension of a system requires increasing the number of representatives chosen in any given individual district, but to do so is generally perceived to weaken local representation. It is just this tension between these two values that is at the heart of classic debates between advocates of proportional representation and 'first-past-the-post'.

---

[3] For instance, voter choice is not listed as a relevant criterion in Bowler et al.'s survey (2005) of electoral system experts.

[4] Again, we tolerate scores that were off the mark by a single point.

In principle, the balance of members' views on these criteria could have been important to their evaluations of systems. If they clearly came to appreciate one dimension over the others, then that priority might have led to a certain outcome. Figure 4.2 illustrates the evolution of the members' appraisals of the importance of these three critical values in British Columbia (data from Table 4.2). Again, it is evident that members were reluctant to choose between the values. High importance was placed on all three dimensions, though voter choice was rated highest, followed by proportionality and then local representation. More centrally, all three criteria fluctuated to some extent over time, but their relative importance was not dramatically altered. This pattern does not in any obvious way concord with a switch in preferences from MMP to STV during the deliberative phase.

So this chapter's major puzzle remains intact. Why did the first citizen assembly alter its comparative judgements of MMP and STV during the course of its activities? The evolution of the importance that members attached to these judgement criteria cannot account for the opinion reversal. This leads us to examine the dynamics of the connections between the criteria and the ratings of electoral systems.

4.4 THE VARYING IMPACT OF CRITERIA ON PREFERENCES?

While assembly members thought all of these values were important, they could still have learned that some were more directly relevant to the decisions their mandates called for. Even a reluctance (or inability) to make sharp distinctions

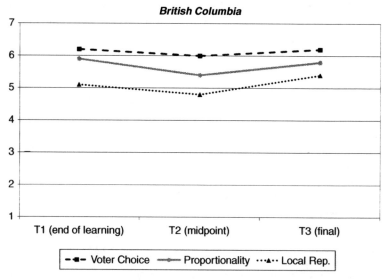

FIGURE 4.2 Evolution of Members' Importance Assessments

among underlying criteria on importance scales does not mean assembly members were confounded and incapable of basing their electoral system choice in terms of clearly defined value priorities. Perhaps members came to realize that opinions on electoral systems ought to be driven by pertinent considerations and trade-offs. Concretely, this logic implies that the effects of the judgement criteria on system preferences might have evolved over time, despite the fact that average importance assessments stayed essentially stable. Such a dynamic could explain why the average ratings of MMP and STV in British Columbia were transformed halfway through to the ultimate advantage of the latter. In fact, it is clear that successive phases of the assembly process saw the relationships between criteria and preferences shift and then crystallize in the final deliberations.

Table 4.3 provides a measure of the members' decision-making by capturing the relative weight of the three criteria on comparative judgements of the two competing systems over time. It reports the results of OLS regression analyses. The dependent variable is the difference between the scores given to STV and MMP respectively. So a positive coefficient indicates the independent variable is positively correlated to ratings of STV. The independent variables range from 1 to 7, while the dependent variables theoretically span from –6 to 6.

None of the three criteria governed the British Columbians' preferences between STV and MMP at the end of the learning phase. This was quite different from the circumstances in the other two assemblies where, by that early stage of their process, proportionality was strongly driving a preference for MMP (over STV) in Ontario and for open-list PR (over MMP) in the Netherlands.[5] Then, as the consultation phase ended in British Columbia, it is evident that the members' electoral system choices were being powerfully driven by both proportionality *and* a concern for identifiable local representation. At that point, both criteria were

TABLE 4.3 *Determinants of British Columbians' Evaluations of STV over MMP*

	T1 (learning)	T2 (midpoint)	T3 (final)
Fair representation of parties	−0.09	−0.39**	−0.05
Choice for the voter	0.14	0.22	0.25
Identifiable local representation	−0.00	−0.17**	0.23**
N	135	137	118
R^2	0.01	0.08	0.16

** Significant at 0.05; * significant at 0.10. Numbers are OLS regression coefficients. The dependent variable is the rating of STV minus the rating of MMP.

[5] Comparable results for the assemblies in Ontario and the Netherlands are not shown here, as their stories are so straightforward. They can be found in Carty and Rose (2007).

leading strongly towards a preference for MMP. Had a decision been forced then, before the members came back to deliberate, it might well have resulted in a recommendation for MMP.

British Columbia's subsequent deliberative phase produced a dramatic shift in assembly members' understanding of these key criteria and how they connect to the two electoral systems. As the results representing views at the end of the process indicate, proportionality basically ceased to be a determining factor, and the impact of local representation was completely reversed so that those believing the latter to be important now supported STV. Both changes can be directly attributed to members' activity during the deliberation period.

Proportionality continued to be a highly rated value for British Columbians, and more highly rated than local representation (see Figure 4.2), but it simply disappears during the deliberative phase as a significant determinant in their choice of which system to recommend. This appears to have been the direct result of the members' examination of each system's proportional dimension. One member prepared a comparative analysis, including several hundred computer simulations, of the likely difference between STV and MMP systems on plausible electoral outcomes for the seventy-nine-seat British Columbia legislative assembly. The discussion of that analysis led members to conclude that there would not be a significant practical difference between the two systems in terms of the proportionality of election results.[6] This had the effect of removing proportionality as an influential consideration in the choice between STV and MMP.

Members completely reversed the linkages on the issue of having an identifiable local representative. Before the deliberative phase started, those who thought it important were inclined to prefer MMP. By the end of the assembly, those committed to it found themselves preferring STV. This shift reflects the difficulty that many members had in dealing with the concept of local representation and its diverse implementation in various systems. It was at once the most familiar aspect of the existing system, and also the source of its non-proportionality. Members' comparatively lower average rating of the importance of local representation testified to that tension and underlay the greater variation among members about its relevance – a variance that did not shrink as a result of the prolonged debate. With proportionality no longer decisive, opinions among members about the salience and very meaning of local representation became the critical issue in the debates of the deliberative phase.

Local representation is an inherent aspect of both alternative systems. MMP maintains single-member districts but, in order to create the party list portion of the system, the absolute number of single-member districts must shrink (unless the legislature increases in size, a prospect ruled out in British Columbia). Concretely,

---

[6] Chapter 6 provides a further consideration of individual members' influence on assembly decision-making.

this meant that the assembly's MMP model was left with individual electoral districts about twice as large as those currently in place. That was hardly unimaginable for it would have made the provincial legislative districts about the same size as those from British Columbia in the national parliament. In contrast, the assembly's proposed STV model did not require any reduction in the total number of locally chosen representatives, although all would now be elected in multi-member districts of varying size. For many members, such districts would have been familiar given that they were a feature of the British Columbia electoral map as recently as 1991.

Through the course of their discussion and debate, the members most keenly committed to local representation came to believe that STV would best serve their interests: all representatives would be locally responsible. By the end of the second deliberation weekend, 66 per cent of the members naming local representation as their first or second most important criterion ranked STV as the best system for the province (only 6 per cent of them identified SMP). These were the individuals who led the assembly to its final choice for the single transferable vote.

4.5 CONCLUSION

This story of the three assemblies as they worked through their learning, consultation, and deliberative phases suggests that, given a focused mandate and carefully structured process, citizens can find their way to decide on complex and technical public policy issues like electoral reform. The members of these similarly structured assemblies all faced the same topic, used similar expertise and parallel proceedings, yet each set of them came up with a different response.

Both the Dutch and Ontario citizens appear to have quickly reached their respective consensus – the former to maintain the essence of their existing system, the latter to recommend a new MMP system – by the end of the learning phase. The early recognition by each assembly's members of these strong electoral system preferences quickly determined their central decision, and thus most of their respective deliberation phases were devoted to discussions of detail rather than a sustained or far-reaching deliberative debate about different system families.

Quite a different path was followed by the members of the British Columbia assembly as they, like their Ontario counterparts, also came to a recommendation for change. They exited the learning phase with divided views and considerable openness to full debate, but their deliberative reflections took a different turn despite the fact that they too were choosing between MMP and STV. With proportionality neutralized, their decision hinged on local representation. During the deliberation phase, many members appear to have changed their minds about just how they understood the very notion of local representation as a working dimension of these two electoral systems. Those debates, coupled with an enthusiasm for the opportunities STV provides to voters for expressing individual preferences, shaped the assembly's eventual choice.

More generally, this chapter has shown that the opinions of ordinary citizens directly involved in an extensive exercise of public decision-making do not evolve chaotically over time. Assembly members' views about electoral systems developed gradually as they were acquiring information about the various options. These attitudes then remained quite stable over the subsequent months. Very little aggregate or individual volatility characterized the consultation and deliberation phases. Only once did a significant movement of opinion occur – the shift from MMP to STV in British Columbia – a preference reversal that was rooted in the understandable reconsiderations fostered by the deliberative process itself.

These findings are also relevant for our understanding of representative and deliberative democracy. Both learning and deliberation matter. First, the acquisition of information had an impact on preferences. Not only are ordinary people able to learn about a difficult policy issue, as they do so their opinions of the current situation and potential alternatives change in consequence. Second, discussion of the issue among assembly members also affected their preferences, but only in British Columbia. There, the deliberative phase generated attitude change and resulted in an outcome different from the one that would have emerged if the decision had been taken earlier.

Having traced the dynamics of citizen judgements across an almost year-long process of learning, consultation, and deliberation, we turn to ask if this all led to them making the 'right' decisions. That question is the focus of Chapter 5.

5

Did the Citizen Assemblies Make the Right Decisions?

[The] audience, tuning in and tuning off here and there, cannot be counted upon to hear, even in summary form, the essential evidence and the main arguments on all the significant sides of a question. Rarely, and on very few public issues, does the mass audience have the benefit of the process by which truth is sifted from error – the dialectic of debate in which there is immediate challenge, reply, cross-examination, and rebuttal.

Walter Lippmann, *Essays on the Public Philosophy* (1955)

One of this book's central concerns is with the competence of citizens. We expect that individuals' political proficiency is not fixed but instead varies in response to context and motivation. Participants in a citizen assembly should be willing to invest much more time and effort in the endeavour precisely because it offers greater prospects for affecting politics than does everyday routine political life. We have already seen that citizens who take part in these policymaking exercises take their role seriously and dedicate themselves to the task. They become interested, engaged, and knowledgeable about electoral systems (Chapter 2). We have also demonstrated that assembly members' electoral system preferences did not fluctuate haphazardly, they emerged as knowledge accumulated and then generally remained constant or moved in reasonable ways (Chapter 4). But that does not mean assembly members became sufficiently competent to make 'good choices'. This chapter investigates a delicate but critical topic: the quality of assembly decisions.

It is not obvious how decision quality is best assessed. What criteria should be used? One possibility is to look at the outcome of the process, at how the proposals were received by those who had to make the final decision – in these cases the governments and publics of the respective political communities. Should we conclude that, since all three reforms failed to be implemented, the assemblies must have made bad choices? We do not think so. After all, the assemblies were charged to propose the best electoral system, not the most acceptable one. Also, less knowledgeable governments and publics may not be the best judges of the decisions rendered by better-informed citizen assemblies. Rather than look at the outcomes, we examine the decision-making process leading up to the choices.

In this chapter, we ascertain whether the selection of electoral systems was consistent with the principles held by the participants. Consistency is a common quality criterion (Converse 1964, 1970; Luskin 1987). It refers to 'the organization of opinions – the extent to which people's opinions are logically or ideologically consistent with other views they hold and with their general values and attitudes' (Price and Neijens 1997: 345).

The standard assumption in the electoral systems literature is that no system is inherently better than another. With many competing goals and principles at stake, there are unavoidable trade-offs (Blais and Massicotte 2002). Particular electoral systems institutionalize goals and principles differently (Farrell 2001). From this perspective, the choice of an electoral system should be related to the principles deemed most important. Since individuals have different priorities, their preferences for electoral systems should differ along those lines. In addition, differences in the collective choices made by groups of individuals seem bound to stem from aggregate differences in priorities. We are interested in both the micro and the macro aspects of assembly decision-making. In the language of social choice theory (List and Pettitt 2002; Pettitt 2003), we want to ascertain both the internal consistency between anterior premises and the final judgement among assembly members, as well as the collective consistency between the aggregate distributions of premises and the final judgement of each assembly. Concretely, we examine both the individual-level correlates of electoral system preferences and the coherence of the ultimate collective decisions reached by the three assemblies.

Focusing on consistency is not unproblematic. To do so successfully requires that there be clear expectations with which to compare the actual behaviour. Fortunately, there are some well-established relationships between principles and preferences in the literature on electoral systems. For instance, a citizen that adheres to the idea of proportional election results should prefer a proportional representation (PR) system over a system with single-member districts.

Specifically, this chapter tackles four questions. First, were individuals' preferences concerning electoral systems consistent with their principles? Electoral systems have consequences for various aspects of the political system. Notably, they shape the proportionality of election results, the presence (or absence) of geographic affiliations for representatives, the selection of candidates within parties, the complexity of the transfer of votes into seats, the number of viable political parties, the party composition of governments (e.g. a coalition versus a single party), and the representation of women and minorities in parliament (Farrell 2001; Van der Kolk and Thomassen 2006). Our task is to determine whether assembly members' evaluations of electoral systems were related to their attitudes towards these topics.

Second, did the consistency between preferences and principles evolve over time? Each assembly worked for almost an entire year on electoral systems. Did they need all this time to master the subject? Deliberation ought to bring about a shared understanding of the topic, but how much time does it take to do so?

We examine whether the relationships between evaluations of electoral systems and relevant attitudes crystallized early or whether they continued to increase in strength during the course of the proceedings.

Third, did members' political sophistication influence the consistency between their preferences and principles? More knowledgeable citizens are thought to be better equipped to deal with complex political issues. But the extensive deliberative process might have levelled the playing field by providing the less knowledgeable with the ability to catch up. We consider whether there were important differences between the decision correlates of the (initially) better informed and those of the less informed.

Finally, were the assemblies' final collective choices reasonable? Ultimately, the three citizen assemblies recommended three different electoral systems. Given that electoral systems constitute trade-offs between competing principles, we assess whether each assembly's proposal was compatible with its particular set of aggregate priorities and values.

5.1 HOW TO GAUGE CONSISTENCY?

To uncover whether members' preferences concerning electoral systems were related to their principles, we explore the correlations between system evaluations and seven relevant objectives and values. The dependent variables are members' ratings of different electoral systems (introduced in Chapter 4). Here, we confine the analysis to the four systems that were seriously considered by the three assemblies: single member plurality (SMP), single transferable vote (STV), mixed member proportional (MMP), and open-list PR (list-PR).

We expect individual preferences about electoral systems to be congruent with views about system features and with general outlooks towards politics and change. Indeed, this is how the judgements of electoral systems by experts have

TABLE 5.1 *Anticipated Relationships between Determinants and System Evaluations*

	SMP	STV	MMP	List-PR
Fair representation of parties	−	+	+	+
Choice for the voter	−	+	+	−
Identifiable local representation	+	+	+	−
Simplicity	+	−	−	+
Anti-party sentiment	−	+	−	−
Aversion to change	+/−	−	−	+/−
Small party support	−	+	+	+

−: Negative relationship; +: positive relationship.

been explained (Bowler et al. 2005; Bowler and Farrell 2006). The anticipated relationships are summarized in Table 5.1.

First, we include assessments of the priorities of assembly members as captured by the importance ratings they give to specific aspects of electoral systems. Four are widely associated with competing systems – *fair representation of parties, choice for the voter, identifiable local representation,* and *simplicity* – and the expected relationships are relatively straightforward.[1] People who care for *fair representation* ought to have less favourable ratings of SMP than the three PR systems, since SMP leads to non-proportional election results (Rae 1969; Lijphart 1994). On *voter choice*, STV and MMP should be favoured since they offer preference ranking and two votes, respectively, while SMP and open-list PR only provide a single vote.[2] In contrast, those who favour *local representation* should like SMP, though they may also be well served by the multi-member districts of STV and by MMP, while open-list PR (especially if based on national lists) clearly delivers the least local representation. Finally, individuals who seek *simplicity* should consider positively SMP and list-PR, two systems where votes are converted into seats in a more straightforward fashion than either STV or MMP.

Then, we have three general political values that ought to be pertinent for views about electoral reform. *Anti-party sentiment* measures dissatisfaction with political parties. Those who score high consider that political parties do not do a good job of 'presenting clear choices on the issues', 'finding solutions to important problems', and 'expressing the concerns of ordinary people'. We would anticipate the most dissatisfied assembly members to be particularly wary of giving too much power to political parties. Thus, they should dislike SMP, a system that tends to be dominated by two strong parties, and systems based on party lists (list-PR and MMP). In contrast, people disappointed by parties should appreciate STV, which allows voters a greater ability to discriminate among party candidates and opens electoral competition to independents.

Aversion to change refers to non-ideological conservatism. Based on McClosky's seminal scale (1958), change-averse individuals think that risky reforms are not worth trying, that 'it's better to stick by what you have', they want to know that 'something really works before taking a chance on it', and they do not like taking risks. Obviously, those who loath change ought to oppose reform, they should instead support the status quo (Nadeau et al. 1999). In these three

---

[1] Three of these objectives had been formally adopted by the two Canadian assemblies as key features they wished to see institutionalized in an electoral system, but we have yet to see evidence that they were actually correlated to preferences.

[2] MMP does not always provide two separate votes, but the alternative MMP systems constructed in British Columbia and Ontario did propose one vote for a local candidate and another for a party list. Open-list PR systems do offer a wide range of vote options between candidates and parties, but most often voters cast only one ballot (though there are a few instances of panachage and vote cumulation).

assemblies, risk-aversion should be positively linked to feelings towards the existing electoral system (SMP in the Canadian assemblies, and list-PR in the Netherlands), and negatively related to alternative systems (STV and MMP).

Finally, participants' *partisan affinities* may well affect their system preferences. The choice of an electoral system is likely to influence the fortunes of political parties. Generally, a more proportional system benefits smaller parties, and a less proportional system advantages larger parties. Members may have been inclined to choose a system that would help the party they prefer. Yet, we do not expect partisan affinities to have a powerful effect in citizen assemblies for two reasons. First, party identification is often considered a shortcut that people use when they do not have much information on a given issue (Sniderman et al. 1991). Since members of citizen assemblies were exposed to an abundance of information, they did not need shortcuts. Second, participants were explicitly invited to think about the system that would be best for the province or country as a whole, they were encouraged to deliberate and to have an open mind, and they were exposed to a diversified set of perspectives. However, in spite of these favourable conditions, we should not rule out the possibility that assembly members, or at least some of them, ultimately preferred the system that would most benefit the party that they personally supported. If that was the case, supporters of smaller parties should be more favourable to PR (in its various forms) than supporters of larger parties, because smaller parties are bound to do much better in PR than in non-PR systems.

5.2 WERE PREFERENCES ABOUT ELECTORAL SYSTEMS CONSISTENT WITH PRINCIPLES?

To establish whether there was, by the end of the assembly processes, clear consistency between these seven principles and the evaluations of electoral systems, we examined the empirical relationships between them. Table 5.2 reports the results from a regression analysis in which data from all three citizen assemblies

TABLE 5.2 *Determinants of Electoral System Evaluations*

	SMP	STV	MMP	List-PR
Fair representation of parties	−0.19**	0.01	0.29**	0.16*
Choice for the voter	−0.23**	0.04	−0.23**	−0.02
Identifiable local representation	0.31**	0.27**	0.16**	−0.15**
Simplicity	0.11**	−0.34**	−0.05	0.17**
Anti-party sentiment	−0.26**	0.28**	0.05	−0.15
Aversion to change	0.02	−0.39**	−0.42**	0.19*
Small party support	−0.05	−0.02	−0.03	0.04
N	276	276	276	276
R^2	0.19	0.32	0.20	0.13

** Significant at 0.05; * significant at 0.10. Numbers are OLS regression coefficients. All variables range from 0 to 1.

were pooled together.[3] The analysis reveals that individual preferences concerning electoral systems were indeed structured by principles. Close to two-thirds of the relationships are statistically significant, despite there being only 276 cases. Also, the model fit statistics are reasonably high for such individual data. Moreover, the relationships make sense, they follow our expectations.

Support for *proportionality* was a significant predictor of three electoral system evaluations. Assembly members who valued it were significantly more likely to give SMP a negative score and to give MMP and open-list PR a positive score. Thus, more proportional systems were more liked by those who considered fair representation an important objective.

Voter choice affected the ratings of two systems. Those who found it important rejected SMP, the system that only offers one vote for a local candidate. They also disliked MMP. They were slightly more likely to have a favourable opinion of STV, the system that allows voters to rank order as many candidates from different parties as they wish, but the impact does not attain statistical significance.

Attitudes towards *identifiable local representation* were linked to preferences for all four systems. This priority is related to lower ratings of open-list PR, while being associated with more positive scores for SMP, STV, and MMP. Considering list-PR often does not provide local representation while the three other systems do deliver it, these links are sound.

Simplicity also had a significant impact on feelings towards three electoral systems. More favourable assessments of SMP and open-list PR were expressed by those preferring a simple system. Conversely, STV was slightly hampered among people who care about simplicity. All three of these relationships fall in line with expectations.

Anti-party sentiment among assembly members was negatively correlated with preferences for SMP. A similar, though not significant, relationship existed for ratings of list-PR. These results are congruous with the interpretation that individuals dissatisfied with parties tend to have lower evaluations of systems that revolve around strong parties. In contrast, anti-party sentiment was positively correlated with assessments of STV, a system that fosters intra-party competition and permits rankings of candidates from various party affiliations.

As expected, *aversion to change* has a negative impact on evaluations of the two systems that constituted departures from the status quo for all three assemblies (STV and MMP). The risk-averse would be expected to favour their existing system. To uncover this behaviour, we need to disaggregate the pooled data. Separate analyses of each assembly confirm that the positive list-PR effect found in Table 5.2 is in fact driven by the Dutch *Burgerforum*, while a parallel relationship emerges for SMP in the Canadian cases.

---

[3] All variables were measured during the final wave of the assembly panel surveys. More details about them can be found in Appendix 2.

Finally, we can ask if the preferences of assembly members were influenced by their *partisan leanings*? The evidence suggests that the answer is no, for there are no significant differences in system evaluations between the supporters of small and large political parties. And this is not due to intervening variables; we find the same lack of a relationship in analyses where controls are dropped. Even among those who voted for big parties, 'first-past-the-post' gets much lower scores than each of the three proportional systems. This is a truly striking finding. It is fair to say that political parties were the actors that would be most directly affected by any change to (or maintenance of) the electoral system. Yet the assembly members appear to have been completely unmoved by their personal partisan inclinations. These results are entirely consonant with our own observation of the process. Members were genuinely struggling to find the 'best' system for their community, and whether any option might benefit or hurt any specific party was not a relevant consideration.

Thus, apart from the exception of partisanship, each of these principles is related to evaluations of some electoral systems. We can tell the story another way – in terms of the electoral systems themselves. Such an account points to members holding sensibly structured preferences. Ratings of SMP regimes were linked to five of the seven factors. SMP was popular among persons who care about local representation and simplicity, who tolerate non-proportionality and restricted voter choice, and who accept political parties. These relationships provide a good depiction of SMP: a simple non-proportional system which, by privileging local representation and offering modest voter choice, is typically dominated by a few strong parties.

Judgements about the STV were governed by two specific dimensions of electoral systems and by two more general dispositions. STV was rated more favourably by assembly participants who care for local representation and those who express partisan disaffection. It was not supported by those adverse to change or in favour of a simple system. This combination reflects quite accurately the characterization of STV within the literature on electoral systems: a relatively complex proportional system that provides particular but extensive local representation and whose ballot structure gives more discretion to voters.

Evaluations of MMP were moulded by four variables. MMP was appraised positively by persons who seek fair election results and those who are interested in local representation. It was not favoured by people who value voter choice or those who fear change. This depiction of MMP also fits with reality: an electoral system which generates proportional outcomes and delivers local representatives, but which offers voters less choice than STV.

Lastly, assessments of open-list PR also hinged upon four considerations. This system received higher ratings from people who desire a faithful translation of votes into seats, simplicity, and (among the Dutch) are risk-averse. It only garnered lower ratings from those who want MPs tied to localities. This is, presumably, what electoral system experts would anticipate, for list-PR is generally understood to be a simple proportional system with little in the way of significant geographic representation.

The results reported in Table 5.2 are derived from an analysis that combines the data from all three assemblies. It is therefore important to ask whether there were important differences between them. Given the small number of cases (100 or less), separate regression analyses inevitably produce much fewer significant effects. Nevertheless, the coefficients are generally in the same direction, though some are inconsistent across assemblies.

Overall, assembly preferences regarding electoral systems were not the product of haphazard reasoning or random guesses. Individual opinions were coherently linked with features of electoral systems and relevant values. Citizen assembly members who liked or disliked particular institutional designs were looking for specific characteristics and outcomes from the voting system.

Of course, as with any correlational evidence, we cannot be sure about the direction of causality. It may be that rationalization was at work. Perhaps assembly participants adjusted their attitudes to fit a particular choice of electoral system. We suggest, however, that preferences and principles did not develop this way. Based on our close observation of the deliberative processes, we believe that assembly members were searching for the design that best accommodated their long-standing objectives and values. Evidence presented in Chapter 4 also supports this view. In British Columbia, opinions about electoral systems changed markedly during the proceedings, while the importance attached to priorities remained essentially intact. Assembly members seem to have brought their preferences in line with their principles rather than the other way around.

In the final section of this chapter, we ascertain whether the final collective choices of the assemblies – their recommendation for the best electoral system for their jurisdiction – were appropriate or not. Beforehand, we investigate the presence of dynamics and heterogeneity in individual decision-making.

5.3 DID THE CONSISTENCY OF PREFERENCES AND PRINCIPLES INCREASE OVER TIME?

Deliberative democracy is assumed to be 'an ongoing activity of mutual reason giving' which induces participants to reflect more thoroughly about the pros and cons of various options (Gutmann and Thompson 2000: 168). As a consequence, we would expect members of deliberative bodies to become more capable of forming opinions on the basis of principles as the process unfolds. Does this logic also apply to citizen assemblies that extend over numerous months? The links between preferences and their determinants might have crystallized as early as the end of the formal learning phase. This would indicate that knowledge acquisition was all that assembly members required to develop an electoral system choice that reflected their personal goals and values. Then again, the level of opinion constraint might have continued to increase during the discussions and debates of the consultation and deliberation phases. Such a pattern would reveal that citizens did benefit from more work in order to gain a better grasp of the topic.

To ascertain whether the consistency between evaluations of electoral systems and principles increased in strength over the life of the citizen assemblies, Table 5.3 compares the structure of opinion at three key junctures: at the end of the learning phase after assembly members had completed their crash-course on electoral systems (T1), during the mid-year break that followed the consultation phase (T2), and at the end of the proceedings after the assemblies had chosen their final recommendation (T3). Thus, the third column for each system simply reproduces the results of Table 5.2.

Clearly, the structure of opinion changed after the learning phase – there were dynamics at work. But it would be inaccurate to assert that all the correlations between principles and preferences simply became stronger over time. Some actually weakened. Nevertheless, the dominant pattern is one of movement towards greater consistency. By and large, preferences exhibited more consistency after the assemblies' deliberations. For each electoral system, the number of significant coefficients was bigger by the end than it had been earlier. The size of the model fit statistics also tended to be larger at the conclusion of the process.

Views about electoral systems were initially constrained by a small number of objectives and values. By the end of the assemblies, more factors mattered. For instance, after the first part of the process, assessments of open-list PR only revolved around notions of proportionality and local representation. Months later, beliefs pertaining to simplicity and aversion to change had surfaced as relevant. Similarly, the other systems saw variables materialize as significant predictors over time: voter choice and partisan disaffection for SMP; anti-party sentiment for STV; voter choice, local representation, and aversion to change for MMP.

An examination of the story in each of the assemblies yields an interesting discrepancy. In the Netherlands, system preferences were more highly structured after the learning phase than at the end of the entire proceedings. Why such a distinct and unexpected pattern? The *Burgerforum* process differed in one major way from the Canadian cases. Since its recommendation would go to the government rather than a binding public referendum, the Dutch assembly was more consultative and less decisive. One could surmise that the lower stakes might have resulted in lower motivations among Dutch participants, and this might explain an overall weaker level of constraint. However, that story cannot account for the pattern actually observed – high opinion consistency at the end of the learning period which then dissipates.

Instead, the discrepancy must stem from the particular manner in which the Dutch assembly unfolded. The *Burgerforum* had essentially disregarded all

TABLE 5.3 *Dynamics over Time, Determinants of System Evaluations*

	SMP			STV			MMP			List-PR		
	T1	T2	T3	T1	T2	T3	T1	T2	T3	T1	T2	T3
Fair repres.	-0.31**	-0.09	-0.19**	-0.02	0.01	0.01	0.21**	0.27**	0.29**	0.39**	0.22**	0.16*
Voter choice	0.01	-0.10	-0.23**	0.07	-0.01	0.04	0.04	-0.16**	-0.23**	-0.02	0.06	-0.02
Local repres.	0.21**	0.26**	0.31**	0.11**	0.20**	0.27**	0.03	0.15**	0.16**	-0.17**	-0.15**	-0.15**
Simplicity	0.20**	0.10*	0.11**	-0.25**	-0.32**	-0.34**	-0.05	-0.06	-0.05	0.04	0.08	0.17**
Anti-party	-0.08	-0.12	-0.26**	0.12	0.13	0.28**	0.00	-0.07	0.05	0.08	-0.01	-0.15
Aversion	0.04	0.03	0.02	-0.18*	-0.20*	-0.39**	0.07*	0.12	-0.42**	0.07	0.17*	0.19*
Small party	0.02	0.02	-0.05	-0.04	-0.02	-0.02	-0.06**	-0.03	-0.03	-0.01	-0.01	0.04
N	247	251	276	247	251	276	247	251	276	247	251	276
R^2	0.18	0.14	0.19	0.12	0.24	0.32	0.06	0.11	0.20	0.15	0.11	0.13

** Significant at 0.05; *significant at 0.10.
Numbers are OLS regression coefficients. All variables range from 0 to 1.

families of electoral systems except variations of list-PR by the time it started its deliberation phase. Thus, all its debates were essentially focused on identifying which form of list-PR would be best for the country. Participants then lost touch with other systems because they were no longer actively discussing them. This case indicates that newly mastered material can quickly fade from memory when people do not reflect on it, when they do not need it anymore. It also means that Table 5.3 understates the increase in belief system consistency that occurred among Canadian assembly members.

In sum, deliberation reinforced the consistency of opinions throughout the citizen assemblies. Even an extensive period of information acquisition did not crystallize the structure of the pertinent belief system. Deliberation continued to strengthen the relationships between preferences and principles during the almost year-long process. In addition, the evidence teaches us that consistency not only increases, it can easily begin to wane, as in the instance of the Netherlands, once certain dilemmas and options are no longer under active consideration.

5.4 ARE THE POLITICALLY SOPHISTICATED MORE CONSISTENT?

One may wonder whether the consistency of electoral system preferences was driven by the most politically sophisticated members of each assembly. There is mounting evidence of inter-individual heterogeneity in political behaviour attributable to political sophistication (Sniderman et al. 1991; Zaller 1992; Miller and Krosnick 2000; Fournier 2006). We know that some assembly participants had been more exposed to politics than others. Was it easier for them to deal with the learning material circulated and to think coherently about the consequences of each electoral system? If that was the case, then perhaps the observed consistency between system evaluations and relevant principles was limited to the more politically engaged citizens.

We can test this idea by determining whether the structure of opinion varies according to assembly members' initial level of political information. Information was measured in the pre-assembly questionnaires using a nine-item battery of factual knowledge questions about political figures and electoral systems.[4] The resulting knowledge scale allows us to separate memberships into thirds, and to compare the decision-making of the least and most informed citizens.

Beforehand, we need to point out that the dependent variables did not differ across information levels. The average evaluations of the four electoral systems

---

[4] This operationalization follows established practice (Zaller 1990; Delli Carpini and Keeter 1993, 1996). The knowledge questions are listed in Appendix 2.

TABLE 5.4 *Comparing Information Levels, Determinants of System Evaluations*

	SMP		STV		MMP		List-PR	
	Low	High	Low	High	Low	High	Low	High
Fair representation	−0.14	−0.10	−0.06	0.17	0.09	0.47**	0.18	0.14
Choice for the voter	−0.35*	−0.28*	−0.05	0.03	−0.18	−0.36**	−0.14	0.02
Local representation	0.19**	0.38**	0.32**	0.16*	0.16**	0.17**	−0.17*	0.00
Simplicity	0.07	0.11	−0.26**	−0.32**	−0.09	0.03	0.18*	0.16**
Anti-party sentiment	−0.37**	−0.16	0.13	0.65**	−0.02	0.24*	0.01	−0.29*
Aversion to change	0.18	−0.02	−0.48**	−0.11	−0.27*	−0.36**	0.11	0.36**
Small party support	−0.06	−0.05	−0.03	−0.03	−0.07	0.02	0.02	0.02
N	109	105	109	105	109	105	109	105
R^2	0.19	0.25	0.31	0.36	0.13	0.31	0.09	0.18

** Significant at 0.05; * significant at 0.10. Numbers are OLS regression coefficients. All variables range from 0 to 1.

among the less and the more knowledgeable participants were very similar, and none of the differences was significant. Next, we examine the correlates of the preferences of the two information groups.

Table 5.4 presents regression results of split-sample analyses for the lowest and highest thirds of the information scale. The decision determinants did vary by knowledge. The effects tended to be in the same direction across both groups, but some coefficients were larger among one group, and some coefficients were only significant among one group. In a few instances, a significant relationship appeared solely among the less informed (anti-party sentiment for SMP, risk-aversion for STV, and local representation for list-PR). However, the reverse – significant effects limited to the more knowledgeable respondents – was twice as common. For instance, MMP was evaluated in terms of local representation and aversion to change across all assembly members, but linked to proportionality, voter choice, and anti-party sentiment only by the more informed. The gap in consistency between the two groups is also revealed by the model fit statistics: the *R*-squared is larger for every electoral system among the high information group.

Overall, electoral system preferences were more consistent among the more politically sophisticated members of citizen assemblies. The decisions of all information groups were constrained by priorities about the consequences of electoral designs and general political outlooks. But the pattern was stronger among the more knowledgeable participants. Thus, political information does aid in structuring reasoning on a complex problem, and this advantage was not completely eliminated by the long deliberative exercise.

5.5 WERE THE ASSEMBLIES' FINAL CHOICES REASONABLE?

To this point, we have seen that evaluations of electoral systems were correlated with relevant principles at the individual level. The discursive dilemma, however, teaches us that individual consistency between premises and judgements can still lead to collectively incoherent conclusions (List and Pettitt 2002; Pettitt 2003). So, to judge collective decision quality, we need to determine whether each assembly's specific aggregate principles were compatible with the electoral system it chose.

Table 5.5 reports the aggregate distribution of views within each of the assemblies on the key evaluative criteria and values that members were using.[5] The scores are simply means, standardized on a 0–1 scale, with high scores indicating high importance for the system features, high disaffection with political parties, and high risk-aversion.

The patterns of aggregate preferences help explain why each assembly ended up with a distinct proposal. All the assemblies attached a high degree of importance to the fair transfer of votes into seats and to greater voter choice (see the first two rows of Table 5.5). Consequently, it is not surprising that all three rejected SMP, a system which entails non-proportional results, little choice, and a few large political parties. Their logical choice was some form of PR.

But each of the three assemblies picked a different form of PR due to its particular set of *other* priorities. In British Columbia, four aspects stand out as comparatively distinctive. Members cared substantially for local representation, were less worried about simplicity, were slightly more dissatisfied with political parties, and were not afraid of change. It is coherent that this assembly would opt for recommending STV. That system delivers locally focused representation, its

TABLE 5.5 *Different Goals for Electoral Systems*

	British Columbia	The Netherlands	Ontario
Fair representation of parties	0.80	0.80	0.89
Choice for the voter	0.86	0.86	0.91
Identifiable local representation	0.73	0.50	0.87
Simplicity	0.54	0.82	0.76
Anti-party sentiment	0.60	0.49	0.51
Aversion to change	0.33	0.46	0.29
Electoral system proposed	STV	List-PR	MMP

Numbers are means of variables that range from 0 to 1.

[5] We have excluded small party support because this factor did not substantially connect to preferences in Table 5.2.

vote counting seems less transparent, and it does weaken the power of party bosses.

The evidence indicates that the Dutch assembly members did not really desire local representation; instead they favoured simplicity and were a little more hesitant towards change than those in the other assemblies. This makes their decision to retain list-PR quite comprehensible. That system uses a single vote to allocate seats proportionally in a straightforward fashion without tying representatives to a precise locality.

Finally, in Ontario, the assembly was not risk-averse and it valued a system that was both simple and locally responsive. It is understandable that it would elect to switch to a mixed system, since MMP balances concerns for local representation and simplicity by keeping many aspects with which SMP voters are familiar, notably having MPs chosen in a traditional 'first-past-the-post' local contest.

Thus, the electoral system reforms put forth by the citizen assemblies were consistent with their respective aggregate goals and values, leading us to believe that their collective decisions were reasonable. They ended up with different proposals because they appreciated and wanted different things.

5.6 CONCLUSION

To evaluate the capacity of citizens to develop and articulate well-reasoned political opinions, this chapter examined the consistency of individual and collective decisions reached within the three citizen assemblies. First, it investigated the relationships between evaluations of electoral systems and several pertinent principles. The analyses showed that individual preferences were indeed anchored by general values and specific objectives of electoral systems. Simply put, the evidence indicates that assembly members developed preferences which were coherent with their particular priorities.

We also explored the dynamics of consistency. The relationships between evaluations of electoral systems and relevant attitudes did change during the course of the citizen assemblies. In the two Canadian cases, the structure of opinions continued to increase throughout the proceedings. In the Netherlands, because the *Burgerforum* stopped debating certain options, the belief systems actually became less constrained.

In addition, there was some heterogeneity in the consistency of preferences. Both the best and least politically informed assembly participants evaluated electoral systems in terms of values and objectives. Nonetheless, the structure of opinions was more robust among the highly knowledgeable members. Our findings suggest that even an extensive deliberative exercise could not entirely level the playing field.

Finally, opinion consistency prevailed at the aggregate level as well. The distribution of general values and specific objectives within each assembly was compatible with their preferences for electoral systems. The three citizen assembly reform proposals reflected each assembly's distinct set of collective principles. Ultimately, they opted for different recommendations because their respective goals differed.

Altogether, these results point to quality decision-making and political competence in the extraordinary context of citizen assemblies. Before reaching a final judgement, however, we must ascertain whether the assemblies' decisions were influenced by insidious external forces. This task is taken up in Chapter 6.

6

Did the Participants Decide by Themselves?

What's the thing people remember about the Gulf War? A bomb falling down
a chimney. Let me tell you something: I was in the building where we filmed
that with a 10-inch model made out of Legos.

Conrad Brean (Robert De Niro), *Wag the Dog* (1997)

In Chapter 5, we explored the extent to which assembly members' preferences about
electoral systems were related to their principles. The evidence demonstrates that
there was indeed a clear link between individuals' objectives and values and the
decisions that they reached, and that those decisions made sense and were reasonable.
The preceding analysis looked at the internal self-reflective process through which
individual participants made up their minds, but there is another dimension to the
decision-making: the external influences imposed on the members. In this chapter, we
are interested in those influences, asking whether participants may have been convinced how to vote for a particular recommendation by other individuals or groups.

One of the underlying fundamental assumptions of the citizen assemblies is that
the members would make independent decisions about which electoral system was
most appropriate for their province or country. But why is independence so
crucial? The basic idea, derived from the Condorcet jury theorem, is that the larger
the group, the more likely it is that a majority of the group will reach a 'correct'
judgement (Grofman 1975; Grofman and Feld 1988). The theorem, however, is
built on the assumption that individuals in the group make up their mind independently. If they were to follow the judgement of an opinion leader within the group,
or some outside expert or lobbyist, the *effective* group size would decrease, and so
would the probability of a 'good' decision (Grofman et al. 1983: 273). This is why
Grofman and colleagues named one of their theorems: 'Think for yourself, John'.

In addition, a lack of independence contradicts pseudorandom selection. Citizen
assemblies, by the way they are composed, represent the public. But the process
can only be legitimate if participants decide autonomously. If the assembly
members were to fall under the sway of some external actors – the chair or staff
of the assembly, interest groups, or some other powerful political actor – they no
longer can be said to represent the public.

We examine some of these possible outside influences in this chapter. The first
possibility is other individuals in the assemblies. Members spent a lot of time

together, not only discussing electoral systems, but also engaging in a wide variety of social exchanges (i.e. schmoozing). How much impact did these exchanges have? Our concern here is not with the full deliberative process, but in the potential effect of particularly influential opinion leaders in the assemblies. Is it possible that the final decision in each assembly was shaped by a few individuals who were particularly trusted or particularly adept at convincing other members?

The second set of potential influences includes the people charged with organizing and directing the assembly activities. On the one hand, there were the experts responsible for educating the members on the substantive issues of their agenda. We focus on the research directors who were in charge of the learning process as well as the experts who were invited to present lectures. They were well positioned to influence, deliberately or involuntarily, the whole process. This could have occurred either because they put too much or too little emphasis on some aspects of the subject or because they framed the information and options in a biased way that made some choices more or less likely. So is there any evidence of this? On the other hand, we also need to examine the role played by the chairs, appointed to manage the organization and run the proceedings. They set the agenda, decided how much or little time to leave for discussions, dealt with whatever issues came up in the meetings, and ultimately established when and how decisions should be reached. We consider the chairs' responsibilities and activities to determine how they might have unduly affected the course of events.

Third, we ascertain the impact, if any, of the public consultations which took place after the learning phase but before the assemblies started their deliberative discussions. That aspect of the process was intended to obtain feedback from the public, informing members about the extent to which there was support for the status quo and how much interest there was for the various reform options. Did those consultations mould the assemblies' final recommendations?

Finally, we turn to political parties. They were, after all, the institutions which were most likely to be directly affected by any modification to the electoral system. They had an obvious and immediate stake in the process and its outcome, so they could be expected to try and influence members. Did parties play a part in the decisions taken by assembly members?

6.1 OPINION LEADERSHIP WITHIN CITIZEN ASSEMBLIES

The first question that we address is whether the final decisions reached by the citizen assemblies may have been shaped by a small number of individual members who moved their colleagues in one particular direction.

Deliberation theorists argue that the process of deliberation contributes to better decisions because it provides the participants with the opportunity to consider a wider array of evidence or facts than they might otherwise confront (Rawls 1971: 359; Fishkin 1995: 28; Page 1996: 2). However, critics of deliberation contend that while this may well be true in theory, practice often differs. They are particularly concerned that the participants in a deliberative setting are themselves far from being equal. Mansbridge goes so far as to suggest that, because communication skills are so crucial in such settings, deliberation actually 'accentuates rather than redress[es] the disadvantage of those with least power in a society' (1980: 277).[1]

This leads us to examine two potential scenarios of unequal influence in the citizen assemblies. The first is the possibility that a few specific individuals with strong preferences on the issue of electoral reform were able to convince the (less committed) majority to choose their option. The second is that the better-educated members of these assemblies had a much greater influence on the final decisions than the less educated.

Ascertaining the power of various actors on a specific issue is not simple, especially because influence can be both direct and indirect, and because some forms of influence are notoriously hard to identify (see Harsanyi 1962; Riker 1964; Dahl 1970; Blais 1974). In these cases, there was a lot of interaction between assembly members. They were all heavily involved in the formal activities of the assemblies: exchanging information and perspectives in the plenary and small-group sessions, and on their website. They socialized a great deal during the meeting weekends, at mealtimes, and in evening get-togethers, and many developed strong friendships that led to continuing relationships between meetings. So there was much opportunity for mutual influence and there is little doubt that many members were affected by conversations with colleagues in the assembly. Inevitably, mutual influence moved in all kinds of directions. Individual A may have been influenced by an important comment made by individual B, but individual B was equally strongly influenced by individual A's argument on another point. In such a process, everyone may be influential but no one is powerful enough to drive the collective outcome.

The question that we are concerned with is whether there is any evidence to suggest that, in these assemblies dealing with complex and unfamiliar issues, a small group of opinion leaders or the better educated in general may have shaped the final decisions that were made. We start with the issue of personal influence.

6.1.1 The influence of a few opinion leaders

We asked assembly members themselves to indicate who they thought were the three members most influential in the final decision of their assembly. The great majority of respondents could and did name three persons, and a total of about thirty individuals were named by at least one respondent in each case, a reflection

---

[1] See also Hibbing and Theiss-Morse (2002: 203). Though assembly members disagree with this point (see Table 2.6).

of the widespread interaction that took place in these assemblies. The main question, however, is whether there was some common perception that a few individuals may have been particularly powerful.

The pattern differed across the assemblies. In British Columbia, one individual member was perceived to be one of the three most influential members by more than 80 per cent of the respondents, and in the Netherlands, two persons were named by about 60 per cent, while no one individual was selected by even half the respondents in Ontario. This suggests that we should be most concerned with the possibility of undue personal influence in British Columbia and least concerned in the case of the Ontario assembly. We supplemented these perceptions with our own close observations of the assemblies' respective deliberative processes. All the evidence leads us to make the following observations about each case.

6.1.2 British Columbia

In the British Columbia assembly, three individuals may have exerted greater influence, though that influence does not seem to have overridden the collective debate. One person declared himself the voter choice spokesperson and kept raising its importance in plenary and small-group sessions as well as on the members' website forum. But voter choice was deemed very important by the whole group from the very beginning (see Table 4.2), and so it is not clear that there was any personal influence there.

A second member appointed himself as an advocate for strong local representation. In formal meetings and social occasions, he kept the issue in the forefront of the members' discussions and debates. This person may have played a critical role in the final discussions and decision.[2] As we saw in Chapter 4, the late move to the single transferable vote (STV) was in part attributable to changing appreciations of how the different options implement local representation. That being said, local representation remained a weaker concern even at the end of the deliberative phase (Table 4.2), and so it is difficult to believe that this person altered the agenda in a significant way.

The third person who appears to have had some direct influence at a key decision point is the individual who was perceived by the great majority of members as the most influential. Widely perceived to be thoughtful and balanced, the individual spent much of the 2004 summer trying to assess the impact of adopting alternate mixed-member and STV electoral systems for the province. He produced a report, based on comparisons of aggregate election outcomes in each system as well as detailed computer simulations, which showed that there was not likely to be much difference in the proportionality either system would produce for the seventy-nine-seat legislature. The paper was widely circulated and increased his credibility, so that the members also came to regard him, by far, as the best

---

[2] For a more thorough analysis of this individual's role, see Lang (2008: 96–8).

informed of their colleagues. The impact of his work was to take proportionality out of the MMP–STV choice by rendering it neutral.

That this individual exerted some influence is undisputable, but it should not be overstated. He did not have a strong preference for STV. In fact, he liked mixed member proportional (MMP) almost as much as STV, both before and after the deliberative phase took place. Also, as we noted in Chapter 4, the late shift to STV in the wider assembly is only partly imputable to changes in the perceived relevance of the proportionality criterion to the MMP–STV choice.

In short, there is evidence that a few individuals played an important role in the British Columbia assembly and particularly during its deliberative period rebalancing of the relevant underlying considerations that led to a late shift towards STV. Yet clearly no one individual swayed the assembly in any particular direction.

6.1.3 The Netherlands

In the Dutch assembly, two persons were named by more than 60 per cent of the members, along with the assembly's experts, as the most influential.[3] The question is whether those two individuals may have led the whole group towards a specific choice.

The assembly's most important decision was to keep the existing national open-list proportional representation (list-PR) system. From the start, however, there was a wide consensus that there was no need to overhaul the existing system; as many as 70 per cent of the participants indicated at the beginning that they were very or fairly satisfied with the Dutch voting system. There is no reason to believe that these two individuals played a major role in the decision to keep nationwide PR.

Perhaps the second most crucial decision concerned the support threshold parties ought to meet in order to win seats in parliament. The question was whether the threshold for party lists should be increased. The issue arose because, with an exceptionally low threshold, the existing Dutch PR system is one of the most proportional systems anywhere and typically returns about ten political parties to the *Tweede Kamer* (Lijphart 1994). By increasing the threshold, the degree of party fragmentation could be reduced. But that proposal did not get much support. The fact is that there was wide approval for strong proportionality from the beginning. Members expressed very little desire to adopt a higher threshold and thus no reason to suppose that any specific individual or small group may have been particularly influential on that issue.

While there is little evidence that the two identified leaders exercised much influence on those major issues, there was one other, relatively minor, decision on which one of the two individuals did make a difference. That was the decision to recommend moving from the D'Hondt to the Hare formula for distributing seats. Among the various proportional formulas, D'Hondt is generally considered to

---

[3] The *Burgerforum*'s expert team included Pien van den Eijden, Hans Klok, and Henk van der Kolk.

produce the least proportional and Hare the most proportional results (Lijphart 1994), though the differences tend to disappear in cases of large district magnitude such as the Netherlands. Still, the Dutch assembly's proposal was to make their system even more proportional. This was a question about which one individual had strong views and about which most other members did not care much. That person did manage to impose his vision on the assembly. It should be pointed out, however, that this change would not have been very consequential, making an already very proportional electoral system only slightly more so.

6.1.4 Ontario

Influence within the Ontario assembly was perceived to have been most dispersed. Based on our close observation of the process, we would say that five or six individuals may have played a more active role and thus may have made a stronger contribution to the final decision. There is little doubt in our mind, however, that these leaders were not decisive in the decision to recommend MMP. In fact, support for MMP was weaker among those individuals than among the assembly as a whole, and some of these people were among the most articulate supporters of either the status quo or STV.

Several of these individuals were particularly influential, though, in some of the secondary decisions that were made. The Ontario assembly recommended increasing the size of the legislature. Some leaders were strong advocates of both sides of the issue, but one individual was particularly influential in making the case for augmenting the size of parliament. His influence was not necessarily personal, however, as support for an increased size came from members of visible minorities and women.

One person played a crucial role in the decision to revisit, and then reverse, an initial choice to allow 'overhangs'. The question of providing overhang seats arises in a mixed-member system when a party wins more seats in the local constituencies than its share of the vote would otherwise entitle it to. In some places, such as Germany and New Zealand, the parties are allowed to keep the extra seats and the others are compensated by increasing the total number of seats in parliament. In other cases, such as Scotland, the total number of seats in the legislature is unaltered. The initial decision of the Ontario assembly was to permit such overhangs, with the prospect of an even larger legislature in some years. But one individual was able to convince the chair to intervene on a substantive issue, something the chair wanted to avoid. The chair agreed to have the assembly revisit this decision. The assembly chose the Scottish approach and recommended a system with no overhang. This was a clear case of strong personal influence, though on a matter of detail that was somewhat subsidiary to the assembly's main agenda.

Thus, all the evidence at our disposal – the members' perceptions tapped in our surveys and our own observations of the assemblies – indicates that no small group of individuals shaped the major recommendations: whether to keep national PR in the Netherlands or to adopt STV in British Columbia or MMP in Ontario. In only one case, British Columbia, is there evidence that one particular individual may have been particularly influential, though that influence was confined to demonstrating that one of the criteria did not help members distinguish between two possible alternate electoral systems. In the other cases, some individual members were decisive, but only on certain secondary issues like the choice of the Hare formula in the Dutch case or the decision not to have overhangs in Ontario.

6.1.5 The influence of members with more education

The second possibility is that the better-educated members of the assemblies may have had a much greater say in the final decisions. It is fair to assume that the better educated generally tend to have better communication skills, and that they are somewhat more likely to intervene, especially in the plenary sessions. And indeed, among the three persons who were named as influential by a majority of the members across all assemblies, one had a doctorate from an elite research university.

The better educated may have been more vocal, and they may also have exercised greater personal influence. Still, they could have had little collective power if they were themselves divided on the issue. In order to conclude that the better educated as a group shaped the decisions that were made, we would need to show that they had some common views and that the less educated converged towards their common position.

There is simply no evidence of such a process going on. Table 6.1 shows the mean rating of the electoral system eventually chosen by each assembly provided by the better and lesser educated (the distinction hinging on the possession of a university education) at the beginning of the process. The ratings are remarkably similar. The same lack of significant difference existed throughout the proceedings.[4] With no trace

TABLE 6.1 *Evaluations of the Electoral System Adopted by Level of Education*

	British Columbia (STV)	The Netherlands (open-list PR)	Ontario (MMP)
Without a university diploma	5.0 (72)	5.6 (43)	5.8 (52)
With a university diploma	5.3 (52)	5.6 (58)	5.9 (40)

Numbers are means of variables that range from 0 to 7. The number of cases is in parentheses. Measures were captured in the first wave of the panel.

[4] There is only one exception, the better educated being more favourable to STV in British Columbia in the middle period; the difference between the two groups was quite small, however.

of an educational cleavage at any point in time, we have no reason to believe that the better educated led their group in any particular direction.

6.2 THE ROLE OF EXPERTS

When they joined the citizen assemblies, most members knew almost nothing about electoral systems. They needed to learn about the variety of options available and about the various criteria by which the impact of different electoral mechanisms could or should be evaluated. This learning exercise was led by academic experts who introduced members to the classification of electoral systems and to the debates about the alleged strengths and weaknesses of different systems. That situation generated a considerable potential for the experts to exert substantial influence, for assembly members were heavily dependent on the educational programme and information the instructors provided. As ordinary citizens, comparatively ignorant of the fine details of electoral institutions, they were not in a position, at least at the beginning of the process, to challenge the observations and claims made by the experts.

At the same time, the potential for assembly teaching staff to dominate the members should not be overstated. Apart from the research directors managing the learning phases, there was a variety of other expert advice available. Members had David Farrell's book and other supplementary materials, and there were many special presentations made by invited experts. So members were introduced to a variety of perspectives. Perhaps as important, the whole process was transparent and completely open as assembly sessions and materials were publicly available.[5] Any expert presenting a view seen to be biased in any way could expect to be criticized. This strengthened the experts' professional instincts to be neutral and objective.

There remains the possibility that the experts' personal views affected, even unconsciously, their presentation of the material and options. The concern is not misplaced. A recent study has shown that deliberative outcomes are vulnerable to the influence of discussion leaders (Humphreys et al. 2006). A bold exercise in deliberative democracy (in Sao Tome and Principe) engaged individuals in 148 small groups to discuss topics related to the country's economic priorities. These small groups were assigned a discussion leader at random. The evidence demonstrates that the leaders had a strong influence on the priorities that their group selected. Humphreys and colleagues conclude 'the preferences recorded in the deliberative meetings to a large extent reflect the preferences of discussion leaders,

---

[5] In the Ontario case, all plenary sessions and some small-group sessions were filmed by TVO, the provincial television network.

not participants' (2006: 620). That finding is a useful reminder that we need to be sensitive to the potential power of those leading deliberation exercises. Nevertheless, it is important to recognize that the São Tomé and Príncipe field experiment involved discussion leaders largely selected in a political process (Humphreys et al. 2006: 596–7). They were rather different from the independent academics who instructed the citizen assemblies. They could in no way be construed as experts.

So what can we say about the influence that the experts may have had on the decisions of the three electoral reform assemblies? The first piece of evidence comes from our surveys of the members. We asked them if they thought that the presentation of the options by the research staff was 'very biased, somewhat biased, somewhat unbiased, or very unbiased'. The great majority of assembly members perceived the research staff to have been remarkably neutral. All in all, only 7 per cent of the participants in the Ontario assembly and only 12 per cent in the British Columbia assembly said that the presentation of the options was somewhat or very biased (this question was not posed in the Netherlands). When asked whether they thought the research staff had an electoral system preference, only a minority said yes (20 per cent in Ontario and the Netherlands, and 31 per cent in British Columbia). And among that minority, there was no consensus about the nature of the preference. In fact, quite a few commented that the research staff must have had an opinion, but that they did not know what it was.

Thus, if the experts had any influence, they used it without the members seeing it, and it must have been subtle and indirect. Is there any indication of such subtle influence? One way that the research staff could have exerted some influence is by defining the options among which the assembly would choose. This raises the question of which typology of electoral systems to use. In the British Columbia and Dutch cases, the materials of the learning phase presented a typology of five 'families' of electoral systems: plurality, majority, PR, STV, and mixed. This standard classification is the one utilized in the major textbook on electoral systems (Farrell 2001). In Ontario, the typology included only four distinct families, on the grounds that the STV should simply be characterized as a specific variety of PR, as noted by other classifications (Blais and Massicotte 2002; Reynolds et al. 2005).

Is it possible that by presenting the choice as one between five rather than four types of systems, the research staff increased the possibility that the assemblies would recommend STV? There cannot be any definite answer to such a hypothetical question. But the available evidence suggests that this is unlikely. First, there is no evidence of a generalized bias in favour of STV across the three citizen assemblies. Second, the greater support for STV in British Columbia can be accounted for by the lesser importance attached to the criterion of simplicity and the more widespread anti-party sentiment (see Chapter 5).

Another way the experts could have shaped the participants' choices is by defining the values and criteria by which the various electoral systems could or should be evaluated. The presentation of these criteria was remarkably similar in the three cases, but some slight differences are noteworthy. In the British Columbia case, the third session of the very first weekend meeting was devoted to 'assessing electoral systems'. The documentation referred to several impacts of electoral arrangements and grouped them under two headings: 'on the system of government' and 'for voters'. In the Netherlands, the third weekend forum focused on eight distinctive consequences of electoral systems, two of them being the number of parties and the role/importance of parties. In Ontario, the research staff prepared, at the beginning of the deliberation phase, a package in which a list of possible objectives were identified, the very first one being that 'our electoral system should produce a legislature with more women and other under-represented groups'. In short, the contrast between the government and voters may have been somewhat more emphasized in British Columbia, the Dutch research staff may have paid more attention to the role of parties, and the under-representation of women and minorities may have been slightly more highlighted in Ontario. We need to ascertain whether those different emphases might have influenced how assembly members thought about the issues.

Did the different assemblies choose different options because they had different objectives and values or was it because they were led to pay greater attention to different criteria by the research staff? Again, there cannot be any definitive verdict on this, but a useful way of addressing the issue is to determine whether there is evidence of substantial value differences among the three assemblies before they started working (and thus before the research staff could exert any influence) and/or whether there is any evidence that the research staff may have primed certain considerations at the expense of others.

First, could it be that the (apparently) more explicit contrast made by the British Columbia staff between voters and governments primed voter choice as a criterion, and facilitated the choice of STV? There seems to be little support for that hypothesis. Populist sentiment was stronger from the start in British Columbia, though our surveys suggest that the differences were quite modest. As many as 61 per cent of the British Columbia assembly members agreed with the statement that 'we would probably solve most of our big problems if decisions could be brought back to the people at the grass roots', but the proportions were only slightly lower in the Netherlands (57 per cent) and Ontario (53 per cent). Furthermore, and most importantly, the correlation between populist sentiment and evaluations of STV as final decisions were made was basically nil (0.06) in British Columbia (as in the other two assemblies). There is thus no evidence that populist feelings were primed in British Columbia. Likewise, there is no indication that voter choice mattered more there than in the other two cases.

The second question that we address is whether the (apparently) stronger emphasis given to parties in the Netherlands programme may have led members of the Dutch assembly to focus more on that dimension and therefore to become more favourable to a list-PR system. This appears very unlikely. On the one hand, as we have seen, a strong majority of the Dutch participants expressed their satisfaction with the existing (open-list PR) system at the very beginning of the process, before hearing the assembly's experts. Also, as many as 89 per cent of the

Dutch members believed, from the time they first met, that 'without political parties there can't be true democracy', a considerably larger proportion than in either British Columbia (61 per cent) or Ontario (73 per cent). They were clearly concerned with parties from the beginning. Moreover, the link between this opinion and ratings of list-PR did not increase in strength during the proceedings – the correlation remained nil throughout (0.02 after the assembly).

Finally, another possibility is that the decision by the Ontario research staff to put the question of women and minorities' representation at the top of the list of 'possible objectives' induced the Ontario members to pay more attention to that particular aspect, and that this may have indirectly helped MMP. There were initially few differences between the three assemblies in the overall distribution of views about women and minorities. The percentage agreeing with the statement that the best way to protect women's interests is to have more women in legislatures is almost identical in Ontario (68 per cent) and British Columbia (67 per cent), though somewhat smaller in the Netherlands (53 per cent). Those expressing support for the view that better representation of minorities is needed in legislatures constituted 47 per cent of the Ontario, 49 per cent of the British Columbia, and 45 per cent of the Dutch membership. The key issue, then, is whether this question might have been primed in Ontario. To check that possibility, we examined the correlation between these views and ratings of MMP among Ontarians. The relationship stayed non-existent (ending up at 0.01). There is thus no evidence that concerns about women and minority representation levels were primed by the Ontario research staff.

Ascertaining the actual influence of experts in a deliberative assembly is a challenging task. In this instance, the task is aggravated by the fact that many of us were ourselves directly involved in steering the process of learning and deliberation. Since the participants initially knew basically nothing about electoral systems and that they had to quickly acquire the necessary information and tools, we recognize that there was a real prospect for influence from the 'teachers'. It is hard to believe that the experts had no influence at all, direct or indirect, on any of the issues that were considered. The fundamental question, however, is whether the experts had a substantial impact on the most crucial decision, that is, the choice of the electoral system. The evidence that we have been able to assemble suggests that the answer is no. The members themselves perceived the research staff to have been neutral. Each staff had a distinctive programme outlining the relevant considerations and criteria, but we have seen no indication of priming effects in the assemblies.

6.3 THE CHAIRS

The experts were not the only actors who could influence the decisions reached by the citizen assemblies. We also need to examine the role played by the externally appointed chairs who were in charge of the process, could decide how much time to devote to various issues, and shape the assemblies' individual decision trees. Their potential for influence was real, and this raises a series of important questions: How did the three chairs conceive of their role? What were their objectives? Did they have any views of their own about electoral systems? Did they have clear conceptions about the process, about how the assembly should reach its decisions? Is there any reason to believe that they had an effect on the final choices that were made?

The chair of the British Columbia Citizens' Assembly was Jack Blaney.[6] He made it very clear from the beginning that he was not an expert on electoral systems and that his goal was to make sure the process was unbiased and fully inclusive. He was very much the leader of the assembly, opening each session with the reminder that 'nothing is decided until everything is decided', so that members should feel free to continue discussing and debating all subjects. Blaney's primary concern was to ensure members established a healthy working environment and he devoted much of his energy towards this. He would constantly 'work the room', talking with people at mealtimes and session breaks, as well as between formal assembly meetings, to see how things were going. He identified individuals who seemed to have the pulse of their colleagues and sought as much feedback from them as possible.

In the actual conduct of the plenary sessions, Blaney's approach could be described as liberal. He preferred to let members talk as much as they wished, even if this meant going over time, until his sense was that most members wanted to move on, and he would then check if that was indeed the feeling of the group. As chair, Blaney was particularly keen to avoid formal votes until the end of the decision-making process. He wanted to keep a good spirit in the assembly and hoped that this would make it easier to reach final decisions. Although he never said so publicly, his worst-case scenario would have been an assembly equally and deeply divided between two options. In the face of that outcome, he probably would have called for more deliberation in the hope of forging a consensus. From that perspective, Blaney was quite successful, since a strong majority supported the recommendation in favour of STV.

It is hard to believe that the chair of the British Columbia citizen assembly had any direct impact on the final electoral system choice. Perhaps his most important decision was to create a deliberation and decision structure that postponed votes until late in the process. This decision kept the assembly united and working forward, and it may have contributed to the near unanimity of the final recommendation, as some indifferent and ambivalent members (between STV and MMP) expressed the view that it was important that the assembly speak with one voice. That outcome might not have been possible if members had been put in

---

[6] For more on the assembly chairs, see Chapter 2 (Section 2.3.1).

the position of expressing their preferences at an early stage of the deliberative debate. Also, Blaney did interpret the assembly's mandate as requiring it to work with the current size of the legislature, and Lang (2008) has raised the possibility that this decision could have advantaged STV, since MMPs might be less attractive to some in a context where local electoral districts grow significantly in size.

The chair of the Dutch assembly, Jacobine Geel, did not have a clear preference for any specific electoral system. In this case as well, we can rule out the possibility of any conscious attempt to influence the outcome of the assembly. Geel's main responsibility was to moderate the plenary sessions, and help to strengthen and maintain the integrity of the process. She was also process oriented. There were, however, some differences in the way Jack Blaney and Jacobine Geel led their groups. Geel appeared more interested in the content of the proposal; she did not prefer any specific option, but she was openly concerned that the *Burger-forum* recommendation be 'workable' and 'consistent'. It was pretty clear, for instance, that she did not like the idea that coalition voting should be studied further. Some members wanted the ballot to offer a vote for a party and a vote for a coalition. This issue was the subject of a vote in the assembly, where sixty-five against sixty-three decided to end discussions about coalition voting. Since some members present did not vote, others were absent that weekend, and the margin was so narrow, certain members asked for a second more formal vote, but Geel refused. Because she agreed to a second vote on another issue later in the process, this refusal suggests the Dutch chair was not interested in coalition voting, which would not be simple to implement in the electoral system. Geel also sometimes expressed the opinion that the forum should recommend some change, even though she would quickly add that a recommendation to keep the existing system would be equally good. She may thus have encouraged the push for recommending a strengthened personal vote element, though support for such change was already relatively widespread among assembly members.

Another difference in the way the British Columbia and Dutch assemblies functioned was the much greater frequency of voting and the greater number of alternatives explicitly considered (seven altogether) in the latter case. The *Bur-gerforum*'s deliberative process was less structured, with no focusing on a limited number of options, and less concerned for building a consensus – a surprise in this quintessential consociational democracy. Issues were to be resolved by voting under an absolute majority rule. These differences in the style of leadership may have affected things at the margin. But, here again, we fail to see how the chair may have even inadvertently influenced the decision to recommend keeping the list system of national PR.

The approach followed by the chair of the Ontario assembly, George Thomson, resembled in many ways the one adopted by Jack Blaney in British Columbia. Great emphasis was given to building strong and positive relationships within the group. This began prior to the assembly's first meeting, as Thomson called each member to discuss what concerns they might have. He was keen to make sure that members felt good about the process and trusted their colleagues. At the same time, he made it very clear that his role was not to get involved in the substance of the matter, and he was quite consistent in this, the only significant exception being his decision to have the assembly revisit the issue of overhang seats.

Thomson decided early on that, unless specifically asked for by members, the assembly would not take a vote on routine matters. Instead, consensus – expressed by a simple show of hands – was adopted as the working decision rule. This reflected the modus operandi of the entire assembly process; unless there was broad agreement, decisions should not be taken.

In all three assemblies, the chair saw his/her role as orchestrating the process. In all cases, they had no clear substantive preferences and so no particular agenda to pursue. Their styles did vary and we cannot dismiss the possibility that some of their decisions may have had some indirect influence on marginal issues. Still, the conclusion seems inescapable that the chairs did not decisively affect the choice of the electoral system.

6.4 THE PUBLIC CONSULTATIONS

In each of the three assemblies, a series of public consultations took place after the learning stage, before the process of deliberation and decision-making started. This consultation phase was meant to inform members about how the public felt about the issue. Was the electorate satisfied or dissatisfied with the existing system? How much appetite was there for reform? What were the major concerns, perceptions, and values at stake? Which potential reform options had greater or weaker support? The question here is whether this public input had any significant impact on the assemblies' recommendations. Our analyses indicate that the consultations did influence the members but did not substantially affect the final outcomes. The most telling sign here is simply the absence of evidence that mean evaluations of the various options changed during the consultations. The most important effect of the consultation exercises was indirect; they strengthened members' confidence that they could meet the expectations vested in them.

British Columbia held the most extensive consultations. They offered assembly members the opportunity to travel, in small groups, to different communities across the province. This sensitized many of them to the vast size of the province and to the representational challenges of rural areas. Perhaps this made them more responsive to the arguments about local representation made by members from those areas. The members learned that most citizens knew far less about electoral systems than they did, and that the great majority they heard from wanted change and some form of proportionality. They also heard many individuals praising the government for setting up the assembly. All this strengthened their sense of legitimacy and competence. The members could also see that there was a concerted attempt by the Green Party and Fair Vote BC (an electoral reform lobby group) to push for the adoption of an MMP system. That campaign was perceived by many to be illegitimate: members believed that the consultative exercise was meant to inform them about the public mood rather than about the views of specific interest groups.

The consultative process in the Netherlands was quite different. Meetings with the public were structured as debates organized around specific questions and propositions, and those attending were invited to cast votes on each of them. The idea was to gauge public reactions to general ideas formulated by the *Burgerforum*, rather than allow the participants to propose explicit options for electoral reform. These meetings were evaluated positively by the assembly members (see Table 2.5), but the consultations did not change their opinions nor did they give them many new arguments. Most felt that those who came were not a representative sample of the population and were not well informed. All in all, then, the Dutch public consultations did not have a major impact.

The Ontario consultative process was similar to the one in British Columbia, though slightly less extensive. As in British Columbia, the main impact was mainly a legitimating one. For most members, it was the first time their work had been recognized and this recognition was empowering. The consultations provided legitimacy not only to the assembly as a whole but also to the positions of members who had aligned themselves with one of the various options. Members rarely heard anything new, but they could later utilize what they heard to support their own positions and to challenge the thinking of other members. Finally, the meetings confirmed that there was appetite for change and broad support for a mixed system.

In short, members in each of the assemblies quickly realized from their experiences in the consultation phase that they knew more about the details and consequences of electoral systems than did the public and that, in British Columbia and Ontario, there was some interest in changing the system. If the consultations had very little impact on the final decisions made, they did provide members with confidence that they were on the right track.

6.5 THE POLITICAL PARTIES

The decision that the assemblies were asked to make was bound to have very direct and substantial consequences for the political parties and the system of party competition in their respective political systems. Most obviously, any proposal to move to a more (or less) proportional system would necessarily benefit small (or large) parties.

From a rational choice perspective, we would expect parties to support the electoral system that maximizes their seat share and/or their chances of being in government (Benoît 2004). Presumably, the parties have compelling incentives to try to convince the respective assemblies that the option that benefits them is the best one for the community.

However, this perspective must be nuanced. Bowler et al.'s survey of candidates and parliamentarians in four countries reveals that their views about electoral institutions are shaped by their values and ideologies as well as by electoral self-interest (2005). As they conclude, pure self-interest is an incomplete explanation for politicians' attitudes towards institutions such as the electoral system. Pilet's detailed analysis of Belgian political parties' positions with respect to three electoral reform proposals also demonstrates that ideas matter, and that parties do not always take the time to think through where their immediate electoral interest lies (2007).

In spite of this, there is little doubt that parties have powerful stakes to protect or to advance on electoral system issues. It is quite clear, for instance, that the principal reason why the single member plurality (SMP) system remains in place in Britain, Canada, and the United States, despite all its shortcomings, is that the major parties have an advantage to keep it (Blais and Shugart 2008). The large parties have a strong interest in maintaining the status quo and this generally goes a long way to explain their behaviour.

From this point of view, one of the most startling features of the events surrounding the three assemblies is that virtually all the parties chose to remain completely silent. This is truly puzzling. It is equivalent to a medical association declining to speak to a commission mandated to propose a system for compensating physicians. Whatever the assemblies proposed could have had huge consequences for the political fate of the parties. How can we explain their decision not to take a position?

In British Columbia, the governing Liberals created the assembly after promising to do so in the manifesto for their successful 2001 election campaign. At the time they launched the assembly (i.e. before its participants had even been selected), the Liberals indicated that they would not make any proposal to the assembly, and they did not. Their rationale was that it was the preserve of citizens to decide which democratic system they wanted, and that it was crucial to maintain distance between the assembly and the government.

The opposition New Democratic Party (NDP) was devastated by the 2001 provincial election in which it won only two seats in the legislature. All its available energy was spent on rebuilding a badly shattered party, and few in the party paid attention to the assembly as it was being set up and started. As a relatively minor party in federal politics, the national NDP has long believed in and campaigned for PR, but the provincial party had a very different perspective. As a major player in the provincial system, it could expect to win office on its own with an SMP electoral system, as it had done in the past. If the provincial party leaders had an incentive to oppose a shift to some form of PR, many of its ordinary individual members strongly believed in it as a matter of principle, and this created the potential for deep internal division at a time when the party was in no condition to manage it. With the Liberals committed to remaining on the sideline, the NDP might also have been accused of undermining the political independence of the assembly process if they had intervened. Clearly, abstaining from the debate was the easiest and safest option.

The only other significant party was the Greens, traditionally a minor player in British Columbia politics, but which had gained some visibility after winning 12 per cent of the vote, but no seats, in 2001. It was a strong advocate of an MMP system, and the party leader Adriane Carr, who had been encouraged by Green success in New Zealand after it adopted MMP in the 1990s, was deeply committed to electoral reform. She made a point of coming to every session of the assembly, sitting prominently in the front row of the public gallery. The party actively campaigned throughout the process in favour of MMP, producing a good deal of written material for the assembly members and appearing at several public hearings.

In British Columbia, then, the two major parties were completely absent from the whole process. Once they had agreed to the principle of citizen decision-making through an assembly and subsequent public referendum, any intervention on their part could have been perceived, or portrayed, as illegitimate.

In the Netherlands, the parties were even more absent from the scene than in British Columbia. The decision to have a citizen assembly was a concession that a minor party (Democrats 66 – D66) extracted from its larger partners as part of the price for its participation in the coalition government. But none of the other parties expressed any interest or concern for the assembly or its work. No party, except D66, had taken any position on the issue of electoral reform in the previous elections, none paid any attention to the assembly, and none presented a brief to the *Burgerforum*.

In short, the assembly was basically a non-event for the Dutch parties, with the notable exception of D66. Because D66 was a pivotal member of the coalition, the other members of the government felt forced to make some accommodation to its priorities, but clearly they considered it only a symbolic gesture. The electoral system was not on any of the major parties' agendas, so they did not take the assembly seriously.

In Ontario, as in British Columbia, the citizen assembly was the result of a series of initiatives on democratic renewal implemented by a newly elected Liberal government after having promised them during the 2003 election campaign. As in British Columbia, premier McGuinty guaranteed complete independence for the assembly, and his party remained completely silent on the question of electoral reform as it worked. The official opposition Conservative party also had little to say. On the few occasions that its leader John Tory was asked about the assembly, he ducked the issue and simply replied that it was up to the public to decide the wisdom of the recommendation. The province's third party, the

New Democrats, took a different stance. Its leader Howard Hampton was an enthusiastic supporter of electoral reform. However, the party accepted the apparent norm of non-intervention and did not present a brief to the assembly in the consultation phase.

In short, almost all the parties in each of the cases refrained from taking a position on a vital issue capable of altering their place in the political system. They did so either because they assumed nothing could come out of the exercise (in the Netherlands), or because they feared any partisan intervention would be deemed to be illegitimate after having agreed to allow ordinary citizens to take ownership of the issue. The surreal outcome was that the actors most likely to be directly affected by a change in the electoral system chose to remain on the sidelines.

6.6 CONCLUSION

In this chapter, we have explored the possibility that assembly members' decisions reflected more than their own values, criteria, or priorities, by having been prejudiced by external forces. We focused on potential influences from leaders within the assembly, experts in charge of informing them, chairs directing the process, the general public through the consultative stage, and the political parties.

With respect to the political parties, our findings are absolutely unequivocal. The parties were strikingly absent from the whole process. This itself raises important questions about the consequences of such a situation. The risk, of course, is that assembly members may not have fully appreciated the problems and opportunities that parties face under different electoral systems.

With respect to opinion leadership within the assemblies, our findings are also pretty clear. There were strong interactions among assembly members, and there was ample opportunity for mutual influence. But all the evidence at our disposal suggests that leadership was widely dispersed. Only in the British Columbia case is there some indication that one particular individual may have played a particularly important part, and then only with respect to one specific dimension of the debate. We can conclude with some confidence that no one person or small group of individuals within the assemblies shaped their final recommendations.

Our conclusions about the role of the chairs are unambiguous as well. The chairs were entirely focused on creating good working relationships within the memberships and making sure that the process was as fair and transparent as possible. They did not have clear personal preferences about electoral systems and they did not have any impact on the content of the decisions.

The same verdict applies to public consultations. They were very helpful in strengthening assembly participants' confidence in their capacity to do the job, but members learned very little from them.

The more difficult question concerns the role of experts, a particularly thorny issue since we, the authors, were among the key members of this group. We are conscious of the fact that we may be prone to downplay the role that we might have played in the process. But again the evidence indicates that the electoral system experts did not define the agenda or govern the choices. Perhaps the most telling fact is that there was initial widespread dissatisfaction with the existing system in Ontario and British Columbia and relatively little in the Netherlands. It was these sentiments which drove the push for reform in the former and the commitment to the status quo in the latter. The most plausible interpretation, it seems to us, is the one advanced in Chapter 5: the specific choice made by each assembly reflected its own particular set of priorities. Different assemblies recommended different electoral systems because their members valued different objectives.

7

Did Participants Become Better Citizens?

> You see this creature with her kerbstone English: the English that will keep her
> in the gutter to the end of her days. Well, sir, in three months I could pass that
> girl off as a duchess at an ambassador's garden party.
>
> Henry Higgins, in Pygmalion by George Bernard Shaw (1913)

The three citizen assemblies provided their members with a unique and unexpected experience. They shared numerous private and public learning and deliberative sessions with people they had never met before, and worked to develop a report which they knew would be widely and critically assessed. Being immersed in an intense political process with the potential to change the functioning of democracy in their province/country was not something easily forgotten. For some individuals, this might have been life changing, for others a source of frustration or disappointment. But none was likely to be unmarked by the opportunity and experience.

Political theorists concerned with issues of public participation and impacts of deliberative democracy claim, just like Henry Higgins, that both can produce 'better' citizens. This assertion can be traced through the works of Aristotle, John Stuart Mill, and Alexis de Tocqueville, with modern versions normally attributed to Arnold Kaufman, Carole Pateman, and Dennis Thompson. Pateman suggests that 'the theory of participatory democracy argues that the experience of participation in some ways leaves the individual better equipped to undertake further participation in the future' (1970: 45). Thompson thinks that participation could 'develop social virtues, such as a sense of cooperation and community', arguing that it increases citizens' political competence and system approval, as well as promotes self-realization including political efficacy (1970: 66). The claim that participation produces better citizens can also be found among recent advocates of deliberative democracy (Gastil 2000; Morrell 2005).

In early work, Pateman and Thompson rooted their assertions in the empirical work of the *Civic Culture*. Almond and Verba had reported the existence of strong relationships between psychological factors like political alienation and levels of political participation (1963: 46). However, these and similar studies only showed correlations between participation and various attitudes, they did not establish a causal connection. Indeed, many scholars interpreted the observed associations the other way around, hypothesizing that it was attitudes like political interest and efficacy that produced or stimulated political participation. This led some researchers to conclude that the empirical investigations used to support the claims of citizenship theorists and participatory democrats could neither prove nor disprove a thesis about the transformational effects of participation (Delli Carpini et al. 2004: 321; Gastil et al. 2008: 351).

While the number of studies explicitly addressing the causal connection from participation to attitudes is still small, some have examined the issue (Finkel 1985, 1987; Leighley 1991; Radcliff and Wingenbach 2000; Mutz 2006). For instance, Steven Finkel analysed the effects of various types of participation on different political attitudes using survey panel data, with mixed results. He found that voting did not have a significant impact on political efficacy, but campaigning did; voting improved regime support, but protesting and aggressive political behaviour did not. Although simple participatory acts like voting, demonstrating, or signing a petition do not seem to be very influential in changing attitudes, Mansbridge suggests that we might expect larger consequences from more demanding activities (1999: 317).

Nevertheless, empirical investigations of the effects of deliberation and other challenging activities on various civic attitudes have also produced largely weak and mixed results. They support the idea that participants in a deliberative setting acquire context-specific efficacy (the feeling that they can influence the outcomes of the process in question), but disagree on whether there is an effect on more generalized efficacy (Gastil and Dillard 1999; Barabas 2004; Carpini et al. 2004). While Morrell (2005) says there is no significant impact, Fishkin and Luskin are more positive. They claim their deliberative poll evidence shows that 'the more citizens deliberate, the more informed, interested, participatory, efficacious, trusting, supportive of democracy, and sociotropic they become' (Fishkin and Luskin 1999: 33; Luskin and Fishkin 2002). For their part, Hibbing and Theiss-Morse are far less optimistic about such processes. They conclude that the positive effects of participation are predominantly limited to situations where people already agree about the topics they discuss. In real politics – where people disagree, where there are distributional problems, and where individuals have to make collective decisions – participation, and especially deliberation, may even have negative effects: 'given the predilections of the people, real deliberation is quite likely to make them hopping mad' (2002: 207).

These conflicting theoretical claims and empirical observations give us good reason to investigate the actual civic effects of citizen assemblies. If we are able to show that the assembly experiences had a considerable impact on the participants, this will strengthen the case of the deliberative democracy advocates. If, on the other hand, we see no impact on attitudes as a consequence of involvement in this most intense form of participation, we will have to be dubious about claims that participation improves citizenship.

7.1 EXPECTATIONS OF CHANGE

To this point, our consideration of the attitudes that political theorists expect to be stimulated by political participation has been cast in general terms. We need to ask what are the expected beneficial effects. Thompson includes: political awareness, knowledge and competence, approval of the political system, efficacy, cooperation, and community (1970: 60–7). Mansbridge mentions four: political efficacy, sense of cooperation, commitment to collective decisions, and democratic character (1999: 314).[1] In this chapter, our analysis is limited to a number of measurable attitudes. We focus on political engagement, political efficacy, opinions towards various political actors and democracy, civic duty, interpersonal trust, populism, and open-mindedness.

Although we start by examining the relationship between participation and attitude change, we also want to enquire into the origins of any such changes.[2] What may be the psychological or social mechanisms generating these effects? While the underlying mechanism may, of course, vary from one effect to another, we anticipate that two key factors explain the acquisition of these attitudes and the differences in the extent to which the assembly participants acquired them. First, members who became heavily involved in the assembly process ought to have changed more than those who attended but were not very active. This is merely an extension of the general expectation that participation makes better citizens – more participation should make them even better. Second, we expect that there was a difference in the acquisition of attitudes between the learning phase and the deliberation phase. On the one hand, if it is indeed deliberative work (discussion, debate, and decision-making) that produces attitude change, then the biggest changes ought to have occurred in the latter part of the assembly proceedings. On the other hand, if it is the learning and social interaction aspects of participation that are mainly responsible for producing attitude movement, then the biggest changes will have been observed in the early stages of the process. With data collected over the life of the assemblies, we are able to compare these two periods and estimate their relative importance in inducing change. As well, we will search for additional explanations in the context of specific attitudes.

7.2 DID ASSEMBLY MEMBERS BECOME MORE POLITICALLY ENGAGED?

In Chapter 3, we saw that the assembly members were typically more interested in politics than the general public at the outset. In order to discover whether members became even more engaged during the process, we look at changes in four measures: subjective political interest ('how interested in politics do you feel?'), political

---

[1] See Luskin and Fishkin (2002: 3) for a list with nine items. Carpini et al. (2004: 320–1) summarize the long list of expectations of deliberative democracy.

[2] See, for example, Barabas who argued that: 'scholars have not clarified how deliberation works' (2004: 687).

TABLE 7.1 *Changing Attitudes: Political Engagement*

	Start	Change	N
Political interest	69.2	+7.8**	318
Attention to political news	74.1	+6.5**	317
Attention to domestic news	58.9	+10.6**	107_n
Informed about politics	60.4	+11.9**	319

All variables range from 0 to 100. n = The Netherlands only.
** Significant at 0.05; *significant at 0.10.

attention ('how much attention do you usually pay to news about politics?', 'how often do you read national news in the newspaper?'), and subjective political information ('how informed about politics do you feel?'). These questions were asked before the first meeting of the assembly, then halfway through the process, and finally after the assemblies completed their work and delivered their reports.

Table 7.1 presents the members' initial average scores on these engagement attitudes and reports the change recorded at the end. The data for all three assemblies were pooled together.[3] All variables have been transformed to a 0–100 scale to simplify comparison. Their direction has also been recoded so that a high value indicates a positive attitude and an increase is the change expected as a consequence of participation.[4] The significance of the differences between T1 and T3 was identified by a (two-sided) *t*-test.

The evidence makes it clear that subjective political interest, attention, and information all increased substantially and significantly over the life of the assemblies. The participants report paying more attention to the news, becoming more interested in, and feeling more informed about, politics at the end of the process than they did at the beginning. Similar changes occurred in all three assemblies. Since the members' initial scores on these attitudes were rather skewed towards the high end, a ceiling effect could be limiting the increases. Indeed, the climb in political interest was much greater among those whose starting levels were relatively low. This logic also accounts for a greater increase of interest among women for, as is the case in the wider population (Verba et al. 1997), their initial interest levels were lower than were those of the men. Once we control for ceiling effects, the gap between the two genders disappears.[5]

---

[3] Some questions were only asked in the Canadian provinces, some were only asked in the Netherlands, as indicated in the column for the number of cases.

[4] If the coding is reversed (as compared to the question wording), this is indicated with an '(r)' in the first column of Table 7.1. Details about the variables can be found in Appendix 3.

[5] In order to control for ceiling (and floor) effects in this chapter's analyses, individual change was taken as the dependent variable and the initial level of that variable was inserted as an independent variable.

To determine whether those with the largest involvement in the assembly experienced the greatest attitudinal shifts, we constructed a measure of involvement based on various assembly activities including visits to the intranet discussion forum, reading the assembly's newsletter, and attendance at consultation meetings. Given the differences in the activities across the three assemblies, we examined each separately. In most cases, differences in the level of involvement do not explain changes in political engagement. The effect of involvement was always positive, but significantly so in only a few instances: political interest and attention in British Columbia, and political information in Ontario.

If the intensity of members' involvement does not systematically account for these differences, it is possible that they were driven by the nature of assembly activity. To consider that possibility, we ask if change occurred during the learning or deliberation phases. The story is ambiguous. The timing of the increase in the attitudes was not the same in all three cases. In British Columbia, the earlier information period clearly led to a larger gain in political interest than the later decision-making stage. But that was not the case in either the Netherlands or Ontario, where the increases seem to have been more gradual, developing over time. This suggests that political interest may have been stimulated in different ways in the different assemblies.

Assembly members did become more politically interested, attentive, and informed than they were at the beginning. They came to appreciate politics even more during the process. However, we are unable to shed much light on how that happened and thus on the precise mechanism that links cause and effect. Involvement played a small role, but the relationship is a very weak one. It is important to note that our data cannot tell us whether these attitude changes were permanent, altering the assembly members' engagement over the longer term, or whether participants, no longer in the grip of the intense learning and deliberative environment, have reverted to their original engagement levels.

7.3 DID ASSEMBLY MEMBERS BECOME MORE SELF-CONFIDENT?

We have three indicators of assembly participants' self-confidence: whether they feel nervous speaking in front of a group, whether they consider themselves a shy person, and whether they think they are able to do things as well as other people. In addition, the members of the Dutch assembly were asked a political efficacy question: whether they thought themselves qualified to play an active role in politics. The results, reported in Table 7.2, indicate that assembly members did not emerge from the proceedings feeling more self-confident. The level of nervousness associated with public speaking was unchanged. Political efficacy also

TABLE 7.2 *Changing Attitudes: Self-Confidence*

	Start	Change	N
I feel nervous when I speak in front of a group (r)	46.5	−1.6	309
In general, I am a shy person (r)	59.1	−5.2**	206_c
I am not able to do things as well as most other people (r)	81.2	−3.8*	204_c
I am well qualified to play an active role in politics	56.0	−0.9	53_n

All variables range from 0 to 100. c = Canada only; n = the Netherlands only.
** Significant at 0.05; * significant at 0.10.

remained static in the Netherlands.[6] The other two items did move significantly, but in a direction that runs contrary to theoretical anticipations. Apparently, participants were shier and less confident about their capacities at the end of the assembly's work. It is unclear to us why this happened.

Aggregate dynamics could mask marked individual differences. For instance, the level of involvement could have fostered positive individual changes in self-confidence. But it did not; assembly involvement was not systematically related to these changes. Another potential mediator is the nature of the experience that each person actually had within the assemblies. More specifically, the beneficial consequences of deliberation could be contingent upon the feeling of having been taken seriously by colleagues. Dutch members were explicitly asked whether other assembly members listened carefully to what they had to say, and whether their political opinions were similar to those of the whole group.[7] There was no significant difference in self-confidence between those who considered that their remarks were respected and those who did not. However, being part of the majority or the minority did matter. The data reveal that those whose opinions deviated from the rest of the assembly became somewhat more positive about their ability 'to play an active role in politics', while those who shared the opinions of the majority came to consider themselves relatively less capable of playing such a role. The difference was small, but it was significant. These results imply that individuals who face widespread disagreement become more efficacious, perhaps because they needed to battle firmly to keep their ground, while those unchallenged by holding dominant views do not develop any increased appreciation of their ability to become active participants.

Nonetheless, the principal conclusion is that most assembly members did not gain in self-confidence and political efficacy. Only the few people with minority opinions seem to have become a bit more efficacious, suggesting that participation

---

[6] The number of Dutch respondents indicating they do not know the answer to this question is substantial. This number does not change substantially between the first and the final surveys.

[7] The percentage with negative perceptions was small in both cases (12–13 per cent).

can stimulate efficacy in instances where individuals are pushed to fight for unpopular views.

7.4 DID ASSEMBLY MEMBERS BECOME MORE POSITIVE ABOUT POLITICS?

Learning to realize the constraints within which individual politicians, political parties, and the government operate, and having an impact on governmental decision-making are generally expected to generate more positive views towards politics (Finkel 1985: 893). Therefore, the information about politics that assembly members acquired ought to have improved their attitudes about political actors. Our data, presented in Table 7.3, show that this was not systematically the case. First, with regard to politicians, the results were mixed. Six of the seven indicators showed a small positive gain, though only half of them were statistically significant. Furthermore, those significant changes did not occur in each assembly. For instance, there actually seems to have been a decline in attitudes about politicians among British Columbians, while there was an increase in Ontario.[8] Thus, any claim that participation improves citizens' attitudes towards the political class is, at best, only modestly substantiated by the data.

With regard to political parties, the findings were again equivocal. There were small positive movements in the beliefs that parties do a good job of presenting clear choices, finding solutions, and expressing people's concerns. But the proportion that accepted the proposition that parties are essential for democracy actually fell a little. Once more, there was some variation in attitude shifts across the three assemblies, with changes in line with expectations being strongest in the Netherlands and Ontario, and weakest in British Columbia.

Views about government also progressed to some limited extent within the assemblies. The idea that the government cares much about what ordinary people think grew significantly among members, particularly in the Netherlands and Ontario.

The most surprising result is the small decline in satisfaction with democracy. Although it increased in the Netherlands, satisfaction deteriorated in both British Columbia and Ontario. These unexpected drops should not be underestimated. Over 30 per cent of Canadian assembly members reported lower evaluations of the democratic system at the end of the proceedings. Part of the explanation for this change may be found in the similar decline of satisfaction with the current

---

[8] Interestingly, Ontario was the only assembly where a group of former politicians made a presentation during the learning phase.

TABLE 7.3 *Changing Attitudes: Opinions about Politics*

	Start	Change	N
Politicians			
Those elected soon lose touch with the people (r)	40.0	−1.0	292
Politicians are ready to lie to get elected (r)	41.3	+2.7	271
Politicians are about as honest as the average person	30.4	+6.9**	313
MPs do not care about opinions of people like me (r)	46.4	+7.2**	83_n
Elected officials are unselfish	48.6	+1.2	311
Elected officials are intelligent	67.4	+2.8**	317
Elected officials are informed	70.0	+1.4	315
Political Parties			
Parties are necessary for democracy	69.6	−6.0**	288
Parties do a good job in presenting clear choices on the issues	44.3	+4.4**	315
Parties do a good job in finding solutions to import. problems	42.6	+4.9**	315
Parties do a good job in expressing the concerns of the people	39.0	+3.8**	315
All parties are basically the same (r)	70.9	−0.3	308
Government			
Government does not care what people like me think (r)	49.7	+5.1**	301
Political System			
Satisfaction with the way democracy works	56.5	−2.5*	317

All variables range from 0 to 100. n = The Netherlands only.
** Significant at 0.05; * significant at 0.10.

electoral system (see the discussion in Chapter 4). Over time, approval of the existing voting systems decreased substantially in Canada while soaring in the Netherlands. The striking parallels in those two patterns suggest that individuals discussing the best way to organize elections may simply come to conceptualize democracy in terms of its specific electoral regime.

Is it actually involvement in the assemblies and, more particularly, the amount of information about politics acquired by the participants that foster positive attitudes towards politics? In order to test this idea, we examined whether attitude change was more pronounced among those who learned more and those who were more involved in the assembly process. These two potential mediators were introduced in Section 7.2. It appears that increased subjective knowledge made a difference, albeit a weak one, for attitudes towards politicians, but not for views about government, democracy, or parties. Those whose reported knowledge of politics improved during the assembly process became slightly more positive towards politicians. By contrast, the level of assembly involvement was inconsequential; it was not related to changes in the attitudes towards any of the four political targets.

All in all, assembly members became somewhat more positive towards politicians, political parties, and the government, but not towards democracy. However, the changes were small, not consistent across all indicators, and not evident in all three assemblies.

7.5 DID ASSEMBLY MEMBERS BECOME MORE CIVIC-MINDED?

According to some democratic theorists, being involved in politics may also improve one's general civic attitudes and values. It is argued, for example, that participation leads to higher levels of interpersonal trust (Brehm and Rahn 1997) and tolerance (Carpini et al. 2004).[9] In Table 7.4, we measure the change on a number of such variables over the assembly process. The first block speaks to members' sense of civic duty and interpersonal trust. Duty to stay informed and to turn out for elections exhibited a very small but significant increase. One of the two conventional trust indicators improved a bit, though not significantly. For such an intensive deliberative experience, this movement appears minuscule.

Participants appear to have become somewhat more positive about other citizens. There were significant, though not substantial, increases on opinions about people's unselfishness, intelligence, information, and capacity to follow political issues and the actions of government. Those changes, however, did not translate into any greater faith in the public's political judgement at the expense of experts and politicians, since the two populism measures did not move.

The last set of attitudes deals with tolerance. Rather than examine traditional indicators (such as the civil liberties that one would allow to unpopular or dissident social groups), we looked at more general measures of open-mindedness/intransigence and authoritarianism. Only a single item was significantly affected: members became less likely to state that most ideas are not worthwhile. The other four did not improve, indicating that the assembly had little impact on these fundamental attitudes.

One might have predicted that civic attitudes would have been fostered among those who had positive experiences with assembly colleagues. In the Dutch case, where we explicitly measured perceptions of these experiences, neither being listened to nor belonging to the majority affected considerably this type of attitude change. Trust was the sole exception. Members who considered that others carefully listened to what they had to say did report slightly enhanced levels of trust.

So, did extensive collaboration towards a common goal alter individuals' opinions of other people and their abilities? The effects of participation in the

---

[9] In most studies of social capital, a reciprocal relationship is hypothesized between participation and trust.

TABLE 7.4 *Changing Attitudes: Duty, Trust, Populism, and Open-Mindedness*

	Start	Change	N
Duty and trust			
It is the duty of every citizen to stay informed	83.8	+2.6*	206$_c$
It is the duty of every citizen to vote in every election	81.6	+2.8**	309
Most people would not take advantage of you	77.4	−1.0	208$_c$
Most people can be trusted	77.2	+3.2	312
People and populism			
People in general are unselfish	50.9	+2.5**	313
People in general are intelligent	60.1	+2.2**	316
People in general are informed	44.9	+2.6**	317
Most people have enough sense to tell gov. is doing a good job	53.3	+7.2**	204$_c$
The major issues are too complicated for most voters (r)	53.5	+3.4**	301
Decisions should be brought back to the people at grass roots	56.5	+1.4	266
I would put my faith in the down-to-earth thinking of the people	55.2	−1.6	276
Open-mindedness			
For most questions there is only one right answer (r)	80.7	−1.6	204$_c$
Most ideas are not worth the paper they are printed on (r)	66.7	+3.2*	187$_c$
Many problems have more than one acceptable solution	85.0	0.0	211$_c$
A person should not be allowed to talk if they do not know (r)	69.1	+0.3	203$_c$
Obedience and respect for authority are most imp. virtues (r)	49.4	+1.0	208$_c$

All variables range from 0 to 100. c = Canada only.
** Significant at 0.05; * significant at 0.10.

assemblies were often in the direction anticipated by advocates for deliberative exercises, but they were not large. Members did become slightly more dutiful, trusting, and positive towards their fellow citizens, but populism and tolerance remained essentially static.

7.6 WERE ATTITUDE CHANGES A CONSEQUENCE OF EXTERNAL FACTORS?

We have attributed the relatively modest changes in attitudes and opinions reported by the members to their participation in the assembly. However, it is possible that other external factors such as the dynamics of the host community's politics drove the observed changes. In the Netherlands, for example, while the *Burgerforum* was taking place, a government coalition fell, an election was called, and the assembly came to an end in the midst of an electoral campaign. Any or all of these events might have been responsible for changing the attitudes of assembly members.

The way to sort out whether assembly participants were affected by other circumstances is to compare them with a group of similar citizens who did not participate in the assemblies. Dutch researchers collected data among a set of individuals who had expressed an interest in taking part in the process (after receiving one of the initial invitation letters), but who were not ultimately selected. These individuals were interviewed both before and after the assembly process. Thus, they provide a control group for *Burgerforum* members.

Table 7.5 presents attitude change results for both the Dutch assembly and the public control group. Differences between the two groups (assembly change minus control change) are reported in the last column, with a positive sign indicating greater improvement among assembly members.

The data indicate that the excluded citizens are not a perfect control. Their baseline attitudes differed somewhat from those of the assembly members: they were slightly more engaged politically and slightly less positive towards political actors than their *Burgerforum* counterparts. These differences may be due in part to selective non-response, which was small in the assembly surveys, but substantial in the control group. We suspect that non-participants particularly interested in politics and the assembly responded more favourably to the survey requests, and that this accounts for some of the differing opinions. In addition, disappointment for not being selected may have caused differences between the assembly and the control group. Nonetheless, given that our central concern is for the dynamics of opinions over time within the two groups, this is not a fatal flaw for the comparison.

For each of the four political engagement attitudes – interest, attention, and information – significant increases were observed among *Burgerforum* members, while they were absent in the general public. Moreover, all four differences between the two groups' changes were significant. Therefore, the changes in political engagement can be attributed to the assembly process. Only one of the two self-confidence items moved significantly in the citizen assembly: the rise of members' confidence in their ability to speak publicly. No such movement took place among the control group, so this change must also have stemmed from participation in the deliberative setting.

In contrast, the same number of significant improvements in opinions about politics occurred among the two groups (seven). Only one of the assembly changes was significantly larger than that of the control group (satisfaction with democracy). As a result, we cannot rule out external factors as the source of the more positive views about politicians, parties, and government in the Netherlands' assembly. The same is true for the increase in the level of interpersonal trust expressed by *Burgerforum* members. The sentiment that most people can be trusted grew more within participants than non-participants, but not substantially so.

Contrary to the general pattern in the pooled analysis (Table 7.4), populism decreased in the Dutch assembly. Most notably, members became less inclined to have faith in the down-to-earth thinking of ordinary people compared with the knowledge of experts and intellectuals. Given that participants were engaged in a process in which they were often said to have become experts themselves, this

TABLE 7.5 *Changing Attitudes: Dutch Assembly versus Interested-Excluded Citizens*

	Assembly members			People not selected			Difference
	Start	Change	N	Start	Change	N	
Political engagement							
Political interest	66.3	+10.0**	106	70.5	0.0	83	+10.0**
Attention to political news	71.0	+9.7**	107	75.2	+2.4	82	+7.3**
Attention to domestic news	58.9	+10.6**	107	66.3	+0.8	83	+9.8**
Informed about politics	61.8	+11.1**	107	67.0	+0.5	83	+10.6**
Self-confidence							
I feel nervous when I speak (r)	45.0	+5.2**	97	57.4	−4.0	83	+9.2**
I am well qualified for politics	56.0	−0.9	53	53.6	−5.2	64	+4.3
Opinions about politics							
Those elected soon lose touch (r)	66.1	+1.1	90	60.9	+3.9	82	−2.8
Politicians are ready to lie (r)	80.6	−6.3*	74	73.2	0.0	82	−6.3
Politicians are about as honest as the average person	35.3	+3.9	102	23.8	+6.1**	82	−2.2
MPs do not care about people (r)	46.4	+7.2**	83	43.8	+2.9	70	+4.4
Elected officials are unselfish	52.9	−2.0	103	48.3	+5.1**	82	−7.1**
Elected officials are intelligent	69.6	+3.3**	106	65.8	+2.9**	80	+0.4
Elected officials are informed	75.9	+1.9	105	73.0	+4.1**	82	−2.2
Parties necessary for democracy	70.1	+1.4	97	72.0	+2.2	75	−0.8
Parties present clear choices	47.7	+7.3**	107	44.3	+2.4	82	+4.9
Parties find solutions to problems	46.4	+5.3**	107	40.2	+3.6	83	+1.7
Parties express people's concerns	36.1	+9.8**	107	29.7	+10.6**	83	−0.8
All parties are the same (r)	71.1	+1.7	98	64.6	+5.7**	82	−4.0
Government does not care (r)	43.7	+9.7**	93	44.3	+8.5**	82	+1.1
Satisfaction with democracy	61.4	+4.9**	108	58.9	−0.4	82	+5.3*
Duty, trust, people, and populism							
It is the duty of everyone to vote	61.6	+3.7	99	69.9	+0.4	82	+3.3
Most people can be trusted	77.7	+7.8*	103	72.3	+3.6	83	+4.2
People in general are unselfish	52.0	−1.4	103	49.3	+4.6*	84	−6.0*
People in general are intelligent	57.0	+0.8	105	54.2	+1.9	81	−1.1
People in general are informed	42.0	+1.4	106	44.8	+3.3*	83	−1.9
Issues are too complicated for most voters (r)	44.0	−1.0	97	42.2	+2.9	79	−3.9
Decisions at the grass roots	55.4	−4.8*	77	61.2	−1.0	67	−3.8
Faith in the thinking of people	58.1	−11.6**	86	59.0	+2.6	78	−14.2**

All variables range from 0 to 100.
** Significant at 0.05; * significant at 0.10.

finding is somewhat ambiguous. Nevertheless, the attitude change does seem to have been produced by experiencing the assembly, since non-participants did not evolve in this way.

Although the results of this comparison of assembly members with Dutch citizens who did not have the same experience need to be treated with caution, they do show that, beyond generating some political engagement, the extended and intense assembly process contributed little, if anything, to making the participants better citizens.

7.7 CONCLUSION

In sum, our analysis indicates that, in general, citizen assembly members became more politically interested, more attentive to political news, and more informed about politics as a result of their participation in the assembly. In addition, their attitudes about politics also improved somewhat, partially a consequence of higher levels of political information. However, the Dutch data denote that these observed changes for views towards political actors could have stemmed from forces external to the assemblies. Among other attitudes, we only uncovered small changes, and they were not consistently in the expected direction across all assemblies and all measures. Civic duty and opinions of citizens may have climbed slightly, but self-confidence, trust, populism, and tolerance did not.

Since citizen assemblies constitute the most intensive participatory and deliberative process yet implemented, this meagre evidence of attitude change will be disconcerting to those who believe political participation improves citizenship. Some, following Mansbridge, may simply claim that the really important changes are too subtle to be measured 'with the blunt instruments of social science' (1999: 291). Other proponents of the idea might suggest that the assemblies were too limited in scope. Another line of defence is that the expected improvements were hampered by a ceiling effect due to relatively positive starting attitudes.

However, in the face of our findings from three distinct cases, these arguments fail to be convincing. Participation in these year-long public policy processes simply did not have a major impact on individuals' general outlooks towards political actors, fellow citizens, and themselves. It may have created more interested and involved individuals, but it did not produce 'better' citizens.

8

Why were the Assemblies' Reform Proposals Rejected?[1]

> The issues are much too important for the Chilean voters to be left to decide for themselves.
>
> Henry Kissinger (1973)

The three citizen assemblies fulfilled their mandates. Each came up with a recommendation for an electoral system and delivered it on schedule and within budget. However, none has resulted in electoral reform. The two Canadian proposals were rejected by the public in referendums, while the Dutch proposal was submitted to the country's cabinet which mostly ignored it. Why? This chapter analyses reactions to these exceptional democratic experiments. It deals with how the citizen assemblies and their proposals were received by governments, political parties, media, and citizens. Empirically, it draws on news content analyses and public opinion surveys to document the views of both elites and masses towards the assemblies and the electoral systems they constructed, and to explain the failure of all three assemblies to result in any system change. To fully grasp the potential of citizen assemblies as policymaking tools, it is essential to study their success, or lack thereof, in finding allies and generating support for their work.

In the Canadian provinces, any account of the ultimate outcome requires a focus on public opinion. Since the death of the electoral reform proposals stems from the choices made by British Columbians and Ontarians voting in the three referendums (2005 and 2009 in British Columbia, 2007 in Ontario), the key to the story lies in uncovering how citizens outside the assembly made up their minds. To understand the voters' responses, we must determine what they knew and thought about the citizen assemblies and the electoral systems they proposed, as well as the factors that drove their referendum decision.

Beyond the account of the actual referendum outcomes, analyses of these cases face some unprecedented theoretical issues. Typically, an electorate confronts a choice defined by politicians and their parties. This time the choice was devised by a group of randomly selected citizens without any discernible connection to

---

[1] Co-written with Fred Cutler.

partisan elites. Did voters appreciate this fundamental difference? Could it have influenced their decision about whether or not to endorse the proposal for reform? On voting day, the people had to grapple with an unfamiliar dilemma: defer to more enlightened peers or follow their own relatively uninformed opinions. The first section of this chapter ascertains how they resolved this dilemma.

Public opinion can obviously be shaped by campaigns and coverage in the mass media. Apart from the handful of individuals who followed the assemblies' deliberations in person or online, most voters could only have been exposed to the subject indirectly through media treatment. Thus, the extent and the nature of the reporting on the assemblies might have been critical to the populations' reactions. We therefore examine the volume of news coverage about the assemblies. It is not clear whether citizen assemblies are a newsworthy subject. On the one hand, they lack features that typically drive political news: conflict, polarization, and official spokesmen vying for attention. On the other hand, they have an aura of novelty and authenticity which might be considered attractive for audiences. Besides the amount of coverage, we also document its tone (positive or negative) to determine how the assemblies were depicted by the media. Section 8.2 is devoted to this topic.

We then analyse the reactions of political elites. Chapter 6 showed that the principal political parties largely kept their distance from the assembly proceedings. They did not want to influence the process while the members were making their decisions. But what happened afterwards? Once the assemblies had made their recommendations and disbanded, what did the parties do? Did governments and political parties become champions of the electoral systems proposed by citizens and try to convince voters of their value and legitimacy? Did they oppose and attack the reform proposals? Did they simply ignore them? The third section tackles these questions.

Finally, the last section deals with the unique Dutch case. The fate of that *Burgerforum*'s recommendation hinged upon the response of the government cabinet to which it was submitted. We present the sequence of events that led to its demise.

8.1 WHY DID THE CANADIAN PUBLICS SAY NO?

In Canada, the implementation of the reform proposals developed by the citizen assemblies was contingent on their approval by the electorate in a public referendum. Voters had to decide whether or not to abandon the existing SMP (single member plurality) electoral system and replace it with a new one. But they had to make up their mind without benefiting from the organizational structure and the motivational culture of the citizen assembly. Most importantly, the general public had not been exposed to the rich background information that assembly participants acquired about the advantages and drawbacks of the multitude of electoral designs used around the world. The assemblies' information on electoral systems (briefing material, lectures, etc.) was made available to everyone interested on the assembly's website, and a summary of their report including a justification for the recommended change was also distributed to all households by mail. It seems unlikely, however, that most voters were sufficiently engaged by the debate on electoral reform to invest the time necessary to reach the level of awareness attained by assembly members.

So how does a less interested and knowledgeable public come to pass judgement on electoral systems? Can it base its choice on fundamental objectives and values as did the members of the citizen assemblies (Chapter 5)? Do knowledge and opinions about the assembly and the proposed reform influence votes? Why did none of the votes reach the 60 per cent threshold that had been set as the standard for success? And just as importantly: why did support drop between the first and second British Columbian referendums (from 58 per cent in 2005 to 39 per cent in 2009), and why was support lower in Ontario (37 per cent) than it had been in British Columbia when the reform proposal first went to the polls?

We captured the views of a random sample of the population in each province during the referendum campaigns. The surveys used a rolling cross-sectional format which allows us to accurately track the evolution of voters' beliefs and opinions over time (Johnston and Brady 2002).[2] Figure 8.1 illustrates the changing average level of support for the reform proposal during the last thirty days of the three referendum campaigns.[3] The opinion surveys slightly overestimated support in each case. In British Columbia in 2005, 64 per cent claimed to be in favour of single transferable vote (STV) at the end of the campaign, while the final vote for it was just 58 per cent. Four years later, British Columbians' approval was overestimated by about 10 percentage points (49 per cent versus 39 per cent). In Ontario, the survey ends up with 47 per cent endorsing mixed member proportional (MMP), rather than the 37 per cent who voted for it. Nevertheless, these surveys reveal much about the general outlook of public opinion regarding electoral system reform and the determinants of referendum preferences.[4]

---

[2] Computer-assisted telephone interviews were conducted by the Institute for Social Research at York University, under the direction of David Northrup. In British Columbia #1, the sample was released as a weekly rolling cross-section from 17 January to 30 April 2005, and then a daily rolling cross-section from 1 May to 16 May (2643 respondents). In Ontario, the daily rolling cross-section spanned from 10 September to 9 October 2007 (1352 respondents). In British Columbia #2, the daily rolling cross-section stretched from 16 April to 11 May 2009 (1039 respondents). The response rates were 51.9, 41.5, and 45.5 per cent, respectively.

[3] We report the proportion of respondents stating they will vote for reform in the referendum (yes/the alternative electoral system/the proposed BC–STV system). The moving average is based on a centred ten-day framework.

[4] For our account of the 2005 referendum, see Cutler et al. (2008).

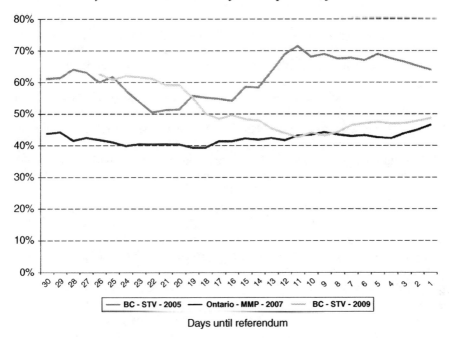

Days until referendum

FIGURE 8.1 Evolution of Support for Reform during the Referendum Campaigns

Figure 8.1 suggests that there were no clear systematic trends over the campaigns: support for reform did not consistently climb or fall in either province. In Ontario, approval of MMP was essentially flat, hovering around the same level for most of the campaign before increasing slightly at the end. The proposal was failing from the beginning of the campaign, and nothing about the campaign itself appears to have affected voters' judgement. In British Columbia, support for STV fluctuated a bit more. During the first referendum, the proportion in favour of reform was constantly above 50 per cent, and it increased substantially halfway through the campaign. The data even suggest that the proposal might have passed the 60 per cent threshold if the vote had been held a week or two earlier. In the province's second referendum, approval of STV appears to have dropped decisively during the second week, before gaining back some ground near election day, but at no point during the campaign did the proposal have the votes to surpass the province-wide threshold.

8.1.1 The determinants of the public's decisions

To ascertain whether the public's verdicts were driven by substance, cues, or whim, we examined the relationships between support for the reform proposals and several potential explanatory factors. Four of these factors reflect the considerations used to explain the preferences of assembly members (Chapter 5). The first is a disposition towards the *fair representation of parties*. Individuals who score high on this variable like proportional election results: they think that 'a party that gets 10 per cent of the votes should get 10 per cent of the seats'. The second is a preference for *coalition governments*, distinguishing those who favour 'governments made up of two or three parties because they are forced to compromise' over 'one-party governments so they can get things done'. Third, *aversion to change* reflects the respondents' admission that they do not 'like taking risks'. We also tap *small party support* by identifying those who voted for a political party that won less than 20 per cent of the vote shares in the previous provincial election.[5] If ordinary referendum voters behaved as assembly members, then more favourable opinions of electoral reform should be found among people who value proportionality and coalitions, those who are adverse to change, and those who vote for minor parties.

Six other variables that could be relevant for public deliberation were explored. One is *satisfaction with the current system*. Referendum voters were faced with a choice between two options: a new electoral system (STV/MMP) or the one that was already in place (SMP). Clearly, an appreciation of the status quo could very well exert some weight on their decision.

The level of general *knowledge about the alternative system* ought to matter as well. As the public learns more about the proposed change, support would be expected to mirror judgements about the quality of the proposal. Given a poorly conceived alternative, the more you know about it, the more reasons you will find to reject it. In this case, we know that the citizen assemblies picked alternatives which reflected their priorities and values (presumably those of the populations from which they were drawn), and that they were not swayed by undue influences. Therefore, greater information about STV/MMP should translate into greater popular support.

We also consider views about *specific features of the alternative systems*. Each reform proposal contained characteristics that could be perceived negatively. In British Columbia, some concern was expressed about the complexity of STV's method of converting votes into seats and about the risk of frequent changes in government. In Ontario, most criticism concerned party control over list seats and the proposed increase in the number of provincial legislators (from 107 to 129). Opinions about both sets of features were operationalized as disapproval measures, so they ought to be negatively correlated to support for reform.

Finally, there are two items dealing with the source of the reform proposals – the citizen assemblies themselves. Deciding which electoral system is best would be challenging without expert information. Instead, *knowledge about the citizen assembly* that designed the alternative system could have served as a useful shortcut. Knowing that a group of randomly selected ordinary citizens came up with the proposal after extensive work independently of government and political

---

[5] In British Columbia, this means the Greens or another party. In Ontario, this includes the NDP, the Greens, or another party.

TABLE 8.1 *Determinants of Public Support for Electoral Reform*

	British Columbia (STV 2005)	Ontario (MMP 2007)	British Columbia (STV 2009)
Fair representation of parties	0.67*	0.31*	0.75*
Coalition governments	0.53*	0.70*	0.81*
Aversion to change	−0.19	−0.18	−0.08
Small party support	0.18	0.33	0.49
Satisfaction with current system	−1.51*	−2.57*	−2.43*
Knowledge about alternative system	1.79*	1.45*	1.68*
Specific features of alternative:			
• complex counting	−0.41*	—	−0.47*
• unstable government	−0.60*	—	−0.69*
• closed party lists	—	−0.88*	—
• more elected delegates	—	−1.15*	—
Knowledge about citizen assembly	1.03*	0.65*	0.09
Trust in citizen assembly	1.23*	0.97*	1.10*
N	1134	1279	979
Pseudo-R^2	0.24	0.20	0.27

* Significant at 0.05. Numbers are logit regression coefficients. All variables range from 0 to 1.

parties could be enough to support the recommendation. This is precisely what we uncovered in the first British Columbia referendum (Cutler et al. 2008). Similarly, *trust in the citizen assembly*'s judgement could substitute for actual knowledge of their proposed electoral system and also lead to support for change.

Table 8.1 presents the results of regression analyses that measure the impact of these ten different variables on public support for electoral reform. Since the dependent variables are dichotomous, either for or against a change to STV/MMP, logistic analyses were performed. The independent variables all range from 0 to 1.[6]

As we hypothesized, most of these factors are indeed associated with public support for electoral reform. General views about electoral systems mattered. In both provinces, individuals who valued proportionality and approved of coalition governments tended to back the proposed changes, which would probably lead to these two consequences.[7] Also, unsurprisingly, people satisfied with the current system were considerably less in favour of reform. Marginal effects reveal that satisfaction reduced support by 26/42/37 percentage points respectively in 2005, 2007, and 2009.

[6] Details about the questions on which the measures are based can be found in Appendix 4.
[7] The effect of fair representation was stronger in British Columbia, however.

Knowledge about the alternative proposal was positively and strongly correlated with reform support. The more voters knew about the recommended system,
the greater their propensity to support it. A person who knew a lot was 31/24/25
percentage points more likely to vote for change than a person who was ignorant.
So the impact of this crucial variable was pronounced in all three cases.

Views about specific aspects of the proposals also affected support for them.
British Columbians concerned about STV's more complex counting method and
the possibility of frequent government changes tended to oppose reform. Ontarians who disagreed with closed party lists and increasing the size of the legislature
were much less prone to vote for MMP. It seems that the negative aspects of MMP
were approximately twice as damaging as those of STV.

Knowledge about the citizen assembly – the creator of the proposal they were
now facing – also contributed to voters' decisions. Knowing more about the
assembly generated higher support for reform. But the impacts of citizens' pro-
fessed familiarity with the assembly varied in strength across the three referendums. The effect was strongest in the first referendum, British Columbia's in 2005,
only half as strong in Ontario, and then negligible in British Columbia in 2009,
five years after the assembly's work. Overall, knowledge of the assembly was less
decisive than information about the new electoral system. Finally, voters who
trusted the assembly were consistently more favourable towards STV/MMP, and
this impact was similar across cases.

Two considerations were irrelevant: neither aversion to change nor small party
support was significantly connected to referendum preferences. Partisans of minor
parties were slightly more likely to vote for the alternative system (by 5 percentage
points on average), but not at a statistically significant level. Citizens, like assembly members, were not swayed by partisan sentiments when it came to passing
judgements on electoral systems.

Thus, citizens' referendum decisions were shaped in predictable and sensible
ways. Their voting behaviour was coherently linked to general predispositions
towards electoral systems, to knowledge and opinions about the specific proposal
put before them, and to information and attitudes about the institution that
proposed the reform. The publics' choices were driven by the same sorts of factors
in both British Columbia and Ontario. And the model fit statistics show that the
structure of opinion was reasonably high for such individual-level data.

Can we say whether the public's decisions were structured to the same extent as
those of the assemblies in Chapter 5? Unfortunately, we cannot easily compare the
analyses of the two groups. First, they dealt with different dependent variables.
The electorates were asked to choose between the status quo and a specific reform
proposal, while assembly members evaluated various electoral system families.
Second, they involved different independent variables. Given ordinary voters'
limited comprehension of the principles underlying electoral systems, we could
not probe their views about the trade-offs between proportionality, voter choice,
local representation, and simplicity. We had to settle for a mixture of cues,

shortcuts, and actual substance. All we can say is that the model fit statistics are similar in both analyses.

8.1.2 The distribution of people's opinions

The preceding evidence identifies the individual correlates of voters' decisions. Due to where people stood on each of these factors, they tended to vote one way or the other. But to understand the overall failures of the three referendums, we need to know where most voters stood on these considerations. Table 8.2 reports the aggregate distribution of the determinants that were relevant among the electorates.[8] It indicates the proportions of respondents who liked proportionality, preferred coalitions, were satisfied with SMP, knew something about STV/MMP, approved of the alternative system's specific features, knew something about the assembly, and trusted the assembly.

The patterns of public opinion shown in Table 8.2 reveal that only three of the considerations made a net positive impact on support for the referendum proposals. Two general values relating to electoral systems did push voters to STV or MMP: solid majorities in both British Columbia and Ontario favoured

TABLE 8.2 *Distribution of Determinants of Public Support for Electoral Reform*

	British Columbia (STV 2005)	Ontario (MMP 2007)	British Columbia (STV 2009)
Fair representation of parties	59	59	54
Coalition governments	63	60	54
Satisfaction with current system	63	74	73
Knowledge about alternative system	31	31	36
Specific features of alternative:			
• complex counting	34	—	33
• unstable government	45	—	44
• closed party lists	—	16	—
• more elected delegates	—	27	—
Knowledge about citizen assembly	25	13	23
Trust in citizen assembly	51	49	50

Numbers are percentages.

[8] We excluded the two factors that did not matter in Table 8.1 (aversion to change and small-party support).

proportional election results and coalition governments. Thus, most citizens in those provinces were predisposed towards the principles behind the recommended proportional representation (PR) systems. In addition, half the people trusted the citizen assembly. This relatively widespread sentiment also helped to establish latent potential support for reform among the populations.

But these advantages were offset by very large hurdles. First, the public was not consumed by an urgent need for change. Most individuals did not think that there was a major problem with SMP: between two-thirds and three-quarters of British Columbians and Ontarians were satisfied with the existing electoral system. Considering the large impact of this variable on individual voting decisions (Table 8.1), such widespread satisfaction may have made reform a non-starter from the beginning. As the saying goes: 'if it ain't broke, don't fix it'.

Second, many people were operating in the dark. Knowledge of the proposed alternative system and the citizen assembly was associated with support for change, but very few voters were actually informed about either. In each province, only a third asserted they knew something about STV/MMP. Besides this self-reported measure, our factual knowledge data also point to low levels of awareness about basic features and consequences of the proposed electoral systems. Information about the agenda-setter was even worse. Only a quarter of British Columbians and just 13 per cent of Ontarians said they knew 'some' or 'a lot' about the citizen assembly. And misconceptions were also rampant: for instance, in Ontario, a majority believed that assembly members had been hand-picked by the government. Given the importance of knowledge in generating enthusiasm for the proposals, the public's lack of it severely hampered the referendums' prospects.

Finally, it must be recognized that some design elements of the new electoral systems were unpopular, particularly in Ontario. The public there was very unhappy about party control over MMP's list seats as well as the proposed addition of more politicians. Only between 16 and 27 per cent agreed with these plans. In British Columbia, many were preoccupied about STV's complexity and potential governmental instability, though substantial minorities reported they were not worried by these features.

Together, these five factors underlay the defeat of the two Canadian proposals: many voters did not mind the current system, they knew little about the citizen assembly and its proposal, and those who knew about the alternative disliked some of its important features.

8.1.3 But why 37 and 39 per cent versus 58 per cent?

The electoral reform proposals were not simply defeated during the 2007 Ontario referendum and the 2009 British Columbia referendum, they lost decisively. Why? And why was support so much lower than in the first British Columbia referendum in 2005? There are two possibilities: either the distributions of the relevant explanatory variables were different or the impacts of the variables were different. We test each of these two possibilities with simulations of the regression results.

The first possibility is that there were different distributions of opinion. When we compare the variables in Table 8.2 for British Columbia 2005 and Ontario 2007, the views of the two voting populations are similar in many regards. Though they do diverge notably on four topics: Ontarians were more satisfied with the current system, more concerned about two features of the alternative, and less aware of the citizen assembly. These differences were all in a direction that could explain lower support for reform in Ontario. To ascertain whether this was actually the case, we conducted a set of simulations: the coefficients of each referendum decision were left the same, while the mean variable values of Ontario 2007 were replaced with the mean values of the 2005 variables. The results indicate how Ontarians would have voted if they had shared the views of British Columbians in 2005 but followed their own decision-making process. The discrepancies of opinion prove to be relatively inconsequential for the final outcome. Had these four attitudes mirrored those found in British Columbia in 2005, support for MMP in Ontario would only have been 4 percentage points higher.

In British Columbia, there are a few differences of opinion that could possibly account for the big gap in support between the two referendums: in 2009, satisfaction with the status quo was higher, and people were slightly less favourable towards proportionality and coalitions. However, the simulations reveal that, if these three considerations had not changed over the four years, support for STV in 2009 would only have been 4 percentage points higher. So the modest disparity of views cannot explain the 19-point gap between the 2005 and 2009 referendum outcomes.

The second possible explanation for the lower reform support in the two most recent referendums is that the determinants did not matter to the same extent as they had in the first referendum. Table 8.1 shows that, during the 2007 Ontario campaign, fair representation and assembly knowledge had weaker effects, while satisfaction with the current system and concerns about the alternative had greater impacts than in British Columbia in 2005. Due to their direction, all these differences could have contributed to the large gap between the two outcomes. To examine this idea empirically, we ran simulations in which the values of the 2007 variables remained intact, but their coefficients were altered to the 2005 levels. These analyses evoke how the Ontario electorate, with its distinctive opinion profile, would have voted had it weighted relevant considerations in the same way British Columbians did in 2005. Three of the five factors turn out to be critical: had satisfaction with SMP and the two opinions about the specific features of the alternative possessed the same influence as in 2005, support for MMP would have been 21 percentage points higher (each variable being responsible for 11, 5, and 5 points respectively). Together, the differing impacts of these three determinants account for most of the gap between Ontario 2007 and the original British Columbia vote. They are clearly the central reason why the MMP proposal ended up with 37 per cent rather than 58 per cent.

In the case of the two British Columbia referendums, two coefficient discrepancies are evident. Satisfaction with the existing electoral system mattered much more in 2009 than in 2005, and knowledge of the citizen assembly no longer affected voting during the second referendum as it had four years earlier in the immediate aftermath of the assembly's existence. Because of their direction, these different impacts could explain why STV support fell from 58 to 39 per cent. Our simulations confirm that the yes side would have garnered 13 more points (9 and 4 points respectively) in 2009 if decisions had been driven by these two variables to the same extent as in 2005. So the shifting effects of decision correlates across the two referendums appear again to be the main cause for the divergent outcomes.

While all three referendums were defeated, some failed more resolutely than others. The evidence demonstrates that the public voted differently partly because they held dissimilar attitudes towards the key issues. But much more importantly, they voted differently because they allocated different weights to the factors that governed their decisions.

Nevertheless, one should not lose track of the fact that a lack of information remains a central explanation for the referendum failures. Our simulations indicate that support for electoral reform would have approached or surpassed the 60 per cent threshold in all three cases if knowledge of the alternative electoral system and of the citizen assembly had been more widespread. If all voters had behaved like those who knew something about MMP/STV and the assembly – not the perfectly informed, just those who were somewhat knowledgeable about the proposal and its source – then the votes in favour of change would have averaged an extra 21 percentage points in the three referendums.

We now know about the state of public opinion which resulted in the three referendum losses. But what led to this state? Why was the judgement about the current electoral system so positive? Why did voters have so little knowledge about the fundamental issues? Why were some views more salient during some campaigns than others? In the next two sections, we consider whether the media and political elites played an important role in shaping public opinion.

8.2 WHAT TYPE OF MEDIA COVERAGE?

To uncover what the mass media were saying about the topic, comprehensive content analyses were conducted by McGill's Media Observatory under the direction of Stuart Soroka. Television/radio/magazine/Internet coverage was not examined, but newspapers should provide a good approximation of total media attention. Articles were collected from all major daily newspapers available in the full-content electronic databanks: seven for British Columbia in 2005, ten for

TABLE 8.3 *Newspaper Coverage during the Last Six Weeks of the Campaign*

	British Columbia (STV 2005)	Ontario (MMP 2007)	British Columbia (STV 2009)
No. of articles per day per paper	0.81	1.15	0.37
% mentioning STV/MMP	96	99	99
% informative about STV/MMP	18	26	47
Tone of STV/MMP coverage (%):			
• neutral	53	38	59
• positive	29	33	29
• negative	18	29	12
% mentioning the assembly	46	32	35
% informative about assembly	8	11	22
Tone of assembly coverage (%):			
• neutral	79	65	70
• positive	20	24	26
• negative	2	11	4

All numbers except those of the first row are percentages.

Ontario 2007, and five for British Columbia in 2009.[9] Searches identified all articles containing any of the following word expressions: electoral reform, electoral system, PR, SMP, 'first-past-the-post', STV, MMP, and citizen assembly (using various spellings). The analyses covered periods of different lengths: seventeen months for British Columbia in 2005, fourteen months for Ontario in 2007, and five months for British Columbia in 2009. In each case, coverage intensified as the referendum date approached. In the interest of comparability, our analysis here focuses on the last six weeks of the campaigns, when most people were discovering that a referendum would take place and were making up their mind. Table 8.3 presents some key evidence.[10]

[9] In the first British Columbia study, the newspapers were: *Globe and Mail*, *Kamloops Daily News*, *National Post*, *Prince George Citizen*, *Province*, *Vancouver Sun*, and *Victoria Times-Colonist*. The Ontario content analysis included: *Brockville Recorder and Times*, *Daily Miner and News*, *Globe and Mail*, *Guelph Mercury*, *Hamilton Spectator*, *Kitchener-Waterloo Record*, *London Free Press*, *Ottawa Sun*, *Timmins Times*, and *Toronto Star*. The second British Columbia study contained: *Globe and Mail*, *National Post*, *Province*, *Vancouver Sun*, and *Victoria Times-Colonist*.

[10] Different coders were used in each case, though for the Ontario and second British Columbia databases, coders were able to 'index' their codes to the preceding datasets. Note that some of the codes used here are purely objective: mentions of electoral systems, assemblies, and so on. These were coded using an automated system (basically, word searches), confirmed by manual coding, and so there is no reason for concern about reliability across articles, or across datasets. There are, however, good reasons to be cautious about the more subjective codes – including tone and quality of information. Tone is coded using a simple positive–negative–neutral scheme, where coders are asked to finish reading the entire article and then make an overall assessment of the tone for the electoral system and/or assembly. Neutral means either the article did not take sides or it was balanced in terms of positive and negative

While media coverage of electoral reform was not widespread anywhere, it did vary across the three referendums. Interestingly, the one case that received the most attention was not the instance where public support proved to be highest. On the contrary, news treatment of the issue was more extensive in Ontario, with slightly more than one article per day per newspaper.[11] The first British Columbia campaign was not far behind, averaging approximately four stories every five days. But the second STV referendum was the clear outlier, with voters seeing only one article every three days dealing with electoral reform.

The vast majority of articles did mention the alternative electoral system that was being proposed (96–99 per cent). These mentions, however, were not very informative. Trained coders evaluated the level of substantive information provided by the articles about STV/MMP (in terms of its functioning and consequences). Most items were rated as low, lacking any basic information. Table 8.3 reports the proportions that were assessed as medium or high. The lowest scores were found in the first British Columbia and Ontario campaigns (18 and 26 per cent), while in 2009 nearly half of the British Columbia reports were judged to be informative (47 per cent). Much of the coverage of the electoral reform issue simply consisted of standard election articles that ended with a comment like: 'On election day, there will also be a referendum on STV/MMP'.

Coders also evaluated the tone of the coverage relating to the proposed electoral system, to gauge whether the treatment left readers feeling more positive, more negative, or neutral about STV/MMP. In British Columbia, both campaigns were similar: the majority of stories were neutral, but among the rest, positive ones clearly outnumbered negative ones. Coverage in Ontario exhibited both less neutrality and more negativity: negative accounts almost matched the numbers of positive ones. The editorial stances of the daily newspapers also indicate that readers in the two provinces were exposed to different perspectives. In British Columbia, editorial desks were split: for instance, the two main Vancouver newspapers (*Province* and *Sun*) supported STV in both campaigns, while the *Victoria Times-Colonist* and the *Globe and Mail* (a national paper published from Toronto) opposed it both times. In contrast, not a single one of the ten main Ontario newspapers endorsed MMP.

Articles were far less likely to mention the source of the proposed electoral reform. Fewer than half of the newspaper items in British Columbia cited the

arguments. Quality of information is somewhat more difficult, but instructions were that 'high' information meant that there was a good deal of substantive information about the system/assembly – you could learn things from these articles; 'medium' information articles offered less information, perhaps in passing; 'low' information articles may have mentioned an electoral system or the assembly, but spent no time explaining things. Overall, inter-coder reliability across the three datasets for these subjective codes is 80 per cent.

[11] Though it should be noted that much of the coverage in the smaller papers was produced by wire services, and therefore duplicated in several papers.

citizen assembly in 2005, while only a third did so in the two other instances. In addition to being less frequent, references to the assembly were also less informative. Any statement that STV/MMP had been designed by a group of ordinary people (not hand-picked by government) would qualify as somewhat informative about the assemblies. Yet only between one article in ten (2005, 2007) and one in five (2009) met this standard. The tone of the coverage about the citizen assemblies was more neutral than that of the electoral systems, and where there was a slant to the story, much more often than not it was favourable.

Are these patterns of media coverage across the three cases compatible with the gaps observed between the referendum outcomes? If public support for electoral change was much weaker in Ontario, it was not because media coverage of the topic was less extensive or less informative there. But, Ontario coverage was somewhat more opinionated and somewhat less supportive of MMP and the citizen assembly. This media context might have contributed to the final result by raising the salience of the status quo and the defects of MMP. In British Columbia, the second referendum fell far short of the first, but newspaper stories were not more negative in 2009, nor were they less informative about STV or the assembly. At the same time, the volume of media coverage on electoral reform was dramatically lower in the second campaign, so that voters saw very few articles about it. This lack of coverage might account for the drop in support between the two referendums. While these patterns are congruent with the divergent outcomes, we cannot offer definitive proof that media coverage was particularly decisive.

8.3 HOW DID THE POLITICAL PARTIES REACT?

The mass media do not build their agenda in a vacuum. Their stories are dictated to a great extent by the reality of current affairs (Bennett 2008; Graber 2009). In politics, the government, major political parties, and other organizations feed the media talking points through a wide variety of means including regular parliamentary business, press conferences, press releases, and informal scrums. If political parties considered electoral reform a campaign priority, they would have pressed the media to serve as a vehicle for those views. Does the lack of media coverage of electoral reform then merely reflect the fact that politicians dodged the issue?

In British Columbia, while the citizen assembly was working to produce its recommendation, the two major political parties remained on the sidelines, hoping to avoid any influence on the deliberations. Once a reform proposal was formulated and a referendum initiated, they both skirted the debate. Neither the Liberals nor the New Democrats took an official position on the issue. Liberal premier Gordon Campbell touted the institution he had created, praising the assembly and the work it accomplished. But he refused to venture an opinion on the merits of the recommended electoral system. Campbell would only say the decision was in the hands of British Columbians: 'This has always been about what citizens want to do, and we will carry out whatever decision they make. If they decide to change to the single transferable ballot, we will do that. If they decide to stay with what we have today, we will follow that, too' (*The Province*, 24 April 2005: A20). The opposition New Democratic Party also assumed a neutral stand. Although its new leader, Carole James, had previously declared that the party supported electoral reform and PR, she declined to come out in favour of STV. Nevertheless, James did commit to enact the proposed system if the referendum was successful: 'If STV passes, we'll implement it' (*The Province*, 12 May 2005: A13). Perhaps signalling its real preference, the party indicated that if public support for reform was high, but failed to meet the double threshold, it would bring forward an alternate model, namely a version of MMP.

The reaction of the minor Green Party was quite peculiar. As the party that suffered the most from the province's SMP regime, it had vigorously promoted electoral reform and had energetically lobbied the citizen assembly to recommend MMP (recall Chapter 6). However, the assembly's decision to pick STV left party leader Adriane Carr fuming, and she hastily announced that her party would join a No camp to campaign against the proposal. She was then quickly forced to reverse her position due to a backlash from Green supporters who recognized that any change was better than the status quo. Officially, the party was neutral, but every local candidate was free to support STV, and many did. Though Carr ultimately acknowledged the Greens would win seats under STV, she never personally endorsed the system nor indicated she would vote for it in the referendum. So even the party that had the most to gain from the assembly's proposal failed to campaign for it.

Four years later, during the second referendum on STV, these parties took quite similar positions. The two dominant parties, led by the same leaders, again remained silent, not campaigning for either side, but promising to respect and implement the public's decision. The Greens, under the direction of a new leader, Jane Sterk, now wholeheartedly embraced the proposal and encouraged voters to vote Yes.

In Ontario, the governing party adopted the same approach as in British Columbia. Premier Dalton McGuinty expressed his government's pride in establishing the citizen assembly. He also urged voters to learn about the two voting systems and to express their views on referendum day. Refusing to say whether he supported MMP or how he would vote, the Liberal leader remained neutral throughout the campaign. He justified this position by stating it was not his place 'to attempt to influence the outcome of the debate' (*Brockville Recorder and Times*, 26 September 2007: A2). For its part, the main opposition party, the Progressive Conservatives, rejected the proposed change. Though the party did not actively campaign against MMP, when asked, the Conservatives did not hesitate to criticize many of its features: the increase in the size of the legislature, the list candidates appointed by 'party bosses', and larger local ridings. 'I will be voting no' said leader John Tory, making this the only instance in the three campaigns where a major party openly argued against the assembly's reform proposal (*Toronto Star*, 5 October 2007: A17). The New Democratic Party, the province's perennial third party, could generally expect to benefit from a switch to PR. Its leader, Howard Hampton, spoke in favour of MMP, though he did not make electoral reform a central focus of the party's campaign. Only the Green Party, which has never won a seat in Ontario, and whose fortunes would improve under PR, was firmly in the Yes camp: 'We'll be yelling from the rooftops (about MMP)' said party leader Frank de Jong (*Ottawa Sun*, 3 September 2007: 8). Although the leaders' positions shaped the parties' provincial campaigns, individual candidates were free to voice their own opinions in local contests. For instance, at a debate in Timmins, all four local competitors said they preferred the current system (*Timmins Times*, 5 October 2007: 12).

Thus, all three Canadian referendum campaigns unfolded without the contending political parties discussing the reform proposals in any meaningful way. None of the major parties endorsed the assembly's recommendation, not even those who had initiated the reform enterprise. And the small parties who could expect better payoffs under PR often did not make a strong campaign push for it. As a result, the issue was essentially absent from elite political dialogue and remained a peripheral item on the media's agenda.

8.4 THE FATE OF THE *BURGERFORUM'S* RECOMMENDATION

The plan for the Dutch citizen assembly, so similar to the Canadian ones in many regards, was different in one crucial respect: it was not to be followed by a referendum. A referendum was not a political option because of the unsettling experience stemming from the popular rejection of the European Treaty in a referendum just before the assembly was established, because nationwide referendums are not common in the Netherlands, and because electoral system change was not a very popular notion in parliament.

Partly as a consequence of this institutional weakness of the *Burgerforum*, the media did not pay a lot of attention to its proceedings. Between September 2005 (months before the start of the assembly) and December 2006 (when the report was published), only 153 stories appeared in the media (Akkerman and Van Santen 2007).[12]

---

[12] The study covered all national newspapers, the larger regional newspapers, and the main news shows on television and radio.

The tone of what coverage existed was predominantly neutral, and the articles that expressed a view were more often negative than positive.

The fate of the *Burgerforum*'s recommendation was, to a large extent, determined by the fall of the cabinet in June 2006, just halfway through the assembly process. The government collapsed because D66 – the political party responsible for launching the assembly – withdrew its support over a different issue. In the following (temporary) minority cabinet, the position of the D66 minister was taken over by a member of the conservative–liberal VVD who was not a proponent of democratic renewal. National elections followed, six months later, just a few days after the assembly chose its recommendation. Of the major parties competing, only D66 and the PvdA (the Labour party) expressed any support for the idea of a citizen assembly. The PvdA even advocated an electoral system similar to that eventually proposed by the assembly. In this election, D66 saw its support decline and its seat share cut in half – from six to three in the 150-seat *Tweede Kamer*.

On 14 December 2006, the chair of the citizen assembly delivered its recommendation to the outgoing VVD minister. The proposal was then sent to parliament, which handed it to a new PvdA–CDA–CU (Labour–Christian Democrat–Christian Union) coalition government for evaluation. In spite of the fact that the new minister of the interior was a member of the sympathetic PvdA, she was not a supporter of the electoral system put forth by the assembly and endorsed by her own party. The responsibility for matters relating to the electoral system was delegated to a junior CDA minister. She discussed the issues with members of the *Burgerforum* in the autumn of 2007, but she had already made it clear that she was not willing to implement the recommended reforms.

It took until April 2008 for the cabinet to make an official reply.[13] The response spoke to both the assembly process and the recommendation. The cabinet began by suggesting that it was difficult to incorporate a representative body separate from parliament into the decision-making process, and deliberately avoided using the word referendum as a possible solution. It went on, in the remainder of the document, to discuss the proposal, but simply argued that there was currently no reason to revise the Dutch electoral system.

It took another five months before the cabinet's response was debated in parliament, yet another sign that the assembly proposal was not high on the politicians' priority list. In September 2008, the Socialist Party complained that almost 6 million euros had been spent on the process, which they considered an enormous amount considering it had led to nothing. The D66 representatives defended the *Burgerforum* and announced that they planned to submit its recommendation via a private bill. Two weeks later, although a motion to evaluate the

---

[13] All relevant documents are filed under dossier #30184 in the Dutch parliament filing system (parlando.sdu.nl). The letter is #20 in this dossier.

assembly process was passed, another to study changing the formula from D'Hondt to Hare (an aspect of the assembly's proposal) was defeated. In May 2009, the junior minister sent an additional report to parliament which again asserted that assemblies are nice instruments but difficult to embed into the existing representative framework. And so the Dutch process came to an end without the politicians asking the citizens what they thought.

8.5 CONCLUSION

The citizen assemblies were followed intensely by some 'anoraks', but they found few allies among the usual political suspects.[14]

In Canada, the public said no to provincial electoral reform, doing so twice in British Columbia. More precisely, public support never met the high standard set by the governments and legislatures. In this chapter, we have sought to understand the reasons for the failures of the three referendums on electoral reform. There is no evidence that the population in each jurisdiction feared PR, for they were rather supportive of the general principles embodied in PR systems. But several obstacles intervened to deny the reform proposals the level of success necessary to pass. First, most voters were satisfied with the existing 'first-past-the-post' system: they did not share the assemblies' verdict on its shortcomings. Second, the public did not have a good understanding of the proposals: they admitted not knowing much about STV/MMP, and they exhibited little factual information. Third, for those with some awareness, particular aspects of the new systems were irritants, especially in Ontario. Finally, knowledge of the source of the reform proposals was slim: few people knew something about the citizen assemblies, and many were misinformed about their nature and composition.

Why did the voters' referendum answers differ across geography and time? Why did they almost say Yes once and soundly vote No twice? Our analysis reveals it had very little to do with the fact that the respective populations held different values and opinions. In reality, the public's views about governance, electoral systems, and citizen assemblies were quite similar in the three areas. Support varied in the referendums not because people relied on different considerations when making up their minds, but rather because they allocated different relative weights to these considerations. Satisfaction with the existing electoral system influenced judgements more strongly in 2007 and 2009, criticisms of the specific proposed reform mattered more in Ontario, and information about the citizen assembly was

---

[14] David Farrell first used the term anoraks – trainspotters in the United Kingdom – to designate the citizen assembly 'groupies' (academics, bloggers, observers, etc.).

not taken into account by British Columbians during their second referendum. The discrepancies between the referendum outcomes can almost entirely be explained by the differences in opinions and, more crucially, by the different weights of the various factors influencing citizens' decisions.

Habitual political decisions, like voting in elections, are set in and influenced by a familiar constellation of media coverage and partisan positioning. The more people hear about an issue, and the clearer are the cues of opinion leaders, the easier it is for them to acquire the information they need to determine where they stand. In these referendums, both elite signals and media attention were lacking. For the most part, politicians ignored the issue. Many parties did not take a position, and those who did were not campaigning vigorously on it. In this situation, the mass media simply followed suit. News items on the referendums, and electoral reform in particular, were infrequent and generally shallow. Without exposure to a substantial public debate about the issue or the different options, it is hardly surprising that citizens ended up knowing little about them.

In the Netherlands, the *Burgerforum* had been initiated despite the fact that few in the political class supported electoral system reform. It came into being as one of the terms of the coalition agreement D66 had managed to extract from its governing partners. But while the citizen assembly was still working, the coalition broke apart, forcing new elections, and no new cabinet had yet emerged when the assembly's recommendation was presented to parliament. Once a government was formed, it did not include D66, was not in favour of changing the electoral system, and refused to implement the proposal. The *Burgerforum* ultimately confronted the harsh reality of a world in which almost none of the established politicians or parties desired electoral reform. Though its birth had defied the political odds, it eventually succumbed to them.

9

Should we Let Citizens Decide?

Whenever the people are well informed, they can be trusted with their own government.

Thomas Jefferson, letter to Richard Price (1789)

It all started with a campaign promise. In its 2001 party platform, the British Columbia Liberal Party pledged to 'appoint a Citizens' Assembly on Electoral Reform to assess all possible models for electing the MLAs, including preferential ballots, proportional representation, and our current electoral system' (BC Liberals 2001: 30). The party declared that a Liberal government would 'give the Citizens' Assembly a mandate to hold public hearings throughout BC, and if it recommends changes to the current electoral system, that option will be put to a province-wide referendum' (BC Liberals 2001: 30). After the Liberals won the election, premier Gordon Campbell kept his promise and asked Gordon Gibson to prepare recommendations on how such an assembly might be organized and operated. In 2002, Gibson delivered his *Report on the Constitution of the Citizens' Assembly on Electoral Reform* that would prove to be a blueprint for a new political institution.

Five years later, not just one but three citizen assemblies had taken place. The concept and process developed in British Columbia was also implemented in the Netherlands (albeit without a referendum) and Ontario. A simple but radical idea that was formulated in the campaign platform of a provincial political party led the way to a series of three bold experiments.

The assemblies constitute the real-world implementation of three fundamental philosophical ideas which had been debated for a very long time but whose practical relevance was still in doubt. The assemblies embody *participatory democracy* because they entail the active involvement of ordinary citizens. Given that they required long periods of education and discussion, they also incarnate *deliberative democracy*. And finally, since all three assemblies interpreted their mandate as a search for the best possible option rather than the sum of individual opinions, they can be seen as instances of *epistemic democracy*.

These democratic ideals all assume capable participants and fair decision-making. But are citizens politically competent? Do they make wise decisions, or are they likely to pursue unworkable or misguided courses of action? By examining three cases in which citizens played an unprecedented policymaking role, we offer valuable insight into the general question of whether or not the people can be trusted with their own government. In this concluding chapter, we review the findings and the theoretical lessons they inspire. We focus on the delegation of political power to citizens, the potential biases of self-selected participants, the quality of citizen judgements, the consequences of large-scale participation, and the legitimacy and acceptability of citizens' political decisions.

9.1 WHY DO GOVERNMENTS DELEGATE POWER TO CITIZENS?

In most contemporary democracies, the ultimate location for legitimate collective decision-making is in legislative assemblies. Legislatures propose, accept, amend, or reject policy initiatives that come either from the government or from individual members of the elected assembly. It can be argued, however, that for some policy domains it is necessary to look for other means to arrive at political decisions. One such area is where members of the legislature find themselves in a conflict of interest because of their direct personal stake in the issue. Obvious examples include policies governing the legislative system itself: notably the size of parliament, the electoral system, term limits, and legislators' salaries.

If most prominent theories of institutional change are true, however, political parties and elected representatives cannot be expected to give citizens a substantial role in institutional design or reform. According to these theories, discussed in Chapter 2, political authorities have preferences about the proper functioning of government, for reasons of self-interest or ideology, and delegating decision-making power to a group of ordinary people is not likely to be in their interest. They will not hand over such power unless they expect delegation to fail or are convinced the outcome will correspond to their preferences. By contrast, politicians are less reluctant to assign advisory power to committees of experts on questions of institutional design. Processes that depend on appointed experts will be more likely to seek politically acceptable proposals, can be shaped by nominating sympathetic experts, or can be more easily ignored if necessary.

Pressure for institutional reform can come from civil society. In our cases, citizen assemblies were instituted after some debate about the electoral system, though not within the public at large. The debate in British Columbia mainly stemmed from a recognition that the electoral outcomes did not always reflect public preferences and, in some cases, even reversed the choice of the largest number of voters. In the Netherlands, the inability of citizens to vote for a government and the failure of the party system to establish a personal bond between voters and representatives lingered but was never combined with a politically viable alternative electoral system. In Ontario, the electoral system was not really seen as a problem in the years preceding the assembly, but concerns were expressed about the wide policy swings that resulted from a succession of ideologically contrasting governments.

These were not pressing problems when the citizen assemblies were announced. On the Canadian west coast, opposition leader Gordon Campbell promised a review of the electoral system as part of a larger programme of democratic renewal after the 1996 election saw his Liberal Party lose despite winning the largest share of the popular vote. But, in 2002, when Campbell established the assembly, his party was in power having won over 95 per cent of the seats in the provincial legislature with less than 60 per cent of the vote. In the Netherlands, a cabinet consisting of Christian Democrats, Conservative Liberals, and the social–liberal Democrats 66 (D66) agreed to initiate the process only because the small D66 made it a condition of their participation in the coalition government. D66 had not managed to generate support for their proposed electoral reform, could not drop the issue, and needed something to justify their continued involvement in the coalition. Thus, the creation of an assembly was an expedient solution to a political quagmire. In this sense, the Dutch *Burgerforum* was a success even though it failed to change the electoral system, for its very existence solved a pressing political predicament. In all cases, the impetus for the citizen assembly experiments came from the political elite, not civil society.

These unprecedented experiments in citizen policymaking were counterbalanced by conditions designed to reduce the risks involved to the political elites. In Canada, the guarantee of a binding public referendum was tempered by the imposition of high hurdles. That decision was partly responsible for the failure of the reform proposal in British Columbia where it initially won over 50 per cent of popular support. In the Netherlands, the decision not to include a referendum as part of the assembly process could be understood in the context of the country's unhappy experience of a failed referendum on the European Treaty, but it considerably undermined the *Burgerforum*'s political power.

What does all this tell us about the debates on explanations of electoral system change? These cases suggest that such institutional decisions should not be studied in a vacuum. Most theories of electoral system change, irrespective of whether they stress seat maximization or ideology, study the issue as if it is separable from ordinary politics. Our examples show it is not. This was most clearly visible in the Netherlands, where the citizen assembly was created to meet the requirements of one of the parties to a coalition agreement. Only the smallest coalition partner was in favour of a substantial change to the electoral system. The extraordinary Dutch assembly was thus the result of ordinary political trade-offs.

More generally, these cases inform us about political power-sharing with citizens. It is important to note that, in all three instances, the establishment of the assembly was driven by political elites. Governments seem to be willing to delegate powers to citizens if they personally think there is a serious problem. But they will make sure that change does not come too easily, and that they can, if necessary, block an unpalatable reform.

9.2 DOES IT MATTER WHO DOES (AND DOES NOT) PARTICIPATE?

In principle, citizen assemblies draw their legitimacy, at least in part, from the way they are selected (combining elements of self-selection and randomness), and from an expectation that they constitute a representative sample of the general public. That accepted, we recognize that it would be unrealistic to expect the processes to fully meet this test. Since the selection phase deliberately included an element of self-selection, and because only about 6 per cent of registered voters responded to the invitation to take part in the citizen assemblies, it was clear that the composition of each assembly would not perfectly mirror the population.

Our analyses in Chapter 3 showed the citizen assemblies indeed were not entirely representative. Assembly members were better educated and, despite efforts to include all age groups, the organizers had difficulties attracting relatively young and relatively old citizens. Those selected seem to have been a bit more negative about current politics (albeit the reverse was true in the Dutch assembly), but at the same time they were much more interested and involved in politics. Non-voters, for example, were virtually absent from the assemblies. Also, at the start of the process, participants were somewhat more negative towards the current electoral system and therefore more eager to change it than the public. This confirms what we have known for a long time: political participation is selective. Once we demand something of citizens, some will abstain. If the demands are relatively light, like voting in elections, representativeness may not be extremely problematic. However, the assembly process made heavy demands on its participants, so it should not come as a surprise that the memberships were not completely representative. Having said this, all groups, apart from non-voters, were to some extent represented.

Those who want to discredit the legitimacy of citizen assemblies will point to this unrepresentative element, arguing that to be legitimate they must not deviate significantly from standard population parameters. However, self-selection is necessary, for only those who are willing to invest time and energy are able to learn, to deliberate, and to make quality decisions. Also, assemblies are substantially more representative than legislatures. Although we did not explicitly make that comparison, there is little doubt that these three citizen assemblies were far closer to a mirror image of their public than were members of the elected legislatures. In addition we have seen that the preferences of better- and lesser-educated participants were essentially identical (Chapter 6), leading us to believe that socio-demographic differences may not have been consequential. Most importantly, the final proposals were all adopted by extremely large majorities. This suggests that a more representative assembly would probably have come to the same recommendation.

We therefore conclude that the composition of the citizen assemblies did not substantially affect deliberations and decision-making. In all likelihood, more representativeness would not have resulted in a very different outcome in any of the three cases.

9.3 HOW GOOD ARE CITIZENS' POLITICAL JUDGEMENTS?

The vast majority of citizens do not possess high levels of political sophistication. They do not care much for politics, they do not pay a lot of attention to it, and they know very little about it. Likewise, their political opinions tend to be unstable, weakly structured, and easily swayed. One can lament the lack of civic responsibility exhibited by people in democratic societies, but it has to be recognized that, in the world of politics as usual, individuals' political actions rarely have a decisive impact. One extra vote, one extra petition signature, or one extra marcher will not make much difference. Beyond the small group of people who find politics an entertaining subject in and of itself – just as others passionately follow sports, soap operas, or music – there is no reason to expect political interest and commitment to be widespread. For most people, the costs simply outweigh the benefits.

We have found, however, that the picture is different when the stakes are higher than in everyday politics. Four chapters at the core of this book offer relevant evidence. Chapter 2 documented the elevated degree of involvement among participants in all three citizen assemblies: only a handful of individuals withdrew from the process, attendance was extremely elevated at each meeting, and participants expressed great enthusiasm for such extensive and challenging activities. Most importantly, they learned about electoral systems. Both quantitative and qualitative observations indicate that knowledge increased tremendously. The bottom line is that a large proportion of assembly members developed a remarkable understanding of the issue they were charged with examining.

Chapter 4 explored the dynamics of preferences about electoral systems and uncovered little movement after the learning phase. As assembly members were building their comprehension of the subject, they gradually developed opinions about the different options. During the following months, these opinions largely stayed the same. At the aggregate level, evaluations of electoral systems and the importance attached to competing goals of electoral reform remained relatively unchanged throughout both the consultation and deliberation phases. At the individual level, there was also little volatility during this period. Most participants gave similar evaluations across the critical months of decision-making. The only notable movement concerned the collectively preferred alternative in British Columbia, which switched from MMP to STV. The analysis of that movement showed it hinged on the difficult question of which system would deliver the best local representation. Thus, assembly preferences on the central issue did not fluctuate haphazardly over time. They emerged progressively during the learning phase and then essentially remained stable or moved in comprehensible ways.

The structure and consistency of citizen assembly preferences was the subject of Chapter 5, which examined the links between evaluations of electoral systems and attitudes towards the desired features and consequences of electoral reform. Those two sets of opinions were strongly correlated at the individual level. Assembly members liked some systems more than others because they favoured certain principles (e.g. proportionality or local representation). The assemblies' learning and deliberative processes were instrumental in improving the structure of members' preferences over time, as the relationships between evaluations and relevant attitudes generally expanded throughout the proceedings. This pattern of consistency was not restricted to the most sophisticated assembly members. Evaluations and attitudes were associated among both more- and less-informed participants, though to a lesser extent in the latter group. The coherence between evaluations and attitudes held when preferences were aggregated at the collective level. The three assemblies picked three different electoral systems because they were looking for different features in and consequences from the electoral politics of their respective political communities.

Finally, Chapter 6 considered whether the decisions of the citizen assemblies were contaminated by extraneous forces. None appears to have had a determining impact on the outcome. The recommendations were not driven by a small number of particularly trusted or influential members. The academic experts in charge of educating the assemblies do not seem to have, voluntarily or involuntarily, influenced the process. The same is true of the chairs who directed the assemblies' proceedings and debates. The members did not blindly follow the somewhat uninformed advice voiced during the public consultations. Lobbying from partisan interests did not have any demonstrable impact. The three reform proposals are best understood as the reflection of the principles to which assembly members subscribed.

In sum, while citizens are generally weakly motivated to become engaged in and informed about political matters, things change drastically when they are presented with the chance to play a decisive role in public decision-making. In spite of the fact that the assemblies dealt with a difficult and technical topic, members were willing to invest the time and effort required to do a good job. Their commitment translated into diligent participation, impressive knowledge acquisition, judgements that evolved non-chaotically, preferences based on principles rather than whim, and reasonable decisions. Citizen political decision-making proved to be of a remarkably high quality.

This transformation did not take place because political junkies stepped forward and got involved in citizen assemblies. Chapter 3 did note that assembly participants were more politically interested than the public at large. But this discrepancy is not sufficiently large to account for the high level of proficiency uncovered among assembly members. Moreover, we have evidence of gains in knowledge and consistency occurring over the course of the process. The main story is that regular folks became extremely motivated, worked hard, and became proficient about the topic of the proceedings. Thus, citizens have the capacity to shed their apathy, overcome their ignorance, and reason conscientiously about an unfamiliar and complex political issue.

It is important, however, to mention some caveats about the quality of citizen decision-making. First, competence is not easily achieved. It took a lot to improve citizen engagement and decisions: it took a multi-million-dollar almost year-long deliberative project to get participants to that point. Individuals needed strong incentives to get involved, and the chance to revise the electoral system was a critical opportunity. But, perhaps even more importantly, to attain high-quality decisions, they required appropriate time, resources, and support. Our analyses suggest that an extensive infrastructure was essential. Also, the level of knowledge about electoral systems and the degree of consistency in preferences continued to climb across the entire assembly process. The informational 'boot camp' that lasted more than six weeks was not enough to get participants to fully master the topic. Assemblies continued to expand their understanding during the consultations and the deliberations. This means that smaller-scale deliberative processes that extend over a shorter period of time may only be revealing the tip of the iceberg. Competence requires a lot of work.

Second, competence is not easily sustained. One of the three citizen assemblies unfolded in a particular manner. The Dutch *Burgerforum* essentially decided to concentrate on a single electoral system family during the deliberation phase (list-PR). In this case where all options except for one were consciously excluded, people rapidly lost touch with the other options. Their knowledge of these systems and the internal structure of their preferences quickly began to disintegrate. So, when the stimulus and the cognitive activation disappear, competence also fades.

Third, competence is not universal. Some assembly members were less competent than others. Even an extensive deliberative process does not wash out the disadvantages associated with a lack of resources and political sophistication. The initially better informed citizens exhibited more structured reasoning and consistency than the less informed. When dealing with complexity, some people are less well equipped, and we cannot completely compensate for these inequalities.

9.4 DOES PARTICIPATION PRODUCE BETTER CITIZENS?

We have already noted that citizen assembly participants learned a lot about the various electoral systems. In Chapter 7, we assessed the impact of the assembly process on various attitudes and values unrelated to electoral systems. Did assembly members become more interested in politics, more active in politics, more civic-minded, more open-minded, more tolerant, and more trusting?

Little is known about the mechanisms that might produce attitude change in participatory settings. Many of the attitudes and values studied are normally seen as rather stable and formed during childhood socialization. The reason why participation would affect these general outlooks is far from clear. So there is little reason to assume that participation improves people's civic views. However, if they do exist, citizen assemblies are the most likely place to discover participation effects on citizenship. First, the process in which assembly members were involved was extremely intense. Second, most participants felt important and listened to. Finally, in each of the assemblies, a wide consensus developed. All three factors should contribute to making citizen assemblies fertile ground for beneficial effects of participation.

Our analysis found that the consequences of this participatory experience, beyond increasing levels of general political interest, were quite small. Despite the favourable circumstances, most attitudes towards politicians, political parties, government, democracy, and fellow citizens did not change significantly, and when they did, these changes were insubstantial and sometimes even in unexpected directions. Therefore, apart from creating more informed and more interested individuals, large-scale participation does not produce better citizens.

9.5 CAN UNINFORMED CITIZENS, PARTIES, AND GOVERNMENTS TRUST INFORMED CITIZENS?

On many grounds, the citizen assemblies were a success. All three managed to deliver a detailed alternative electoral system on schedule and within budget. They convinced a quite representative group of citizens to sacrifice much of their personal time to this cause, and virtually all those recruited stayed until the very end. Assembly participants expressed satisfaction for the learning, discussion, and deliberation activities that were organized, and they clearly benefited from them. Moreover, assemblies worked intensely and produced sensible decisions and recommendations. Yet, for all these accomplishments, none of the reform proposals was implemented. One was ignored by government. Two were turned down by voters. Why? This was explored in Chapter 8.

In the Netherlands, the story is simple. The proposal, born out of politics, died the same way. The *Burgerforum* was created as a concession to a minor coalition partner. But while the assembly was working, the Dutch political world was overturned: the coalition broke apart, and a new cabinet was formed without the party that was a driving force behind the institution of the assembly. When the assembly's report was released, an election had just taken place and a new government was still a few months away. Electoral reform was simply not a priority for the other political parties. So the proposal fell on deaf ears.

What about Canada? Did the problem lie with the citizen assemblies themselves? Did they suffer from a lack of legitimacy in the eyes of the public? This was not the case. Trust of the assembly was quite widespread, and assembly trust translated into votes for change of the electoral system. Could it be that the recommendations put forward were not that reasonable? Were the alternative electoral systems unacceptable because they were at odds with the values of the wider citizenry? This account is also not corroborated by the evidence. Canadian voters largely supported the principles behind proportional representation (e.g. fair election results, coalition governments), and these were linked to support for electoral reform.[1]

Most of the story for the two referendum failures revolves around information, or rather lack thereof. First, as assembly members learned about single member plurality, its consequences, and other possibilities, their evaluations of the current system declined. Ordinary voters, however, knew little about the existing electoral system. Devoid of this knowledge, voters continued to like 'first-past-the-post' and objected to change, despite their support for proportionality. Second, knowledge of the proposal was related to support for reform: the more people knew about MMP/STV, the more they voted for that system. The problem is few people were actually informed about the proposals. Third, awareness of the citizen assembly also led to votes for change: those who recognized that common people were behind this project tended to endorse it. But again, only small numbers were acquainted with that fact. In Canada, the central impediments to electoral reform stemmed from low levels of information among the electorate.

In addition, the fact that most political parties largely ignored the assembly and the referendum campaign – some even explicitly opposed the proposal – also contributed to its public rejection. Furthermore, the high referendum thresholds did not help either. In British Columbia, a clear majority supported reform in the first referendum. It only failed because the rules allowed an uninformed minority to block the proposal.

This brings us back to Thomas Jefferson's remark that opened this chapter. It is in fact accurate. When well informed, citizens do a good job. The critical issue concerns the existence of that information precondition. The participants of citizen assemblies had become knowledgeable and they were able to produce well-

---

[1] Though some particular features of the specific PR proposals antagonized many voters, especially in Ontario.

reasoned decisions. The general public, however, was not very informed and so it failed on the second count. Precisely what made the assembly work was absent in the population. Citizen policymakers rose above the usual apathy and unsophistication to design a coherent policy proposal, but that proposal then came to the voters, hit the wall of uninformed support for the status quo, and was rejected.[2]

This paradox exposes a fundamental contradiction in the combination of a citizen assembly with a public referendum. If one attaches great importance to the necessity of education and preparation before deliberation and decision-making for the former, why disregard that logic for the latter? If assembly members need a good deal of information to come to an enlightened decision, how can we then rely on voters who lack knowledge? Does it make sense to give the final say to individuals who have not carefully studied the topic? This goes against the rationale at the very heart of the assembly process.

In these cases, the promise of a binding public referendum undoubtedly served several important purposes. It was a key motivator for the Canadian assemblies, assuring members of the seriousness of the task and of the real power they possessed. The referendum also added legitimacy to the final outcome by involving the population in a fundamental political decision. And given the novelty of the institutional design, it was probably a reassuring safeguard for these first test runs of the citizen assembly model.

Nevertheless, coupling a citizen assembly with a plebiscite may never actually result in policy change, since an unsophisticated public who lack awareness of the issues, the alternatives, and the process may systematically fall back on the less risky status quo.

9.6 WHEN SHOULD CITIZENS DECIDE?

Are there lessons to be drawn from these three experiments about the conditions under which it does or does not make sense to ask a citizen assembly to decide what needs to be done on a given issue? Before directly addressing the question, two preliminary observations must be made. First, ordinary citizens are able to deal with complex issues in a reasonable manner, provided they are given the appropriate time and resources. As we have seen, the three citizen assemblies performed remarkably well and came up with proposals that were consistent with the goals that they sought to achieve. At the same time, however, we need to

---

[2] We are not blaming voters for being in the dark. That is their natural (and rational) political habitat. Political parties and mass media also contributed by not talking much about the referendum, failing to dispel myths, or promoting inaccuracies (e.g. assembly members were hand-picked by the government).

recognize that existing constitutional principles leave most public decisions to elected representatives. The reason we have elections is to delegate the power to decide to a group of people that we trust (or do not distrust too much!). A citizen assembly is an expensive instrument that ought to be used sparingly, and under exceptional circumstances.

These three assemblies all dealt with the choice of an electoral system. Citizen assemblies are particularly appropriate for this kind of issue. Politicians are in a conflict of interest when it comes to choosing an electoral system, because their chances of being re-elected are linked to the way votes are transformed into seats. More precisely, small parties are bound to benefit from a PR system, while large parties will be disadvantaged. A normative case can be made that this type of issue should be removed from politicians' authority. The same would apply to electoral laws broadly conceived, in particular the regulation of money and media in election campaigns, and to constitutional issues.

Electoral and constitutional regimes are thus obvious candidates for the establishment of citizen assemblies. But they are neither a sufficient nor a necessary condition. We would argue that citizen assemblies should be created only when there is a relatively large consensus that there is a real 'problem'. In the absence of such a consensus, there is unlikely to be any momentum for reform nor support for citizen delegation. It is striking that such a consensus did not exist in the Netherlands or Ontario. We suggest then that the optimal circumstances for creating a citizen assembly are when there is widespread recognition of the existence of a problem and the perception that the political system has failed to produce a satisfactory solution.

In turn, this does mean that citizen assemblies will be dealing with the most challenging issues facing a society, that there might not be appropriate solutions for some of these problems, and that citizen assemblies may not often succeed. But our analyses suggest that ordinary citizens can accomplish a lot when they are sufficiently motivated and can benefit from expert information. The citizen assembly is a 'last resort' instrument that has the potential to improve the way we address some of our most pressing conundrums.

Presuming citizen assemblies are only to be used under exceptional circumstances for important problems, politicians may want their proposals to be approved by the population in a referendum. We see no clear normative reason to establish a super majority threshold for the approval of a citizen assembly proposal. In fact, the benefit of the doubt should be given to any suggestion made by a set of citizens after deep and extensive examination of all the possible options.

That being said, the fact is that in two of the three referendums examined here, most voters did not endorse the citizen assembly's recommendation. Our evidence indicates that this was largely due to voters' lack of knowledge about the assembly and its proposals, and to their resulting attachment to the status quo. We would argue that much more information needs to be provided to the electorate both before and during the campaign. This extra information should increase the probability of a thoughtful public vote.

FIGURE 9.1   Raphael's *The School of Athens* (1509/10) © INTERFOTO / Alamy.

And citizen assemblies themselves need to play a more extensive role in the public discussion on their recommendations. The assemblies should not be dissolved at the end of the decision-making phase. Their members should be actively involved in the debate, making the case for their proposals. It seems that their task should not be limited to simply finding the 'best' solution to the problem at hand; they should also then work to educate the population about their reasoning and conclusions. Of course, it is important that those who are opposed to whatever proposal the citizen assembly makes be allowed to contribute to the public debate as well. But assembly members should be fully engaged in the political process that follows their deliberations.

9.7   THE THIN LINE BETWEEN . . .

The School of Athens, Raphael's beautiful fresco, was painted during the early days of the sixteenth century. Though unequivocally secular, it is located in the Apostolic Palace of the Vatican, where the Pope resides. It depicts Plato and

Aristotle walking through a great hall, surrounded by countless renowned philosophers from ancient Greece (see Figure 9.1). The two protagonists are debating. Perhaps they are arguing about art, mathematics, medicine, religion, rhetoric, or science. But we like to think that they are quarrelling over the political competence of citizens, the ageless dispute which opened this volume.

Plato may be launched into this classic line:

> When they meet together, and the world sits down at an assembly, or in a court of law, or a theatre, or a camp, or in any other popular resort, and there is a great uproar, and they praise some things which are being said or done, and blame other things, equally exaggerating both, shouting and clapping their hands, and the echo of the rocks and the place in which they are assembled redoubles the sound of the praise or blame – at such a time will not a young man's heart, as they say, leap within him? Will any private training enable him to stand firm against the overwhelming flood of popular opinion? Or will he be carried away by the stream? Will he not have the notions of good and evil which the public in general have? He will do as they do, and as they are, such will he be? (*The Republic: Book VI*)

And Aristotle may be countering with:

> there are some artists whose works are judged of solely, or in the best manner, not by themselves, but by those who do not possess the art; for example, the knowledge of the house is not limited to the builder only; the user, or, in other words, the master, of the house will even be a better judge than the builder, just as the pilot will judge better of a rudder than the carpenter, and the guest will judge better of a feast than the cook. (*Politic: Book III*)

We have sought to offer a new empirical perspective on this age-old debate. Not surprisingly, the lessons are mixed. On the one hand, during extraordinary circumstances, collectives of ordinary people are indeed capable of giving guidance on the design of part of the democratic house in which they live. They can develop a profound understanding of a complex topic, they can evaluate options based on relevant principles, they can come to a decision that reflects their specific priorities, and they can avoid falling prey to biases and pressures.

On the other hand, all the effects we observed occurred in a particular context where motivated citizens were promised a powerful political role and were supported by a resource-rich and balanced infrastructure that promoted proficiency and diligence. Moreover, the positive effects hardly spilled over to the public at large. When individuals who had not benefited from the unique environment of citizen assemblies turned their attention to the same issue, the usual limitations surfaced. Most crucially, many voters lacked the contextual background information that could allow them to recognize the option that conformed to their interests.

So, even when citizen assemblies prove to be an instance of intense participatory, deliberative, and epistemic democracy, the setting in which assemblies exist may undo all the good they are able to achieve.

Appendix 1: Description of Electoral Systems

Throughout this book, we refer to several different electoral systems. For readers not familiar with them, and the language used to describe them, this brief description provides a basic introduction. For a more detailed account, as well as where they fit in the world of electoral systems and an assessment of their impact on the politics of political systems using them, the reader ought to consult David Farrell's *Electoral Systems: A Comparative Introduction*, a book used by members of all three citizen assemblies.

Electoral systems are conventionally described in terms of three properties. The *ballot structure* refers to the form of choice that voters have when they come to cast their vote. It may involve simply placing an X beside a name of a candidate or a party, but it may also offer more complex possibilities such as ranking choices in order of preference. The *district magnitude* refers to the number of legislative seats to be filled from the area: it may range from one to the total number in the legislature. The third characteristic is the *electoral formula*, which refers to the mathematics of translating votes into seats.

SINGLE MEMBER PLURALITY (ALSO KNOWN AS FIRST-PAST-THE-POST)

This is the system that was in place in both British Columbia and Ontario at the time of their assemblies. A simple system, it involves the election of a single representative from each electoral district. Voters place an X beside the name of the candidate they prefer and the candidate with the most votes is declared elected.

Under this system there is no specified number of votes necessary for election – it depends on the number of candidates and the fragmentation of electoral support. With only two candidates, a majority is required, but with more than two candidates, representatives may be elected with far less than a majority of the votes. Since each district produces different results, there is no necessary connection between a political party's vote and seat shares across the entire system. In extreme cases, a party may even win a majority of seats despite the fact that it received fewer votes than another party.

PROPORTIONAL REPRESENTATION – PARTY LIST

Proportional list systems distribute seats to political parties in terms of their vote shares: a party with 10 per cent of the votes will receive about 10 per cent of the seats. In 'closed' list systems, voters cast a ballot for the party per se, and seats are awarded to the appropriate number of individuals working down from the top of the list of candidates. In 'open' list systems, voters express a preference for an individual candidate, a process that may alter the party's candidate ordering and thus the identity of those elected. The degree of proportionality can be affected by the exact formula used to calculate vote shares, the number of seats to be distributed, and the existence of a minimum threshold that may be required for a party to take part in the seat distribution.

The list-PR system in the Netherlands was highly proportional, as the entire country was effectively one electoral district with 150 seats and the threshold was very low. Citizens vote for one individual on one party's list but, given the counting rules, the parties' candidate orders normally prevailed.

MIXED MEMBER PROPORTIONAL

This is a dualistic system: one part is a conventional single member plurality arrangement in which individual local representatives are selected; the other part involves a vote for a party at a regional or system level. The seats from this second part of the system are assigned to ensure that parties receive the same overall proportion of seats as they did votes. The formal organization of such systems can vary considerably: the relative size of each part may vary, the counting rules of the second part may differ, and electors may cast either one vote or one for each part. In this system, some of the elected officials represent distinct geographic constituencies, while the others simply come from a predetermined party list. Whatever the specifics of the design, the common feature is that the results are proportional to the votes cast. A variant of this kind of system was recommended by the Ontario Citizens' Assembly on Electoral Reform.

SINGLE TRANSFERABLE VOTE

The single transferable system provides voters with the opportunity to rank order (1, 2, 3, etc.) their preferences of all the candidates standing for election in electoral districts that return several members. A sequential vote-counting procedure that involves initially tallying first preferences, but then assigning second and subsequent preferences, is employed to determine which candidates have the support necessary (the electoral quota) for election. Given that most votes fall along party lines, the outcomes are generally proportional, with party seat shares reflecting their vote shares. This system maximizes the choice offered to voters, who can differentiate between candidates and parties, and so generates both intra- and inter-party electoral competition. A variant of this type of system was recommended by the British Columbia Citizens' Assembly on Electoral Reform.

Appendix 2: Question Labels, Wordings, and Codings for Chapter 5 (British Columbia/the Netherlands/Ontario)

Single member plurality (0–1):

- Please rate each system on a scale from 1 to 7 in terms of how good you personally think each system would be (1 = very bad, 7 = very good). [w12_l1_c/v548/ds4.m1.c]

(1 if very good; 0 if very bad)

Single transferable vote (0–1):

- Please rate each system on a scale from 1 to 7 in terms of how good you personally think each system would be (1 = very bad, 7 = very good). [w12_l1_g/v551/ds4.m1.g]

(1 if very good; 0 if very bad)

Mixed member proportional (0–1):

- Please rate each system on a scale from 1 to 7 in terms of how good you personally think each system would be (1 = very bad, 7 = very good). [w12_l1_e/v555/ds4.m1.e]

(1 if very good; 0 if very bad)

Open-list proportional representation (0–1):

- Please rate each system on a scale from 1 to 7 in terms of how good you personally think each system would be (1 = very bad, 7 = very good). [w12_l1_h/v553/ds4.m1.h]

(1 if very good; 0 if very bad)

Fair representation of parties (0–1):

- Please rate each criterion on a scale from 1 to 7 in terms of how important you personally think each criterion is (1 = not important, 7 = extremely important). [w12_l2_d/v536/ds4.m2.d]

(1 if extremely important; 0 if not important)

Choice for the voter (0–1):

- Please rate each criterion on a scale from 1 to 7 in terms of how important you personally think each criterion is (1 = not important, 7 = extremely important). [w12_l2_f/v538/ds4.m2.f]

(1 if extremely important; 0 if not important)

Identifiable local representation (0–1):

- Please rate each criterion on a scale from 1 to 7 in terms of how important you personally think each criterion is (1 = not important, 7 = extremely important). [w12_l2_g/v539/ds4.m2.g]

(1 if extremely important; 0 if not important)

Simplicity (0–1):

- Please rate each criterion on a scale from 1 to 7 in terms of how important you personally think each criterion is (1 = not important, 7 = extremely important). [w12_l2_j/v542/ds4.m2.j]

(1 if extremely important; 0 if not important)

Anti-party sentiment (0–1) [alpha = 0.72]:

1. How good a job do political parties generally do in presenting clear choices on the issues: a very good job, quite a good job, not a very good job, or not a good job at all? [w12_b1/v513/ds4.b1]
2. How good a job do political parties generally do in finding solutions to important problems: a very good job, quite a good job, not a very good job, or not a good job at all? [w12_b2/v514/ds4.b2]
3. How good a job do political parties generally do in expressing the concerns of ordinary people: a very good job, quite a good job, not a very good job, or not a good job at all? [w12_b3/v515/ds4.b3]

(1 if not a good job at all on all three items; 0 if a very good job on all three items)

Aversion to change (0–1) [alpha = 0.59]:

1. Reforms to improve society are worth trying even though they can be risky. Do you strongly agree, somewhat agree, somewhat disagree, or strongly disagree? (reverse) [w12_f5/v560/ds4.f5]

2. It is better to stick by what you have than to be trying new things you really do not know about. Do you strongly agree, somewhat agree, somewhat disagree, or strongly disagree? [w12_k4/v564/ds4.j4]
3. I would want to know that something would really work before I would be willing to take a chance on it. Do you strongly agree, somewhat agree, somewhat disagree, or strongly disagree? [w12_k7/v565/ds4.j7]
4. In general, I like taking risks. Do you strongly agree, somewhat agree, somewhat disagree, or strongly disagree? (reverse) [w12_k11/v566/ds4.j11]

(1 if strongly agree to items #2 and #3 and strongly disagree to items #1 and #4; 0 if strongly disagree to items #2 and #3 and strongly agree to items #1 and #4)

Small-party support (0/1):

- Which party did you vote for in the last provincial election? [w12_s5/ds4.s1]
- Which party did you vote for in the last national election? [v577]

(1 if supported a party which obtained less than 15 per cent of the votes; 0 otherwise)

Political information (0–1) [alpha = 0.62]:
(British Columbia/Ontario)

- Do you recall the name of the first woman to be prime minister of Canada? [w1_i1/ds1.h1]
- Do you recall the name of the Canadian prime minister who signed the free trade agreement with the United States? [w1_i3/ds1.h3]
- Do you recall the name of your present provincial MLA/MPP? [w1_i4/ds1.h4]
- Do you know a country which has the same voting system as in Canada, that is, the candidate with the most votes wins? [w1_i6/ds1.h6]
- Do you know a country where they have proportional representation, that is, the percentage of seats a party gets is about the same as the percentage of the votes it got? [w1_i9/ds1.h9]

(British Columbia)

- Do you recall the name of the first member of a visible minority to become a premier in British Columbia? [w1_i2]

(The Netherlands)

- What is Mr. Weisglas' position in the Dutch constitution? [v100]
- What is the name of the Minister of Home Affairs? [v101]
- How many seats does the first-chamber have? [v102]
- Which political parties make up the current government coalition? [v104]

- Do you know a country which has a voting system where the candidate with the most votes wins? [v056]
- Do you know a country which has the same voting system as in the Netherlands, that is, a system where the percentage of seats a party gets is about the same as the percentage of the votes it got? [v059]

(Ontario)

- Do you recall the name of a female minister in the provincial government? [ds1.h2]

(All)

- Do you recall which level of government has the primary responsibility for health, education, and social welfare? [w1_i5/v103/ds1.h5]
- Do you know a country where people have two votes, one for the party they prefer and one for the local candidate they prefer? [w1_i7/v057/ds1.h7]
- Do you know a country where voters get to rank the candidates in their order of preference? [w1_i8/v058/ds1.1h8]

(1 if answered all questions accurately; 0 if answered all questions inaccurately)

Appendix 3: Question Labels, Wordings, and Codings for Chapter 7 (British Columbia/the Netherlands/Ontario)

Political involvement (0–100):

- How interested in politics do you feel? [w1_c1, w12_c1/V002, V503/DS1.C1, DS4.C1]

(100 if very interested; 0 if not interested)

- How much attention do you usually pay to news about politics: a lot, somewhat, a little, or none? [w1_e8, w12_e8/V001, V502/DS1.E8, DS4.E10]

(100 if a lot; 67 if somewhat; 33 if a little; 0 if none)

- When there is domestic news in the newspaper, for example, about problems in the government, how often do you read that: nearly always, often, now and then, seldom, or never? [V004, V505]

(100 if nearly always; 75 if often; 50 if now and then; 25 if seldom; 0 if never)

- How informed about politics do you feel? [w1_c2, w12_c2/V003, V504/DS1. C2, DS4.C2]

(100 if very informed; 0 if not informed)

Self-confidence (0–100):

- I feel nervous when I speak in front of a group. Do you strongly agree, somewhat agree, somewhat disagree, or strongly disagree? [w1_k13, w12_k13/V080, V567/DS1.J13, DS4.J13]

(100 if strongly disagree; 67 if somewhat disagree; 33 if somewhat agree; 0 if strongly agree)

- In general, I am a shy person. Do you strongly agree, somewhat agree, somewhat disagree, or strongly disagree? [w1_k3, W12_k3/DS1.J3, DS4.J3]

(100 if strongly disagree; 67 if somewhat disagree; 33 if somewhat agree; 0 if strongly agree)

- I am not able to do things as well as most other people. Do you strongly agree, somewhat agree, somewhat disagree, or strongly disagree? [w1_k5, w12_k5/ DS1.J5, DS4.J5]

(100 if strongly disagree; 67 if somewhat disagree; 33 if somewhat agree; 0 if strongly agree)

- I am well qualified to play an active role in politics. Do you strongly agree, somewhat agree, somewhat disagree, or strongly disagree? [V225, V568]

(100 if strongly agree; 67 if somewhat agree; 33 if somewhat disagree; 0 if strongly disagree)

Opinions about politics, politicians (0–100):

- Those elected soon lose touch with the people. Do you strongly agree, somewhat agree, somewhat disagree, or strongly disagree? [w1_a6, w1_a5/V036, V523/DS1.A6, DS4.A6]

(100 if strongly disagree; 67 if somewhat disagree; 33 if somewhat agree; 0 if strongly agree)

- Politicians are ready to lie to get elected. Do you strongly agree, somewhat agree, somewhat disagree, or strongly disagree? [w1_a9, w12_a8/V025, V517/ DS1.A9, DS4.A9]

(100 if strongly disagree; 67 if somewhat disagree; 33 if somewhat agree; 0 if strongly agree)

- On the whole, would you say that politicians are more honest, less honest, or about as honest as the average person? [w1_b5, w12_b5/V024, V516/DS1.B4, DS4.B4]

(100 if more or as honest; 0 if less honest)

- MPs do not care about opinions of people like me. Do you strongly agree, somewhat agree, somewhat disagree, or strongly disagree? [V032, V521]

(100 if strongly disagree; 67 if somewhat disagree; 33 if somewhat agree; 0 if strongly agree)

- On a scale of 0 to 10, where 0 means very selfish and 10 means very unselfish, where would you place elected officials? [w1_g1_b, w12_g1_b/V083, V570/ DS1.G2, DS4.G2]

(100 if very unselfish; 0 if very selfish)

- On a scale of 0 to 10, where 0 means very unintelligent and 10 means very intelligent, where would you place elected officials? [w1_g2_b, w12_g2_b/ V085, V572/DS1.G4, DS4.G4]

(100 if very intelligent; 0 if very unintelligent)

- On a scale of 0 to 10, where 0 means very uninformed and 10 means very informed, where would you place elected officials? [w1_g3_b, w12_g3_b/ V087, V574/DS1.G6, DS4.G6]

(100 if very informed; 0 if very uninformed)

Opinions about politics, political parties (0–100):

- Without political parties, there can't be true democracy. Do you strongly agree, somewhat agree, somewhat disagree, or strongly disagree? [w1_a1, w12_a1/ V012, V507/DS1.A1, DS4.A1]

(100 if strongly agree; 67 if somewhat agree; 33 if somewhat disagree; 0 if strongly disagree)

- How good a job do political parties generally do in presenting clear choices on the issues: a very good job, quite a good job, not a very good job, or not a good job at all? [w1_b1, w12_b1/V020, V513/DS1.B1, DS4.B1]

(100 if a very good job; 67 if quite a good job; 33 if not a very good job; 0 if not a good job at all)

- How good a job do political parties [in this country] generally do in finding solutions to important problems: a very good job, quite a good job, not a very good job, or not a good job at all? [w1_b2, w12_b2/V021, V514/DS1.B2, DS4.B2]

(100 if a very good job; 67 if quite a good job; 33 if not a very good job; 0 if not a good job at all)

- How good a job do political parties [in this country] generally do in expressing the concerns of ordinary people: a very good job, quite a good job, not a very good job, or not a good job at all? [w1_b3, w12_b3/V522, V515/DS1.B3, DS4.B3]

(100 if a very good job; 67 if quite a good job; 33 if not a very good job; 0 if not a good job at all)

- All parties are basically the same, there isn't really a choice. Do you strongly agree, somewhat agree, somewhat disagree, or strongly disagree? [w1_a13, w12_a13/V029, V519/DS1.A13, DS4.A13]

(100 if strongly disagree; 67 if somewhat disagree; 33 if somewhat agree; 0 if strongly agree)

Opinions about politics, government (0–100):

- I don't think the government cares much what people like me think. Do you strongly agree, somewhat agree, somewhat disagree, or strongly disagree? [w1_a3, w12_a3/V014, V509/DS1.A3, DS4.A3]

(100 if strongly disagree; 67 if somewhat disagree; 33 if somewhat agree; 0 if strongly agree)

Opinions about politics, democracy (0–100):

- On the whole, how satisfied are you with the way democracy works in British Columbia/the Netherlands/Ontario: very satisfied, fairly satisfied, not very satisfied, or not satisfied at all? [w1_e1, w12_e1/V011, V506/DS1.E1, DS4.E1]

(100 if very satisfied; 67 if somewhat satisfied; 33 if not very satisfied; 0 if not satisfied at all)

Duty and trust (0–100):

- It is the duty of every citizen to stay informed about what is going on in British Columbia/Ontario. Do you strongly agree, somewhat agree, somewhat disagree, or strongly disagree? [w1_d2, w12_d2/DS1.D2, DS4.D2]

(100 if strongly agree; 67 if somewhat agree; 33 if somewhat disagree; 0 if strongly disagree)

- It is the duty of every citizen to vote in every election. Do you strongly agree, somewhat agree, somewhat disagree, or strongly disagree? [w1_f2, w12_f2/ V071, V558/DS1.F2, DS4.F2]

(100 if strongly agree; 67 if somewhat agree; 33 if somewhat disagree; 0 if strongly disagree)

- Do you think that most people would take advantage of you if they got the chance, or would they try to be fair? [w1_j4, w12_j1/DS1.I4, DS4.I1]

(100 if they would try to be fair; 0 if they would take advantage of you)

- Generally speaking, would you say that most people can be trusted, or that you can't be too careful in dealing with people? [w1_j8, w12_j5/V076, V563/DS1. I8, DS4.I5]

(100 if most people can be trusted; 0 if you can't be too careful)

People and populism (0–100):

- On a scale of 0 to 10, where 0 means very selfish and 10 means very unselfish, where would you place people in general? [w1_g1_a, w12_g1_a/V082, V569/ DS1.G1, DS4.G1]

(100 if very unselfish; 0 if very selfish)

- On a scale of 0 to 10, where 0 means very unintelligent and 10 means very intelligent, where would you place people in general? [w1_g2_a, w12_g2_a/ V084, V571/DS1.G3, DS4.G3]

(100 if very intelligent; 0 if very unintelligent)

- On a scale of 0 to 10, where 0 means very uninformed and 10 means very informed, where would you place people in general? [w1_g3_a, w12_g3_a/ V086, V573/DS1.G5, DS4.G5]

(100 if very informed; 0 if very uninformed)

- Most people have enough sense to tell whether a government is doing a good job. Do you strongly agree, somewhat agree, somewhat disagree, or strongly disagree? [w1_d8, w12_d8/DS1.D8, DS4.D8]

(100 if strongly agree; 67 if somewhat agree; 33 if somewhat disagree; 0 if strongly disagree)

- The major issues of the day are too complicated for most voters. Do you strongly agree, somewhat agree, somewhat disagree, or strongly disagree? [w1_f1, w12_f1/V070, V557/DS1.F1, DS4.F1]

(100 if strongly disagree; 67 if somewhat disagree; 33 if somewhat agree; 0 if strongly agree)

- We would probably solve most of our big problems if decisions could be brought back to the people at the grass roots. Do you strongly agree, somewhat agree, somewhat disagree, or strongly disagree? [w1_f8, w12_f8/V074, V561/ DS1.F8, DS4.F8]

(100 if strongly agree; 67 if somewhat agree; 33 if somewhat disagree; 0 if strongly disagree)

- I'd rather put my faith in down-to-earth thinking of ordinary people than the theories of experts and intellectuals. Do you strongly agree, somewhat agree, somewhat disagree, or strongly disagree? [w1_f4, w12_f4/V072, V559/DS1. F4, DS4.F4]

(100 if strongly agree; 67 if somewhat agree; 33 if somewhat disagree; 0 if strongly disagree)

Authoritarian values (0–100):

• For most questions there is only one right answer. Do you strongly agree, somewhat agree, somewhat disagree, or strongly disagree? [w1_d4, w12_d4/ DS1.D4, DS4.D4]

(100 if strongly disagree; 67 if somewhat disagree; 33 if somewhat agree; 0 if strongly agree)

• Most of the ideas which get printed nowadays aren't worth the paper they are printed on. Do you strongly agree, somewhat agree, somewhat disagree, or strongly disagree? [w1_d6, w12_d6/DS1.D6, DS4.D6]

(100 if strongly disagree; 67 if somewhat disagree; 33 if somewhat agree; 0 if strongly agree)

• Many problems have more than one acceptable solution. Do you strongly agree, somewhat agree, somewhat disagree, or strongly disagree? [w1_f3, w12_f3/ DS1.F3, DS4.F3]

(100 if strongly agree; 67 if somewhat agree; 33 if somewhat disagree; 0 if strongly disagree)

• A person ought not to be allowed to speak if he/she doesn't know what he's/ she's talking about. Do you strongly agree, somewhat agree, somewhat disagree, or strongly disagree? [w1_f7, w12_f7/DS1.F7, DS4.F7]

(100 if strongly disagree; 67 if somewhat disagree; 33 if somewhat agree; 0 if strongly agree)

• Obedience and respect for authority are the most important virtues children should learn. Do you strongly agree, somewhat agree, somewhat disagree, or strongly disagree? [w1_k10, w12_k10/DS1.J10, DS4.J10]

(100 if strongly disagree; 67 if somewhat disagree; 33 if somewhat agree; 0 if strongly agree)

Appendix 4: Question Labels, Wordings, and Codings for Chapter 8 (2005/2007/2009 Referendums)

Public support for electoral reform (0/1):

- The referendum question will be: 'Should British Columbia change to the BC-STV electoral system as recommended by the Citizens' Assembly on Electoral Reform?'. Do you think you will vote YES or NO? [V4]

(1 if yes; 0 otherwise)

- The referendum question will be. 'Which electoral system should Ontario use to elect members to the provincial legislature? The existing "first-past-the-post" electoral system or the alternative electoral system proposed by the Citizens' Assembly, mixed member proportional?'. If you vote in the referendum, do you think you will vote for the existing system or the alternative, or are you not sure? [REFV3]

(1 if the alternative system; 0 otherwise)

- The referendum question will be: 'Which electoral system should BC use to elect members to the provincial legislative assembly? The existing system, "first-past-the-post", or the single transferable vote system (BC-STV) proposed by the Citizens' Assembly on Electoral Reform?' Do you think you will vote for the existing system or the proposed BC-STV system? [V4]

(1 if the proposed system; 0 otherwise)

Fair representation of parties (0–1):

- A party that gets 10 per cent of the votes should get 10 per cent of the seats. Do you agree or disagree? [G4/REFG4/G4]

(1 if agree; 0.5 if DK; 0 if disagree)

Coalition governments (0–1):

- In your opinion, which is better: one-party governments so they can get things done, or governments made up of two or three parties because they are forced to compromise? [C1/REFC1/C1]

(1 if governments made up of two or three parties; 0.5 if DK; 0 if one-party governments)

Aversion to change (0–1):

* In general, you like taking risks. Do you agree or disagree? [P1/REFG10/J2]

(1 if disagree; 0.5 if DK; 0 if agree)

Small-party support (0/1):

* Will you vote for the Liberal Party, the NDP, the Green Party, or another party? [V2/V2]

    (1 if Green Party or another party; 0 otherwise)

* If you vote, which party do you think you will vote for: the Liberal Party, the Conservative Party, the NDP, the Green Party, or another party? [REFV2]

(1 if NDP, Green Party, or another party; 0 otherwise)

Satisfaction with current system (0–1):

* And how satisfied are you with the way the current electoral system works in British Columbia: very satisfied, somewhat satisfied, not very satisfied, or not at all satisfied? [G11/G10]
* On the whole, how satisfied are you with the system we use to choose our members of the provincial parliament: very satisfied, somewhat satisfied, not very satisfied, or not at all satisfied? [REFG14]

(1 if very satisfied; 0.67 if somewhat satisfied; 0.5 if DK; 0.33 if not very satisfied; 0 if not at all satisfied)

Knowledge about alternative system (0–1):

* The Citizens' Assembly has proposed a change to the way we elect the BC Legislature in Victoria. The system they proposed is called BC-STV. Would you say you know a lot, some, not very much, or nothing about this proposal? [B1/B1]
* The Citizens' Assembly has proposed a change to the way we elect our representatives to the Ontario Legislature. The system they proposed is called mixed member proportional, or MMP for short. Would you say you know a lot, some, not very much, or nothing about this proposal? [REFB1]

(1 if a lot; 0.67 if some; 0.33 if not very much; 0 if nothing or DK)

[Concern for] Specific features of alternative (0–1):

* Under the proposed BC-STV system it will be hard to follow how the ballots are counted. Are you very concerned, somewhat concerned, not very concerned, or not at all concerned about this? [C3/C3]

- Some people say that with the BC-STV voting system the parties in power will change too often. How concerned are you about this? Are you very concerned, somewhat concerned, not very concerned, or not at all concerned about this? [C4/C4]

(1 if very or somewhat concerned; 0.5 if DK; 0 if not very or not at all concerned)

- Under the MMP system, parties will get top-up seats so the number of seats matches the number of votes they got. Each party will put forward a list of people to fill these seats. These people will fill 30 per cent of the total seats. Do you think the parties choosing these people [top-up seats] is a good thing, a bad thing, or does it not matter? [REFC4]
- Under the proposed system there would be 129 members elected to the provincial legislature. That's 22 more than we have now. Is this a good thing, is it a bad thing, or does it not matter? [REFC7]

(1 if a bad thing; 0.5 if DK or does not matter; 0 if a good thing)

Knowledge about the citizen assembly (0–1):

- How much would you say you know about the BC Citizens' Assembly on Electoral Reform? Would you say a lot, some, not very much, or nothing? [A1]
- How much would you say you know about the Ontario Citizens' Assembly on Electoral Reform? Would you say a lot, some, not very much, or nothing? [REFA1]
- How much would you say you know about the BC Citizens' Assembly on Electoral Reform which was in operation in 2004? Would you say you know a lot, some, not very much, or nothing? [A1]

(1 if a lot; 0.67 if some; 0.33 if not very much; 0 if nothing or DK)

Trust in citizen assembly (0–1):

- Because the members of the Citizens' Assembly are people like me, I trust their judgement. Do you agree or disagree? [J1/REFG2/J1]

(1 if agree; 0.5 if DK; 0 if disagree)

References

Aarts, K., & van der Kolk, H. (2006). Understanding the Dutch 'No': The Euro, the East, and the Elite, *PS: Political Science and Politics, XXXIX*, 243–6.

Achen, C. H. (1975). Mass Political Attitudes and the Survey Response. *American Political Science Review, 69*(4), 1218–31.

——Bartels, L. M. (2002). Blind Retrospection: Electoral Responses to Drought, Flu, and Shark Attacks. *Paper presented at the Annual Meeting of the American Political Science Association*, Boston.

Akkerman, T., & van Santen, R. A. (2007). *Burgerforum Kiesstelsel in Het Nieuws. Analyse Van De Berichtgeving in De Media*. Amsterdam: Onderzoekscentrum PERFORM.

Almond, G. A., & Verba, S. (1963). *The Civic Culture: Political Attitudes and Democracy in Five Nations*. Newbury Park, CA: Sage Publications, Inc.

Althaus, S. L. (1998). Information Effects in Collective Preferences. *American Political Science Review, 92*(3), 545–58.

——(2003). *Collective Preferences in Democratic Politics: Opinion Surveys and the Will of the People*. Cambridge. Cambridge University Press.

Amar, A. R. (1983). Choosing Representatives by Lottery Voting. *Yale Law Journal, 93*(7), 1283–308.

Ansolabehere, S., Rodden, J., & Snyder, J. M. (2008). The Strength of Issues: Using Multiple Measures to Gauge Preference Stability, Ideological Constraint, and Issue Voting. *American Political Science Review, 102*(2), 215–32.

Arnstein, S. R. (1969). A Ladder of Citizen Participation. *Journal of the American Institute of Planners, 35*(4), 216–24.

Barabas, J. (2004). How Deliberation Affects Policy Opinions. *American Political Science Review, 98*(4), 687–701.

Barber, B. R. (1984). *Strong Democracy: Participatory Politics for a New Age*. Berkeley, CA: University of California Press.

Bartels, L. M. (1996). Uninformed Votes: Information Effects in Presidential Elections. *American Journal of Political Science, 40*(1), 194–230.

——(2008). *Unequal Democracy: The Political Economy of the New Gilded Age*. Princeton, NJ: Princeton University Press.

Bawn, K. (1993). The Logic of Institutional Preferences: German Electoral Law as a Social Choice Outcome. *American Journal of Political Science, 37*(4), 965–89.

BC Liberals. (2001). *A New Era for British Columbia: A Vision for Hope and Prosperity for the Next Decade and Beyond*, Campaign Platform.

Bennett, W. L. (2008). *News: The Politics of Illusion*. New York: Longman.

Benoit, K. (2004). Models of Electoral System Change. *Electoral Studies, 23*(3), 363–89.

Blais, A. (1974). Power and Causality. *Quality and Quantity, 8*(1), 54–63.

——(2000). *To Vote or Not to Vote?: The Merits and Limits of Rational Choice Theory*. Pittsburgh, PA: University of Pittsburgh Press.

Blais, A., & Massicotte, L. (2002). Electoral Systems. In L. LeDuc, R. G. Niemi & P. Norris (Eds.), *Comparing Democracies 2: New Challenges in the Study of Elections and Voting* (pp. 40–69). London: Sage.

——Shugart, M. S. (2008). Conclusion. In A. Blais (Ed.), *To Keep or to Change First Past the Post: The Politics of Electoral Reform* (pp. 184–226). Oxford: Oxford University Press.

——Blake, D., & Dion, S. (1993). Do Parties Make a Difference? Parties and the Size of Government in Liberal Democracies. *American Journal of Political Science*, *37*(1), 40–62.

————————(1996). Do Parties Make a Difference? A Reappraisal. *American Journal of Political Science*, *40*(2), 514–20.

——Carty, R. K., & Fournier, P. (2008). Do Citizens' Assemblies Make Reasoned Choices. In M. E. Warren & H. Pearse (Eds.), *Designing Deliberative Democracy: The British Columbia Citizens' Assembly* (pp. 127–44). Cambridge: Cambridge University Press.

——Gidengil, E., Fournier, P., & Nevitte, N. (2009). Information, Visibility and Elections: Why Electoral Outcomes Differ When Voters are Better Informed. *European Journal of Political Research*, *48*(2), 256–80.

Boix, C. (1999). Setting the Rules of the Game: The Choice of Electoral Systems in Advanced Democracies. *American Political Science Review*, *93*(3), 609–24.

Bowler, S., & Donovan, T. (2002). Democracy, Institutions and Attitudes About Citizen Influence on Government. *British Journal of Political Science*, *32*(2), 371–90.

——Farrell, D. M. (2006). We Know Which One We Prefer but We Don't Really Know Why: The Curious Case of Mixed Member Electoral Systems. *British Journal of Politics and International Relations*, *8*(3), 445.

——Farrell, D. M., & Pettitt, R. T. (2005). Expert Opinion on Electoral Systems: So Which Electoral System Is 'Best'? *Journal of Elections, Public Opinion & Parties*, *15*(1), 3–19.

——Donovan, T., & Karp, J. A. (2008). Why Politicians Like Electoral Institutions: Self-Interest, Values, or Ideology? *The Journal of Politics*, *68*(2), 434–46.

Brehm, J., & Rahn, W. (1997). Individual-Level Evidence for the Causes and Consequences of Social Capital. *American Journal of Political Science*, *41*(3), 999–1023.

British Columbia Citizens' Assembly on Electoral Reform. (2004). *Making Every Vote Count, the Case for Electoral Reform: Technical Report*. Victoria, BC: Citizens' Assembly on Electoral Reform.

Brown, M. B. (2006). Survey Article: Citizen Panels and the Concept of Representation. *Journal of Political Philosophy*, *14*(2), 203–25.

Burgerforum Kiesstelsel. (2006). *Procesverslag Burgerforum, Also Available in English on the DVD Accompanying the Final Proposal of the Burgerforum*: Burgerforum Kiesstelsel.

Butler, D., & Stokes, D. E. (1974). *Political Change in Britain: The Evolution of Electoral Choice*. New York City: St. Martin's Press.

Button, M., & Ryfe, D. M. (2005). What Can We Learn from the Practice of Deliberative Democracy? In J. Gastil & P. Levine (Eds.), *The Deliberative Democracy Handbook: Strategies for Effective Civic Engagement in the Twenty-First Century* (pp. 20–34). San Francisco, CA: Jossey-Bass.

Cabannes, Y. (2004). *72 Frequently Asked Questions About Participatory Budgeting*. Nairobi: UN Habitat.

Carty, R. K., & Rose, J. (2007). Citizens' Criteria for Choosing an Electoral System: Evidence from the Electoral Reform Assemblies in British Columbia, the Netherlands and Ontario. *Paper presented at the Annual Meetings of the American Political Science Association*.

——Blais, A., & Fournier, P. (2008). When Citizens Choose to Reform SMP: The British Columbia Citizens' Assembly on Electoral Reform. In A. Blais (Ed.), *To Keep or to Change First Past the Post?: The Politics of Electoral Reform* (pp. 140–62). Oxford: Oxford University Press.

Catt, H., & Murphy, M. (2003). What Voice for the People? Categorising Methods of Public Consultation. *Australian Journal of Political Science, 38*(3), 407–21.

Cohen, J. (1989). Deliberation and Democratic Legitimacy. In A. Hamlin & P. Pettit (Eds.), *The Good Polity* (pp. 17–34). Oxford: Blackwell.

——(1996). Procedure and Substance in Deliberative Democracy. In S. Benhabib (Ed.), *Democracy and Difference* (pp. 95–119). Princeton, NJ: Princeton University Press.

Colomer, J. M. (2005). It's Parties That Choose Electoral Systems (or, Duverger's Laws Upside Down). *Political Studies, 53*(1), 1–21.

——(Ed.). (2004). *Handbook of Electoral System Choice*. London: Palgrave Macmillan.

Converse, P. E. (1964). The Nature of Belief Systems in Mass Publics. In D. E. Apter (Ed.), *Ideology and Discontent* (pp. 206–61). New York City: Free Press.

——(1970). Attitudes and Non-Attitudes: Continuation of a Dialogue. In E. Tufte (Ed.), *The Quantitative Analysis of Social Problems* (pp. 168–89). Reading: Addison-Wesley

——(1980). Comment: Rejoinder to Judd and Milburn. *American Sociological Review, 45*(4), 644–6.

Crosby, N. (1995). Citizens Juries: One Solution for Difficult Environmental Questions. In O. Rwnn, T. Webler & P. Wiedemann (Eds.), *Fairness and Competence in Citizen Participation: Evaluating Models for Environmental Discourse* (pp. 157–74). Dordrecht: Kluwer.

——Nethercut, D. (2005). Citizens Juries: Creating a Trustworthy Voice of the People. In J. Gastil & P. Levine (Eds.), *The Deliberative Democracy Handbook. Strategies for Effective Civic Engagement in the Twenty-First Century* (pp. 111–19). San Francisco, CA: Jossey-Bass.

Cutler, F., Johnston, R., Carty, R. K., Blais, A., & Fournier, P. (2008). Deliberation, Information, and Trust: The British Columbia Citizens' Assembly as Agenda Setter. In M.E Warren & H. Pearse (Eds.), *Designing Deliberative Democracy: The British Columbia Citizens' Assembly* (pp. 66–91). Cambridge: Cambridge University Press.

Dahl, R. A. (1970). *Modern Political Analysis*. Englewood Cliffs: Prentice Hall.

Dalton, R. J. (2004). *Democratic Challenges, Democratic Choices: The Erosion of Political Support in Advanced Industrial Democracies*. Oxford: Oxford University Press.

Delli Carpini, M. (2005). An Overview of the State of Citizens' Knowledge About Politics. In M. S. McKinney, L. Lee Kaid, D. G. Bystrom & D. B. Carlin (Eds.), *Communicating Politics: Engaging the Public in Democratic Life* (pp. 27–40). New York City: Peter Lang.

——Keeter, S. (1993). Measuring Political Knowledge: Putting First Things First. *American Journal of Political Science, 37*(4), 1179–206.

———(1996). *What Americans Know About Politics and Why It Matters*. New Haven, CT: Yale University Press.

Delli Carpini, M., Cook, F. L., & Jacobs, L. R. (2004). Public Deliberation, Discursive Participation, and Citizen Engagement: A Review of the Empirical Literature. *Annual Review of Political Science*, *7*, 315–44.

de Sousa Santos, B. (1998). Participatory Budgeting in Porto Alegre: Toward a Redistributive Democracy. *Politics & Society*, *26*(4), 461–510.

Dienel, P. C., & Renn, O. (1995). Planning Cells: A Gate to 'Fractal' Mediation. In O. Renn, T. Webler & P. Wiedemann (Eds.), *Fairness and Competence in Citizen Participation: Evaluating Models for Environmental Discourse* (pp. 117–40). Dordrecht: Kluwer.

Downs, A. (1957). *An Economic Theory of Democracy*. New York City: Harper.

Druckman, J. N. (2004). Political Preference Formation: Competition, Deliberation, and the (Ir)Relevance of Framing Effects. *American Political Science Review*, *98*(4), 671–86.

——Nelson, K. R. (2003). Framing and Deliberation: How Citizens' Conversations Limit Elite Influence. *American Journal of Political Science*, *47*(4), 729–45.

Dryzek, J. S. (1990). *Discursive Democracy: Politics, Policy, and Political Science*. Cambridge: Cambridge University Press.

——(2000). *Deliberative Democracy and Beyond: Liberals, Critics, Contestations*. Oxford: Oxford University Press.

——(2001). Legitimacy and Economy in Deliberative Democracy. *Political Theory*, *29*(5), 651–69.

Elster, J. (1998). *Deliberative Democracy*. Cambridge: Cambridge University Press.

Erikson, R. S. (1979). The SRC Panel Data and Mass Political Attitudes. *British Journal of Political Science*, *9*(1), 89–114.

——MacKuen, M. B., & Stimson, J. A. (2002). *The Macro Polity*. Cambridge: Cambridge University Press.

Farrell, D. M. (2001). *Electoral Systems: A Comparative Introduction*. New York City: Palgrave Macmillan.

Fearon, J. D. (1998). Deliberation as Discussion. In J. Elster (Ed.), *Deliberative Democracy: Cambridge Studies in the Theory of Democracy* (pp. 44–68). Cambridge: Cambridge University Press.

Feldman, S. (1989). Measuring Issue Preferences: The Problem of Response Instability. *Political Analysis*, *1*(1), 25.

Finkel, S. E. (1985). Reciprocal Effects of Participation and Political Efficacy: A Panel Analysis. *American Journal of Political Science*, *29*(4), 891–913.

——(1987). The Effects of Participation on Political Efficacy and Political Support: Evidence from a West German Panel. *The Journal of Politics*, *49*(2), 441–64.

Fishkin, J. S. (1991). *Democracy and Deliberation*. New Haven, CT: Yale University Press.

——(1995). *The Voice of the People*. New Haven, CT: Yale University Press.

——Luskin, R. C. (1999). Bringing Deliberation to the Democratic Dialogue. In M. E. McCombs & A. Reynolds (Eds.), *The Poll with a Human Face: The National Issues Convention Experiment in Political Communication* (pp. 3–38). Mahwah, NJ: Lawrence Erlbaum Associates.

————(2005). Experimenting with a Democratic Ideal: Deliberative Polling and Public Opinion. *Acta Politica*, *40*(3), 284–98.

Fournier, P. (2002). The Uninformed Canadian Voter. In J. Everitt & B. O'Neill (Eds.), *Citizen Politics: Research and Theory in Canadian Political Behaviour* (pp. 92–109). Oxford: Oxford University Press.

——(2006). The Impact of Campaigns on Discrepancies, Errors and Biases in Voting Behavior. In H. E. Brady & R. Johnston (Eds.), *Capturing Campaign Effects* (pp. 45–77). Ann Arbor, MI: University of Michigan Press.

Franklin, M. N. (2004). *Voter Turnout and the Dynamics of Electoral Competition in Established Democracies since 1945*. Cambridge: Cambridge University Press.

Gastil, J. (2000). Is Face-to-Face Citizen Deliberation a Luxury or a Necessity? *Political Communication*, *17*(4), 357–61.

——(2006). How Balanced Discussion Shapes Knowledge, Public Perceptions, and Attitudes: A Case Study of Deliberation on the Los Alamos National Laboratory. *Journal of Public Deliberation*, *2*(1), 1–35.

——Dillard, J. P. (1999). Increasing Political Sophistication through Public Deliberation. *Political Communication*, *16*(1), 3–23.

——Deess, E. P., Weiser, P., & Meade, J. (2008). Jury Service and Electoral Participation: A Test of the Participation Hypothesis. *The Journal of Politics*, *70*(2), 351–67.

Gibson, G. (2002). *Report on the Constitution of the Citizens' Assembly on Electoral Reform*. Victoria, BC: Government of British Columbia.

——(2008). Notes for a Presentation: 'When Citizens Decide: Challenges of Large Scale Public Engagement'. University of British Columbia.

Graber, D. (2009). *Mass Media and American Politics*. Washington: CQ Press.

Gray, M., & Caul, M. (2000). Declining Voter Turnout in Advanced Industrial Democracies, 1950 to 1997: The Effects of Declining Group Mobilization. *Comparative Political Studies*, *33*(9), 1091–121.

Grofman, B. (1975). A Comment on 'Democratic Theory: A Preliminary Mathematical Model'. *Public Choice*, *21*(1), 99–103.

——Feld, S. (1988). Rousseau's General Will: A Condorcetian Perspective. *American Political Science Review*, *82*(2), 567–76.

——Owen, G., & Feld, S. (1983). Thirteen Theorems in Search of the Truth. *Theory and Decision*, *15*(3), 261–78.

Gutmann, A., & Thompson, D. (1996). *Democracy & Disagreement*. Boston, MA: Harvard University Press.

————(2000). Why Deliberative Democracy is Different. *Social Philosophy & Policy*, *17*(1), 161–80.

————(2004). *Why Deliberative Democracy?* Princeton, NJ: Princeton University Press.

Habermas, J. (1989). *The Structural Transformation of the Public Sphere: An Inquiry into a Category of Bourgeois Society*. Cambridge, MA: Massachusetts Institute of Technology.

——(1996). *Between Facts and Norms: Contributions to a Discourse Theory of Law and Democracy*. Cambridge, MA: Massachusetts Institute of Technology.

Harsanyi, J. C. (1962). Measurement of Social Power, Opportunity Costs, and the Theory of Two-Person Bargaining Games. *Behavioral Science*, *7*(1), 67–81.

Hendriks, C. M. (2005). Consensus Conferences and Planning Cells: Lay Citizen Deliberations. In J. Gastil & P. Levine (Eds.), *The Deliberative Democracy Handbook. Strategies for Effective Civic Engagement in the Twenty-First Century* (pp. 80–110). San Francisco, CA: Jossey-Bass.

Hetherington, M. J. (1998). The Political Relevance of Political Trust. *American Political Science Review*, *92*(4), 791–808.

Hibbing, J. R., & Theiss-Morse, E. (2001). *What Is It About Government That Americans Dislike?* Cambridge: Cambridge University Press.

————(2002). *Stealth Democracy: Americans' Beliefs About How Government Should Work*. Cambridge: Cambridge University Press.

Humphreys, M., Masters, W. A., & Sandbu, M. E. (2006). The Role of Leaders in Democratic Deliberations: Results from a Field Experiment in Sao Tome and Principe. *World Politics*, *58*(4), 583–622.

Hurwitz, J., & Peffley, M. (1985). A Hierarchical Model of Attitude Constraint. *American Journal of Political Science*, *29*(4), 871–90.

————(1987). How are Foreign Policy Attitudes Structured? A Hierarchical Model. *American Political Science Review*, *81*(4), 1099–120.

Institute on Governance. (2007). *Citizen Deliberative Decision-Making: Evaluation of the Ontario Citizens' Assembly on Electoral Reform*. Ottawa: Institute on Governance.

Irvin, R. A., & Stansbury, J. (2004). Citizen Participation in Decision Making: Is It Worth the Effort? *Public Administration Review*, *64*(1), 55–65.

James, M. R. (2008). Descriptive Representation in the British Columbia Citizens' Assembly. In M. E. Warren & H. Pearse (Eds.), *Designing Deliberative Democracy: The British Columbia Citizens' Assembly* (pp. 106–26). Cambridge: Cambridge University Press.

Johnston, R., & Brady, H. (2002). The Rolling Cross-Section Design. *Electoral Studies*, *21*(2), 283–95.

Joss, S., & Durant, J. (1995). *Public Participation in Science: The Role of Consensus Conferences in Europe*. London: British Science Museum.

Judd, C. M., & Milburn, M. A. (1980). The Structure of Attitude Systems in the General Public: Comparisons of a Structural Equation Model. *American Sociological Review*, *45*(4), 627–43.

Katz, R. S. (1997). *Democracy and Elections*. New York City: Oxford University Press.

Kinder, D. R. (1998). Opinion and Action in the Realm of Politics. In D. T. Gilbert, S. T. Fiske, & G. Lindzey (Eds.), *The Handbook of Social Psychology* (pp. 778–867). Oxford: Oxford University Press.

Kuklinski, J. H., & Quirk, P. J. (2000). Reconsidering the Rational Public: Cognition, Heuristics, and Mass Opinion. In A. Lupia, M. D. McCubbins, & S. L. Popkin (Eds.), *Elements of Reason: Cognition, Choice, and the Bounds of Rationality* (pp. 153–82). Cambridge: Cambridge University Press.

Lang, A. (2008). Agenda-Setting in Deliberative Forums: Expert Influence and Citizen Autonomy in the British Columbia Citizens' Assembly. In M. E. Warren & H. Pearse (Eds.), *Designing Deliberative Democracy: The British Columbia Citizens' Assembly* (pp. 85–105). Cambridge: Cambridge University Press.

Le Bon, G. (1896). *The Crowd: A Study of the Popular Mind*. London: T. Fisher Unwin.

Legislative Assembly of Ontario. (2005). *Report of the Select Committee of Electoral Reform*. Toronto: Legislative Assembly of Ontario.

Leighley, J. (1991). Participation as a Stimulus of Political Conceptualization. *The Journal of Politics*, *53*(1), 198–211.

Lijphart, A. (1994). *Electoral Systems and Party Systems: A Study of Twenty-Seven Democracies, 1945–1990.* New York City: Oxford University Press.

List, C., & Pettit, P. (2002). Aggregating Sets of Judgments: An Impossibility Result. *Economics and Philosophy, 18*(1), 89–110.

Lodge, M., McGraw, K. M., & Stroh, P. (1989). An Impression-Driven Model of Candidate Evaluation. *American Political Science Review, 83*(2), 399–419.

——Steenbergen, M. R., & Brau, S. (1995). The Responsive Voter: Campaign Information and the Dynamics of Candidate Evaluation. *American Political Science Review, 89*(2), 309–26.

Lupia, A. (1994). Shortcuts Versus Encyclopedias: Information and Voting Behavior in California Insurance Reform Elections. *American Political Science Review, 88*(1), 63–76.

——McCubbins, M. D. (1998). *The Democratic Dilemma: Can Citizens Learn What They Need to Know?* Cambridge: Cambridge University Press.

Luskin, R. C. (1987). Measuring Political Sophistication. *American Journal of Political Science, 31*(4), 856–99.

——(1990). Explaining Political Sophistication. *Political Behavior, 12*(4), 331–61.

——Fishkin, J. S. (2002). Deliberation and 'Better Citizens'. *Paper presented at the Workshops of the European Consortium for Political Research*, Turin.

——Jowell, R. (2002). Considered Opinions: Deliberative Polling in the UK. *British Journal of Political Science, 32*(3), 455–87.

McClosky, H. (1958). Conservatism and Personality. *American Political Science Review, 52*(1), 27–45.

McCormick, J. P. (2006). Contain the Wealthy and Patrol the Magistrates: Restoring Elite Accountability to Popular Government. *American Political Science Review, 100*(2), 147–63.

Madsen, D. (1978). A Structural Approach to the Explanation of Political Efficacy Levels under Democratic Regimes. *American Journal of Political Science, 22*(4), 867–83.

Manin, B. (1987). On Legitimacy and Political Deliberation. *Political Theory, 15*(3), 338–68.

——(1997). *The Principles of Representative Government.* Cambridge: Cambridge University Press.

Mansbridge, J. J. (1980). *Beyond Adversary Democracy.* Chicago, IL: University of Chicago Press.

——(1999). On the Idea That Participation Makes Better Citizens. In S. E. Elkin & K. E. Soltan (Eds.), *Citizen Competence and Democratic Institutions* (pp. 291–328). University Park, PA: Pennsylvania State University Press.

——(2003). Rethinking Representation. *American Political Science Review, 97*(4), 515–28.

Mendelberg, T., & Karpowitz, C. (2007). How People Deliberate About Justice: Groups, Gender, and Decision Rules. In S. W. Rosenberg (Ed.), *Deliberation, Participation and Democracy. Can the People Govern?* (pp. 101–29). London: Palgrave Macmillan.

Miller, N. R. (1986). Information, Electorates, and Democracy: Some Extensions and Interpretations of the Condorcet Jury Theorem. In B. Grofman & G. Owen (Eds.), *Information Pooling and Group Decision Making* (pp. 173–92). Greenwich: JAI Press.

Miller, J. M., & Krosnick, J. A. (2000). News Media Impact on the Ingredients of Presidential Evaluations: Politically Knowledgeable Citizens are Guided by a Trusted Source. *American Journal of Political Science, 44*(2), 295–309.

Morrell, M. E. (2005). Deliberation, Democratic Decision-Making and Internal Political Efficacy. *Political Behavior, 27*(1), 49–69.

Mueller, J. E. (1973). *War, Presidents, and Public Opinion*. New York City: John Wiley & Sons.

——(1994). *Policy and Opinion in the Gulf War*. Chicago, IL: University of Chicago Press.

Mutz, D. C. (2002). Cross-Cutting Social Networks: Testing Democratic Theory in Practice. *American Political Science Review, 96*(1), 111–26.

——(2006). *Hearing the Other Side: Deliberative Versus Participatory Democracy*. Cambridge: Cambridge University Press.

Nadeau, R., Martin, P., & Blais, A. (1999). Attitude Towards Risk-Taking and Individual Choice in the Quebec Referendum on Sovereignty. *British Journal of Political Science, 29*(3), 523–39.

Nevitte, N. (1996). *The Decline of Deference: Canadian Value Change in Cross-National Perspective*. Peterborough: Broadview Press.

Norris, P. (1999). *Critical Citizens: Global Support for Democratic Government*. Oxford: Oxford University Press.

Novy, A., & Leubolt, B. (2005). Participatory Budgeting in Porto Alegre: Social Innovation and the Dialectical Relationship of State and Civil Society. *Urban Studies, 42*(11), 2023–36.

Nye, J. S., Zelikow, P., & King, D. C. (1997). *Why People Don't Trust Government*. Cambridge, MA: Harvard University Press.

Ontario Citizens' Assembly on Electoral Reform. (2007a). *Democracy at Work: A Record of Ontario's First Citizens' Assembly Process*. Toronto: Ontario Citizens' Assembly on Electoral Reform.

——(2007b). *Public Consultation Reports*. Toronto: Citizens' Assembly Secretariat.

Ottati, V. C., Riggle, E. J., Wyer, R. S., Schwarz, N., & Kuklinski, J. (1989). Cognitive and Affective Bases of Opinion Survey Responses. *Journal of Personality and Social Psychology, 57*(3), 404–15.

Page, B. I. (1996). *Who Deliberates? Mass Media in Modern Democracy*. Chicago, IL: University of Chicago Press.

——Shapiro, R. Y. (1992). *The Rational Public: Fifty Years of Trends in Americans' Policy Preferences*. Chicago, IL: University of Chicago Press.

Pateman, C. (1970). *Participation and Democratic Theory*. Cambridge: Cambridge University Press.

Pettit, P. (2003). Deliberative Democracy, the Discursive Dilemma, and Republican Theory. In J. S. Fishkin & P. Laslett (Eds.), *Debating Deliberative Democracy* (pp. 138–62). Oxford: Blackwell.

Pharr, S. J., & Putnam, R. D. (2000). *Disaffected Democracies: What's Troubling the Trilateral Countries?* Princeton, NJ: Princeton University Press.

Pilet, J. B. (2007). *Changer Pour Gagner?: Les Réformes Des Lois Électorales En Belgique*. Brussels: Université de Bruxelles.

Pitkin, H. F. (1967). *The Concept of Representation*. Berkeley, CA: University of California Press.

Popkin, S. L. (1991). *The Reasoning Voter: Communication and Persuasion in Presidential Campaigns*. Chicago, IL: University of Chicago Press.

Price, V., & Neijens, P. (1997). Opinion Quality in Public Opinion Research. *International Journal of Public Opinion Research*, *9*(4), 336–60.

Putnam, R. D. (2000). *Bowling Alone: The Collapse and Revival of American Community*. New York City: Simon and Schuster.

Radcliff, B., & Wingenbach, E. (2000). Preference Aggregation, Functional Pathologies, and Democracy: A Social Choice Defense of Participatory Democracy. *The Journal of Politics*, *62*(4), 977–98.

Rae, D. W. (1969). *The Political Consequences of Electoral Laws*. New Haven, CT: Yale University Press.

Rahat, G. (2004). The Study of the Politics of Electoral Reform in the 1990s: Theoretical and Methodological Lessons. *Comparative Politics*, *36*(4), 461–79.

Rawls, J. (1971). *A Theory of Justice*. Cambridge, MA: Belknap Press of Harvard University Press.

Remington, T., & Smith, S. (1996). Political Goals, Institutional Context, and the Choice of an Electoral System: The Russian Parliamentary Election Law. *American Journal of Political Science*, *40*(4), 1253–79.

Reynolds, A., Reilly, B., & Ellis, A. (2005). *Electoral System Design: The New International Idea Handbook*. Stockholm, Sweden: International IDEA.

Riker, W. H. (1964). Some Ambiguities in the Notion of Power. *American Political Science Review*, *58*(2), 341–9.

Rosenberg, S. W. (2007). Types of Discourse and the Democracy of Deliberation. In S. W. Rosenberg (Ed.), *Deliberation, Participation and Democracy: Can the People Govern?* (pp. 130–59). London: Palgrave Macmillan.

Rowe, G., & Frewer, L. J. (2005). A Typology of Public Engagement Mechanisms. *Science, Technology & Human Values*, *30*(2), 251–90.

Salisbury, R. H. (1975). Research on Political Participation. *American Journal of Political Science*, *19*(2), 323–41.

Schuman, H., & Presser, S. (1981). *Questions and Answers in Attitude Surveys: Experiments on Question Form, Wording and Context*. New York: Academic Press.

Schwarz, N., & Sudman, S. (1992). *Context Effects in Social and Psychological Research*. New York City: Springer-Verlag.

Shepsle, K. A. (2001). A Comment on Institutional Change. *Journal of Theoretical Politics*, *13*(3), 321–5.

Shugart, M. S. (1992). Leaders, Rank and File, and Constituents: Electoral Reform in Colombia and Venezuela. *Electoral Studies*, *11*(1), 21–45.

——(2008). Inherent and Contingent Factors in Reform Initiation in Plurality Systems. In A. Blais (Ed.), *To Keep or to Change First Past the Post: The Politics of Electoral Reform* (pp. 7–60). Oxford: Oxford University Press.

Smith, G., & Wales, C. (2000). Citizens' Juries and Deliberative Democracy. *Political Studies*, *48*(1), 51–65.

Sniderman, P. M., Brody, R. A., & Tetlock, P. (1991). *Reasoning and Choice: Explorations in Political Psychology*. Cambridge: Cambridge University Press.

Soroka, S., & Wlezien, C. (2010). *Degrees of Democracy: Politics, Public Opinion and Policy*. Cambridge: Cambridge University Press.

Thompson, D. F. (1970). *The Democratic Citizen*. Cambridge: Cambridge University Press.

Thompson, D. F. (2008). Who Should Govern Who Governs? The Role of Citizens in Reforming the Electoral System. In M. E. Warren & H. Pearse (Eds.), *Designing Deliberative Democracy: The British Columbia Citizens' Assembly* (pp. 20–49). Cambridge: Cambridge University Press.

Tourangeau, R., Rips, L. J., & Rasinski, K. A. (2000). *The Psychology of Survey Response.* Cambridge: Cambridge University Press.

Van der Kolk, H. (2007). Electoral System Change in the Netherlands: The Road from PR to PR (1917–2006). *Representation, 43*(4), 271–87.

——Thomassen, J. (2006). The Dutch Electoral System on Trial. *Acta Politica, 41*(2), 117–32.

Van Deth, J. W., & Elff, M. (2004). Politicisation, Economic Development and Political Interest in Europe. *European Journal of Political Research, 43*(3), 477–508.

Van Schagen, J. (2007). *Electoral System Civic Forum Process Report.* The Hague: Burgerforum Kiesstelsel.

Verba, S., Schlozman, K. L., & Brady, H. E. (1995). *Voice and Equality: Civic Voluntarism in American Politics.* Cambridge, MA: Harvard University Press.

——Burns, N., & Schlozman, K. L. (1997). Knowing and Caring About Politics: Gender and Political Engagement. *The Journal of Politics, 59*(4), 1051–72.

Walsh, K. C. (2003). *Talking About Politics: Informal Groups and Social Identity in American Life.* Chicago: University of Chicago Press.

Warren, M. E. (2008). Citizen Representatives. In M. E. Warren & H. Pearse (Eds.), *Designing Deliberative Democracy: The British Columbia Citizens' Assembly* (pp. 50–69). Cambridge: Cambridge University Press.

——Pearse, H. (2008). *Designing Deliberative Democracy: The British Columbia Citizens' Assembly.* Cambridge: Cambridge University Press.

Wolfinger, R. E., & Rosenstone, S. J. (1980). *Who Votes?* New Haven, CT: Yale University Press.

Zaller, J. (1990). Political Awareness, Elite Opinion Leadership, and the Mass Survey Response. *Social Cognition, 8*(1), 125–53.

——(1992). *The Nature and Origins of Mass Opinion.* New York City: Cambridge University Press.

——Feldman, S. (1992). A Simple Theory of the Survey Response: Answering Questions Versus Revealing Preferences. *American Journal of Political Science, 36*(3), 579–616.

Index